Interdisciplinary Curriculum

CHALLENGES TO IMPLEMENTATION

Published by Teachers College Press, 1234 Amsterdam Avenue, New York, NY 10027

Library of Congress Cataloging-in-Publication Data

Interdisciplinary curriculum : Challenges to implementation / edited by
  Sam Wineburg & Pam Grossman.
        p. cm.
    Includes bibliographical references and index.
    ISBN 0-8077-3988-X (cloth : alk. paper)—ISBN 0-8077-3987-1 (pbk. : alk.
paper)
      1. Interdisciplinary approach in education—United States. 2.
Curriculum planning—United States.   I. Wineburg, Sam S. II. Grossman,
Pamela L. (Pamela Lynn), 1953–
    LB2806.15.I568 2000
    375'.001'0973—dc21   00-044332

ISBN 0-8077-3987-1 (paper)
ISBN 0-8077-3988-X (cloth)

Printed on acid-free paper

Manufactured in the United States of America

07 06 05 04 03 02 01 00   8 7 6 5 4 3 2 1

Interdisciplinary Curriculum

CHALLENGES TO IMPLEMENTATION

SAM WINEBURG & PAM GROSSMAN
Editors

Foreword by John Goodlad

Teachers College, Columbia University
New York and London

Contents

Foreword

JOHN GOODLAD

Education and schooling are not the same thing. Education takes place in schools but encompasses much more. Indeed, education is a ubiquitous presence, for good or ill, in one's surround. Whereas schooling is a public, political enterprise, education is of the self and, therefore, private even though stimulated by social contexts.

The fundamental differences between education and schooling create tensions, most obvious in the conduct of schooling because of its public, political nature. The tensions in the individual learner's education, because of its private nature, are much less obvious. Insightful, caring parents and teachers, close to children in classrooms, are sensitive to the tensions that arise in individual students when schools are called upon to serve public purposes, such as promoting the national economy.

Policymakers frequently are frustrated with the sluggish response of educators to school reform proposals claiming to be in the public interest. Frequently, however, teachers' hesitation stems from perceiving the reforms not to be in the children's best interests. There is plenty of evidence to show the readiness of most teachers to respond to proposals that clearly connect with their responsibilities to students' learning. Failure to implement what appears to make sense is likely to result from the sheer weight of effecting change under circumstances already formidable in their demands on time and energy. Talk of needed change comes easily; the challenge of effecting significant change is vastly underestimated.

Because schooling is a large, public enterprise, it carries with it a considerable organizational apparatus and commitment of federal, state, and local dollars. Consequently, *efficiency* ranks high as an evaluative criterion. Because education has to do with the shaping of individual human character and dispositions, *morality* ranks high as an evaluative criterion. Clearly, we see the potential tension between a criterion of "goodness" that favors orderliness and fiscal accountability and one that has only to do with what is "right" in seeking to shape the self. For example, grade promotion policies were little affected in response to the eloquently expressed concerns of Presidents Elliot of Harvard University and Harper of the University of Chicago, in the late 19th century, regarding the damaging effects of high failure rates on children and youths. But, when Leonard Ayres pointed out, in his 1909 report, the added financial costs of pupils' grade repetition, the order went out to schools, especially in big cities, to drop practices of nonpromotion. Perhaps it will be the argument of economic efficiency that will slow the current propensity to retain in their present grades children who fail a test or two.

Some of the literature on school change leaves one with the impression that there are successive eras of struggle among conflicting ideas for educational improvement, each seeking to outdo the other in regard to what is best for children. Yes, there is such a struggle at what might be termed the ideological or idealistic level of educational discourse. Almost invariably, however, these ideas share a much larger struggle—that of securing a firm place in practice. The organizational apparatus of schooling and the array of practices it sustains are far more powerful adversaries to a proposal for change than are alternative proposals in the same domain of schooling, be it teaching, the structure of the curriculum, reporting to parents, or whatever. Consequently, studies of school change are quite consistent in their findings and recommendations, regardless of the substantive nature of the initiatives studied.

The reality is that there are *not* cycles of change during which differing ideologies and accompanying practices of schooling succeed one another, each dominant for several decades before yielding to another. In the United States, there is a grade-by-grade pattern of student grouping, curriculum organization, tests, textbooks, pupil promotion policies and practices, remedial learning activities, and more that effectively resists intrusions that do not fit comfortably into the whole. Many of the ideas and accompanying proposed practices that fail to gain entry have much to commend them, and so they return later, sometimes with sufficient rhetorical massaging to suggest, for a time, some success. What goes around comes around.

This cycling and recycling of good ideas, with limited implementation, is commonly referred to as failure. The charge is superficial and shortsighted. Clusters of good ideas commonly share concepts and principles backed by research that speaks to the essence of education, teaching, and learning. Consequently, over time, they tend to sensitize the system of schooling to its responsibility to the human beings it is supposed to educate, serving as a brake on the excesses of efficiency. This certainly was the case over a relatively long period of time with Progressive Education, which certainly modified a good many traditional practices while substituting few for them. A stunning example of the above is found in the influence of the twelfth-century scholar Chu Hsi. He set out to modify the utilitarian careerism of the subject-and-examination Chinese schools of the time through emphasizing his educational aim of "learning for the sake of oneself." What he succeeded in doing was infusing into Chinese culture the three equally indispensable aims of Confucian education: transmission of culture, service to society, and moral self-transformation.

The issue of curriculum and teaching that Wineburg, Grossman, and their colleagues address in what follows is not new (nor is it their primary issue, as I shall point out later). Indeed, it is a much recycled one. I have little doubt that Chu Hsi addressed it. The significant characteristic of the many alternatives to the prevailing single subject or discipline pattern of curriculum organization is their common focus on how best to connect school learning and the developing self of the learner. Wisely, Wineburg and Grossman did not set out to argue the virtues of one pattern over another—a much-debated topic in the literature of the curriculum field. Their interest, rather, is in the much more transcendent issues of what connects with educators' beliefs about learning and of effecting these connections in teaching.

The revisitation of educators in relatively modern times to alternatives in curriculum organization has been driven largely by increasing understanding of human development, of learning as the essence of being human. Little-challenged early in the 20th century was the view of the mind as a muscle that improved with exercise through the study of subjects derived from the classical trivium and quadrivium. Edward L. Thorndike's "scientifically designed textbooks" assured that the separate subject disciplines would be around for a while. One is awed, then, by the sheer radicalism of Harold Rugg's proposal in Part I of the Twenty-sixth Yearbook of the National Society for the Study of Education (1926): Perhaps at least part of the school curriculum should be organized around the large issues of American life and the global context. Rugg opened the door for the proposal of his colleague George Counts to be walked through it: Youths in school might well be immersed in the shortcomings and necessary reconstruction of the social order (1932).

By the middle of the century, the teachings of Rugg and Counts were still controversial but only moderately radical in the existing social order. Whereas changing the behavior of nations occupied public attention in the aftermath of World War I, faith in the power of education to shape individual and collective human behavior caught public attention following World War II—significantly influenced perhaps by the Holocaust and the atomic bombing that brought closure to the fighting but not peace of mind.

The postwar flurry of interest in child study and children's schooling was unprecedented. Proposals for schooling fostered careers in educational journalism. The carefully designed and orchestrated child study program of Daniel Prescott (deeply moved and scarred by his own war experiences) swept east and west, north and south across the United States from the late 1940s well into the 1960s, first out of the University of Chicago and then the University of Maryland. His trained "disciples"—and they were virtually that—carried the three-year sequence of summer seminars and in-between studies of children to tens of thousands of classroom teachers. His colleague Carolyn Tryon joined with Prescott in defining a sequence of children's "developmental tasks," suggesting curricular experiences that teachers might construct to assist the young in coping with and mastering these tasks in growing toward adulthood (in the 1960 Yearbook of the Association for Supervision and Curriculum Development). The organizing elements of her curriculum were not derived from the subject disciplines but were the developmental tasks of life primarily outside of school.

My memory of those years is that Prescott's scheme of studying one child and then a group of children over a year impacted participating teachers' relationships with their students. But one would have been hard-pressed to find many deeply immersed in classroom activities addressed to Tryon's developmental tasks during the years that her book was showing up in the reading lists for prospective and practicing teachers. From the perspective of what colleagues and I have referred to elsewhere as the ideological or idealistic curriculum as contrasted with the operational or experiential (Goodlad et al., 1979), the decade from 1947 to the launching of Sputnik in 1957 might well be called "the golden age of curriculum theorizing." Much of it addressed the problem of connecting school curricula to the lives and surrounding circumstances of children and youths, as Tryon was endeavoring to do.

What was referred to then as "the core curriculum" was not even a distant cousin of today's convention: a core of high-status subjects—English, mathematics, science, and social studies—required for graduation from high school and admission to college. Rather, the "core" was to be comprised of socially relevant topics such as juvenile delinquency, selected by student agreement, that would stimulate inquiry: development of a list of key issues, determination of the relevant data to be gathered, conduct of the necessary research, discussion, and the writing and presentation of a report or reports. Part of most days were to be devoted to the conventional subjects. The target was the junior high school, still in an embryonic, unsettled stage of development. Nelson Bossing's 1949 estimate of such core curricula existing in about 10 % of all junior high schools may be exaggerated. One must be careful in accepting the estimates of advocates.

The work of Florence Stratemeyer and her associates at Teachers College, Columbia University, shares close kinship with that of Tryon and had a wide dissemination during the decade and beyond. Her organizing elements were "persistent life situations." The centers of learning and instruction were activities that students could readily connect with their daily experiences so as to mitigate their fears, profit from their failures and successes, and reconstruct their lives in the recommended Deweyan fashion. The concepts were first laid out in a 1947 book, *Developing a Curriculum of Modern Living.* The 1957 revision was much more explicit with respect to the organizing elements and the centers of activity selected for dealing with them.

The book provided evidence that the many teachers who studied with Stratemeyer and her colleagues were struggling, sometimes quite successfully, with implementation. But, one more time, the road from eager identification with provocative ideas to matching them in practice was cluttered with the obstacles of too little time, too few committed colleagues, limited resources, the burden of district and institutional requirements, and the sheer difficulty of lifting the ideas from the pages of a book and having wonderful classroom experiences. But who can confidently say that little or no good came through and from it all?

It is to having wonderful educational experiences—by teachers as well as their students—that my colleagues Sam Wineburg and Pam Grossman and their associates address their efforts in what follows and in their professional work. There is little here that connects with the repetitive litany of school reform: things gone wrong, people and practices to be fixed, carrots as incentives, sticks as warnings, and consequential accountability. There is a great deal here, however, about individual and institutional renewal.

About educational renewal, another colleague, Ken Sirotnik, has this to say:

> Thinking about renewal as the operative change model instead of reform suggests a major deconstruction of traditional accountability notions. Responsibility is a more useful concept; it suggests, for example, the moral obligations of educators as stewards of their schools to create and nurture learning environments for their students as well as for themselves. And it suggests that educational and political leaders should provide the necessary resources and time to make this happen. In a renewing educational organization, then, the "program" to be "evaluated" becomes the renewal process itself; and "evaluation" becomes the ongoing process of rigorous and active self-examination, reflection, and critical inquiry." (1999, p. 608)

Interdisciplinary curricula is a worthy concept that has come around once more to challenge the supremacy of separate subjects as *the* way to organize curricula. Whether or not they gain parity or even triumph in some schools for a period of time is of less import than whether they help stimulate and sustain an ethos of continuous renewal—a condition which by its very essence nourishes having and implementing wonderful ideas.

REFERENCES

Ayers, L. P. (1909). *Laggards in our schools: A study of retardation and elimination in city school systems.* New York: Charities Publication Committee.

Bossing, N. L. (1949). *Principles of secondary education.* New York: Prentice-Hall.

Counts, G. S. (1932). *Dare the school build a new social order?* New York: John Day Company.

Goodlad, J. I., & Assoc. (1979). *Curriculum inquiry: The study of curriculum practice.* New York: McGraw-Hill.

Prescott, D. A. (1957). *The child in the education process.* New York: McGraw-Hill.

Rugg, H. O. (1926). *The foundations and technique of curriculum construction.* Part 1, Yearbook of the National Society for the Study of Education (vol. 26). Bloomington, IL.: Public School Publishing Company.

Sirotnik, K. A. (1999). Making sense of educational renewal. *Phi Delta Kappan, 80* (8), 606–610.

Stratemeyer, F. B. (1957). *Developing a curriculum for modern living.* New York: Teachers College Press.

Stratemeyer, F. B., Forkner, H. L., McKim, M. G., & Assoc. (1947). *Developing a curriculum for modern living.* New York: Teachers College Press.

Tryon, C. (1960). *Yearbook of the Association for Supervision and Curriculum Development.* Washington. DC: The Association for Supervision and Curriculum Development; National Education Association.

Introduction

When Theory Meets Practice in the World of School

PAM GROSSMAN, SAM WINEBURG, AND SCOTT BEERS

I need help with ideas that would form legitimate projects to integrate science and math at the high school level. I teach in a high school that will soon be visited with an edict from the state for teachers to design multidisciplinary projects that would accomplish this.
—Siskin, chapter 9, this volume.

This SOS call recently went out over a national E-mail bulletin board for teachers. It and many messages like it testify to the urgency teachers feel regarding interdisciplinary curriculum. Schools and districts from coast to coast have rushed to adopt these curricula. The topic perennially tops teachers' and principals' lists of concerns (Brandt, 1991). Discussions about interdisciplinary curricula are regular features in the pages of the *Phi Delta Kappan, Educational Leadership, Education Week,* and other publications with wide readerships. Interdisciplinary curriculum, it seems, has become synonymous with school reform; three-quarters of the "restructuring schools" in one recent study were engaged in interdisciplinary curriculum reorganization (Little, 1997).

This trend is national. A survey of more than 10,000 schools found that nearly two-thirds had implemented or planned to implement interdisciplinary curricula (Cawelti, 1994). And the phenomenon reaches beyond American borders. To the north, British Columbia's blueprint for school renewal, *British Columbia Year 2000,* places "curriculum integration" at the core of its reform agenda (Brandes & Seixas, chapter 8, this volume; Case, 1994).

On the face of it, there are many good reasons for the popularity of interdisciplinary curriculum. As advocates observe, the world does not come neatly packaged in bundles, each wrapped in a separate discipline. Rather, the issues that engage and sustain our interest require the skillful orchestration of multiple concepts and bodies of knowledge. Tasks such as building a house or building a stock portfolio, negotiating a pay raise or negotiating the craggy foothills of the Rockies all require the coordination of different skills and kinds of knowledge. The Atlanta bomb squad that defused an explosive device during the 1996 Summer Olympics didn't say to itself, "Now we are using chemistry, now we are using physics, now we are using psychological and sociological notions of crowd control" but combined these bodies of knowledge in fluid and lightning-quick ways. Advocates of interdisciplinarity promise a curriculum imbued with a similar spirit.

Furthermore, with the knowledge explosion that has accompanied the computer age, interdisciplinarity promises to counterbalance narrow specialization. In theory, interdisciplinary curricula allow students to see patterns in chaos, transcend surface details, and see "the big picture" that so often eludes us as moderns. Discerning patterns across diverse bodies of content can be motivating to students as well as to the adults who teach them. As Judith Rényi notes in chapter 2, the "subjects in silos" school day has as much meaning to children as "first we do science, then we do math, and then we do lunch." For teachers, the opportunity to pool talents and plan joint curricula offers a chance to overcome the culture of privatism that pervades many schools. By reaching beyond their own specializations to work with others, teachers have the chance to remain intellectually alive, always close to the excitement of new learning. Unlike other reform strategies that tinker at the margins, the creation of interdisciplinary curriculum promises to provide teachers with opportunities to come together over what matters most: what actually gets taught and learned in classrooms.

Together these many promises make a compelling case. But across this century attempts to change schools by breaking down subject matter walls have met with checkered and mostly short-lived success. In the face of a steady stream of curriculum innovations, traditional disciplines and subject matters have shown a surprising resiliency, suggesting perhaps that they might be part of what Tyack and Tobin (1994) have called the "grammar of schooling." Subject matters represent deep institutional structures that, like the arms of a starfish, have a way of regenerating soon after amputation.

There are several reasons for this resiliency. First, subjects like math, science, English, and history possess a certain intuitive quality. Dissecting a frog is not the same as dissecting the Coolidge presidency; understanding math's commutative property bears little resemblance to understanding whether Truman should have commuted the death sentences of Julius and Ethel Rosenberg. In Rényi's words, rocks, trees, poems, and kingships *are* different. That the study of rocks gives rise to geology, of trees to botany, of kingships to diplomatic history, with each field possessing its own means of inquiry, methods of verification, and criteria of judgment, is more than mere coincidence. Instead, these differences reflect the intrinsic complexity of the varied phenomena of human life. Recognition of this complexity is reflected, at least implicitly, by even the most adamant proponents of interdisciplinarity when they seek to combine, first, disciplines with family resemblances—history with English or math with science—rather than rushing to integrate the calculus course with the AP history survey. Beliefs about similarities across subjects implicitly speak to common ways of knowing—narrative forms of argument in history and literature versus "paradigmatic" forms of proof and verification in math and science (Bruner, 1986).

The issue of disciplinary structure goes well beyond ways of organizing knowledge. Disciplines provide a social matrix for people with common interests, joint commitments, and certain commonalities in viewing the world. As children progress through the educational system, their interests naturally begin to narrow. One student's passion for computer games leads to an interest in programming languages, Boolean logic, and advanced mathematics, while another's gift in mediating social conflicts leads to interests in the sociology of groups and aspects of organizational management. Accompanying the knowledge gleaned in advanced study are new social relationships with like-minded individuals who have traveled similar paths. It is not only that we might be more likely to find voracious readers of fiction among English than, say, chemistry teachers. But as Grossman and Stodolsky have shown (1995), subject matter departments themselves provide crucial but often overlooked contexts for the development of a host of attitudes and beliefs about schooling and its purposes. And as we ascend the educational ladder, these disciplinary affiliations become more and more powerful (Becher, 1989).

It makes sense, then, that the sites where interdisciplinary curricula have made the greatest inroads have been at the elementary- and middle-school levels, places that support a generalist ethos and to which teachers often come without strong disciplinary commitments. Indeed, the much repeated slogan of the elementary school teacher, "I teach children, not subject matters," is often held up as justification for an approach that speaks to children's needs, not the arcane and developmentally questionable commitments of disciplinary associations.

However, many curricula developed at these grade levels, while called interdisciplinary, are actually "pre-disciplinary," organized around common-sense themes that draw little on disciplinary ways of knowing (Gardner & Boix Mansilla, 1994). Sometimes the label "interdisciplinarity" simply means that the curriculum possesses a common theme but lacks an overarching framework or connecting structure. In one elementary classroom observed by Applebee, Burroughs, and Cruz (chapter 5, this volume), the teacher darted from the topic of libraries to farms to street signs to No Smoking signs to an activity engaging students in their own "don't wants," all in the space of a mid-morning lesson. No wonder that when a youngster was asked by the researcher why his teacher "mixes up" different subjects, his response registered bafflement: "I don't know how she mixes it up, she just mixes it up." What tends to happen with such curricula is that disciplines become storehouses containing topics for classroom activities; typically, however, only one part of a disciplinary storehouse is raided while another is systematically ignored. So, for example, in an interdisciplinary history and English curriculum, history becomes the site to explore information about events such as the American Revolution, the Great Depression, or the Civil Rights movement but not the place to learn about the evidentiary nature of historical knowing, the ever-present tension between historical continuity and change, the tentative nature of historical claims, or how and why historians change their minds about the past. English, in contrast, often becomes the storehouse for fictional works related to these events or for writing assignments, but rarely for discussions of why certain texts have attained canonical status or for understanding multiple critical perspectives on a single text. In other words, the "disciplined" part of *disciplinary* tends to fall away, leaving a body of information without the tools for evaluating its quality or warrant.

Such concerns, however, are rarely the ones that make it to the top of the list when teachers or administrators deliberate over interdisciplinary curriculum. Often the choice to implement a new curriculum is based on symbolic factors, such as a desire to be seen as progressive and in the forefront of reform (Hammerness & Moffett, chapter 7, this volume). Other times the fuel behind the interdisciplinary push is the desire to solve problems of fragmentation in the school curriculum and to address the psychological and social needs of students and teachers (Brandes & Seixas, chapter 8, this volume). Sometimes the choice is hardly a choice at all, as is the case when teachers respond to an administrative mandate to implement curricula chosen by others (Siskin, chapter 9, this volume).

In the world of school, as Boix Mansilla, Miller, and Gardner (chapter 1, this volume) note, it is the structural and organizational features of interdisciplinarity—issues of blocking schedules or coordinating joint planning periods—that too often overshadow what interdisciplinarity offers as *an intellectual experience*, especially what it offers that traditional disciplinary approaches do not.

A BRIEF HISTORICAL CONTEXT

As John Goodlad points out in the Foreword to this volume, movements to create interdisciplinary curriculum have ebbed and flowed in American education across the entire century, both in higher education as well as at K–12 levels. At the university level, enormous bursts of energy surrounded "general education" movements during the first part of this century; influential innovations such as Robert Maynard Hutchins's "Great Books" curriculum at the University of Chicago, the Western Civilization courses at Columbia, or the "Social and Economic Institutions" courses developed at Amherst College in years prior to World War I provided models for the rest of the country (Klein, 1990). These courses and their imitators responded to deep fears of increased specialization that accompanied the explosion of scientific knowledge in the first quarter of the 20th century. At the heart of this movement was the belief that an educated person needed synoptic frameworks for understanding advances in knowledge that seemed to multiply at exponential rates. Interdisciplinarity, particularly in the guise of general education, became a pedagogical response for helping students construct these synthetic frameworks, as well as discouraging them from becoming fixated on one narrow corner of the academic curriculum.

Many of the earliest attempts at interdisciplinarity took the form of "borrowing," in which techniques used in one field were appropriated by another. So, for example, psychology, as it came to take shape in the American research university, became increasingly mathematical, borrowing mathematical techniques from statistics and methods of experimentation from the natural sciences. (This borrowing, however, was typically one-sided, with soft sciences borrowing much more frequently from the hard sciences, in part to improve their own status within the university.) Borrowing paved the way for the creation of hybrid fields, based largely on common areas of interest rather than fidelity to a single discipline. By the 1950s, new academic areas, majors, and centers, organized around "area studies," began to appear on college campuses. These new arrangements did not constitute a rejection of traditional disciplines per se but were based on the belief that a given problem could be better illuminated by applying multiple disciplinary lenses to it. Particularly in the social sciences, it was widely believed that issues of social life were simply too complex to be captured by a singular way of knowing. At Harvard, for example, this led to the creation of the Department of Social Relations, which brought together psychologists, sociologists, anthropologists, and other interested "behavioral" scientists. These models, however, did not reject disciplinarity but rather sought to build upon disciplinary achievements.

More recently, interdisciplinary movements in higher education have taken a less respectful stance toward the traditional disciplines. Indeed, the disciplines have come under particular attack from postmodern scholars. From the vantage point of postmodernism, the disciplines are viewed as communities of power whose members seek to protect their own interests rather than pursue the disinterested advance of knowledge (Messer-Davidow, Shumway, & Sylvan, 1993). Gaining support from Foucault's studies of culture and society, postmodern scholars reject the argument that the traditional disciplines represent natural or intuitive ways of carving up the world. Instead, the disciplines are viewed as one of a host of oppressive social arrangements that systematically privilege one group over another—excluding women and minorities, elevating the Western experience over others, all the while proclaiming objectivity but seeking in actuality to control and dominate (Foucault, 1977).

The postmodern turn has left its imprint on the face of the modern university, with a host of new areas and fields—feminism, multiculturalism, gay and lesbian studies, cultural and gender studies—clamoring for space alongside traditional academic departments. Yet, as Robert Scholes (1985) has argued, those who seek to problematize disciplines must first be deeply rooted in them. A successful or persuasive act of deconstruction requires more than a passing acquaintance with the issues of how disciplines are put together (Messer-Davidow et al., 1993). The ability to discern a weak from a strong disciplinary beam is something that only comes after sustained disciplinary apprenticeship. Rather than being erased by the postmodern assault, traditional disciplines have increasingly integrated aspects of this critique, and have emerged as conversation partners rather than arch enemies. For many postmodern scholars, such as the critic of anthropology who himself was a specialist in anthropological methodology or the postmodern textualist who was an expert in Shakespeare (Brandes & Seixas, chapter 8, this volume), the disciplines continue to serve as unavoidable points of departure.

K–12 SETTINGS

The history of interdisciplinary curriculum in K–12 settings offers both parallels with and divergences from the contexts of higher education. Like their colleagues in universities, K–12 curriculum developers have been concerned with the overspecialization of knowledge and the fragmentation of the curriculum and have looked to interdisciplinary curricula as a unifying and integrating force. On the one hand, such innovations as the "core program" of the Oak Ridge, Tennessee schools in the 1950s (Capehart, 1958), which focused on common understandings and general problem-solving strategies, offered direct parallels to trends at the university level. On the other hand, there is a different flavor to the discussions of interdisciplinarity depending on whether they occur in a university seminar or a middle school teachers' lounge. While university discussions take diverse disciplinary ways of knowing and the use of different disciplinary tools for granted, such issues may get little air space in an elementary- or middle-school conversation (cf., Shaw, 1993, cited in Black, 1997). Interdisciplinarity is not viewed so much as an intellectual problem but as a practical solution, a means to increase motivation among students and teachers and create a more healthy social and psychological environment in the school setting.

This different focus has its roots in the earliest forms of interdisciplinary curricula in school settings. Klein (1990) cites, in particular, the "correlation" theories of the Herbartians, and their belief that the child's ability to make connections across diverse intellectual areas was the secret to intellectual growth. Notions of correlation and the parallel concept of "integrative education" stimulated enormous interest in the first half of this century. In 1935, the yearbook for the National Education Association focused on "Integration: Its Meaning and Application." Over 20 years later, in 1958, interest was unabated with the publication of the National Society for the Study of Education (NSSE) Yearbook, *The Integration of Educational Experiences*.

But it is a mistake to assume that these earlier uses of the words "interdisciplinary" and "integrative" bear the same meaning as they do today. To cite one example, Benjamin Bloom's use of the term "integrative" in his chapter in the 1958 NSSE Yearbook carried with it no particular cross-disciplinary meaning. Rather, Bloom was concerned with how experiences *within* a single course, such as high school American history, might be integrated, as when a teacher who discussed the Dred Scott decision linked this event to issues that motivated the Constitutional Convention or played a role in the authoring of the Federalist Papers.

Similarly, as John Goodlad noted in a chapter in the same 1958 volume, interdisciplinary curricula could stray away from any particular disciplinary tradition, as was the case with the "child study movement," which dominated teacher education in the 1940s and 1950s, or even the movement to create nongraded schools. Indeed, in the classic conflict between a "child-centered" or a "subject-centered" curriculum, the interdisciplinary banner was typically hoisted by the self-proclaimed advocates of children, and sometimes led to such curricular nonstarters as "family living," "health and safety," or "personality and etiquette."

One aspect that has showed stability across the century has been the difficulty of implementing and sustaining interdisciplinary interventions over the long haul. For example, many of the conflicts that arise in the settings described in this volume, such as the tendency of one discipline to be subservient to another in interdisciplinary marriages (Hamel, chapter 4; Roth, chapter 6; Wineburg & Grossman, chapter 3, all this volume), have long-standing roots in American curricular history. The experience of the Eight-Year Study (Aiken, 1942/1991), one of the largest educational innovations in this century, vividly illustrates this point.

The attempt to integrate subjects was only one of a bundle of innovations that were put into effect in the 30 schools participating in this study. But according to Wilford Aiken, chairman of the Progressive Education Association committee charged with evaluating the study and the author of its final report, it was a feature that looked good on paper but proved disastrous in practice. Then, as now, the impetus behind innovation was the desire "to break down walls" that separated "broad field from broad field" and created "artificial barriers" separating teacher from teacher. However, attempts to merge mathematics and science were "usually abandoned early" because most teachers perceived that the union was unnecessary and had "no sound basis." Hopes were higher for the successful integration of history and English until it was discovered that:

> English became "the handmaiden" of history, that the literature of some periods was too scarce to warrant spending much time on it, and that it became necessary to resort to artificial integration which was deemed worse than the evils which fusion sought to eliminate. Many teachers began to suspect that there was something fundamentally wrong in attempting to "put subjects together." . . . The visitor would have found in 1933 enthusiasm for fusion of subjects, but had he come again in 1936 he would have found doubt, discouragement, and a search for something better. (Aiken, 1942/1991, p. 53)

INTERDISCIPLINARY CURRICULUM TODAY

In another instance of educational amnesia, today's push to create interdisciplinary curricula is largely unburdened by a historical perspective on potential challenges and obstacles. Typical of contemporary calls to create interdisciplinary curricula is the how-to approach of Tchudi and Lafer (1996), who base their advice on a series of distinctions between "traditional instruction" and the approach they advocate, interdisciplinary knowing. They argue that interdisciplinary knowing offers an alternative to the "stranglehold of disciplinary knowledge" which provides students with "canonical" or "standard knowledge." In its stead, their approach would offer a curriculum of "constructed knowledge" pursued by invigorated students working "in the service of inquiry" (Tchudi, 1994; Tchudi & Lafer, 1996). Their language suggests the tendency to conflate what is taught with how it is taught; interdisciplinary knowing stands not only for curriculum innovation but as an antidote to "traditional instruction." Similarly, interdisciplinary curriculum is automatically equated with a student-centered classroom.

The problem with these kinds of statements (besides their idealized images and either-or thinking) is that advocacy has far outpaced careful description of what happens when new curricula are put into practice. Despite the popularity of interdisciplinary curricula across the nation, there is no body of evidence that attests to greater learning in high-quality interdisciplinary versus high-quality disciplinary classrooms. The problem goes well beyond the lack of data on student achievement. The existing literature on this topic (cf., Adler & Flihan, 1997) is almost entirely comprised of idealized descriptions of programs and how to put them in place, and almost entirely devoid of descriptions of what actually happens when theory meets school practice. We know nearly nothing about what occurs when teachers from different walks of life and different academic backgrounds join together to thrash out programs for student learning. We know even less about what happens when integrated curricula, hatched in well-funded educational "hothouses," are let loose across sprawling urban districts with competing interests and educational traditions. We don't even have a good idea of how children across different grade levels make sense of teachers' attempts to merge different subjects and curriculum. In light of these gaps, claims about the salutary effects of new curricula should be viewed with caution.

The chapters in this volume begin to address these gaps in our understanding. Together they shed light on how teachers' different understandings of the disciplines—different from each other, different from university scholars, different from administrators, and different from students—must be taken into account before the success of any intervention can be guaranteed. The chapters take up questions across an array of educational settings, from elementary- and middle-school settings to high schools to school-university partnerships and new forms of teacher interaction using technology. Despite this variety, several common themes cut across the individual chapters. Some of these themes refine our understanding of problems in the interdisciplinary movement, while others simply reflect the state of the field.

Issues of Definition

The lack of common definitions about what constitutes interdisciplinarity, for example, falls into the latter category. When people hold different meanings of the same words they end up talking past each other, thinking they agree (or disagree) when in fact they have failed to understand each other in the first place. The problem here is not a shortage of schemes that have sought to differentiate among curricular integration, fusion, integrative, cross-disciplinary, or interdisciplinary, approaches but rather the inability of any one of these schemes to impose conceptual order among multiple audiences. Even in this volume similar terms are used in different ways.

For example, Boix Mansilla, Miller, and Gardner (chapter 1) see interdisciplinary work resting on the use of intellectual tools from more than one discipline. Rényi (chapter 2), on the other hand, would view this approach as "multidisciplinary" and would reserve the term "interdisciplinary" for the *simultaneous* use of several disciplinary tools. In their chapter, Hammerness and Moffett don't engage in a definitional process but instead describe the conflicting definitions of those who enact interdisciplinary curricula in schools. Similarly, Brandes and Seixas (chapter 8) show how the lack of shared definitions across educational levels brought teachers to the university expecting one thing only to be offered another. In chapter 5, Applebee and colleagues make an attempt at conceptual housekeeping and offer a typology that plots interdisciplinary curriculum on a continuum from correlated to reconstructed approaches. But the last 50 years have witnessed dozens of typologies (cf., Henry, 1958), and the meanings given to these terms have seemed to proliferate, not narrow, in the face of these typologies. As editors we have resisted any attempt to codify or impose a singular set of definitions in this volume. The lack of agreement over the terms of the debate simply reflects the disorderly state of the art.

Disjunctures Between Levels

One theme that echoes across these chapters is the gulf between notions of interdisciplinarity in university settings and how these notions are understood in K–12 contexts. Particularly in the humanities, the issue of interdisciplinarity on university campuses becomes "problematized," and reflects the postmodern awareness about the positionality of knowledge, its construction and use. Debates about these issues are heady and result in the organization of conferences, the production of monographs, and the development of fresh perspectives that challenge traditional disciplinary communities. Even with these newer perspectives, the nature of knowledge—who controls, disseminates, and regulates it—remains in the forefront (e.g., Messer-Davidow et al., 1993). But as several of the chapters here demonstrate, issues of knowledge can be quite distant from the concerns of those who enact interdisciplinary curricula in schools. While a university geographer and literary critic might ask, What is a map, and how do maps reflect the unequal distribution of resources, school teachers have different concerns (Brandes & Seixas, chapter 8, in this volume). The question more typically asked when social studies is combined with language arts tends to be, Can the language arts teacher teach "mapping skills"?

In schools, the motivational and emotional concerns of students often dictate curriculum choice. And so, historical fiction is used to excite students and "make history come alive," rather than as an opportunity for students to think hard about what makes one story "fictional" and another "historical" (Applebee et al., chapter 5, this volume). Whereas interdisciplinarity at the university level typically follows from an intellectual impulse, the push at the school level, as Siskin shows (chapter 9, this volume), is often an administrative mandate. The frantic response to these dictates leads naturally to a focus on the most immediate concerns, such as which materials to use on Monday. Other times it leads to curriculum selection based less on sound educational practice and more on what fits a preselected theme (Roth, chapter 6, this volume). One English teacher, interviewed by Black (1997), chose to teach Conrad Richter's novel *The Light in the Forest* because her interdisciplinary team had selected forests as their theme, and the book had the word "Forest" in the title.

The Role of Dialogue

It is clear from the approaches described here that time for teachers to talk and debate issues of curriculum is central to the success of any curriculum intervention. Teachers' ability to understand one another comes only after sustained engagement with ideas, as well as the time and space to talk about them openly. The notion that teachers can sit down in a 2-hour planning meeting and easily convey to one another the pillars of their disciplines ignores the nature of disciplinary socialization, where ideas and conceptions become part of a working vocabulary that over time becomes tacit and assumed. In other words, disciplinary assumptions become a taken-for-granted aspect of thought. As we note in chapter 3, even when teachers are provided with a forum for putting disciplinary differences on the table, the sheer novelty of the forum and the lack of experience in this form of talk leads people to label their disagreements in terms of personality conflicts and other personal issues, rather than seeing them as a set of more or less systematic epistemological differences about how to read texts. This process may be even more difficult in the elementary school context in which teachers may not undergo a strong disciplinary socialization in any one discipline, making issues of disciplinarity all the more distant from their own experiences as learners. Even in the secondary school context, many departments house teachers with diverse disciplinary backgrounds; social studies, for example, brings together teachers with a wide array of college specializations, from geography to history, sociology to political science.

Making disciplinary assumptions explicit is not necessarily a linear process easily depicted on a flowchart. Particularly when people care deeply about the issues involved, the process invariably engenders disagreement, misunderstanding, and conflict. Even when teachers have the opportunity to talk through these differences, the ability to forge new understandings of another's discipline, and understand how it differs from one's own (rather than being a slightly different version of one's own) is a partial process measured in terms of degree. As Hamel notes in chapter 4, while some scholars might claim that the world doesn't come carved up in disciplines, it is clear that for many teachers disciplines provide powerful lenses for interpreting the world of schooling. As adults, we abandon our existing ways of seeing only after much struggle, and even then with much reluctance. Without extended time to engage each other as learners and the space to thrash out differences, there is little chance that joint planning sessions will go beyond collaborations of convenience.

But what happens when talk is aborted and dialogue silenced, as in the high school studied by Hammerness and Moffett (chapter 7, this volume)? There, the implementation of an interdisciplinary curriculum at the high school level took on symbolic meaning, pitting teacher against teacher. Because teachers on the different sides of the divide—those committed to what traditional disciplines had to offer students and those willing to create new interdisciplinary experiences—had no forum in which to discuss their differences, a polarization resulted. Like a dysfunctional family with well-known but unspoken secrets, the faculty brokered an uneasy truce. In this case, as in so many others like it, students were the unlucky beneficiaries of this stalemate.

The Discipline in Interdisciplinary

The final theme which arises from these chapters is the extent to which solid interdisciplinary work does not seek a flight from the disciplines but rather uses them as resources upon which to create opportunities for children's learning. As Rényi points out in her account of New Mexico's Zia Elementary School (chapter 2, in this volume), this interdisciplinary architecture project could have easily degenerated into yet another diorama of model pueblos. What prevented this was the commitment by teachers to their *own* learning. Years before embarking on a project with students, teachers took up a sustained program of study to make sure that they understood the underlying principles of mathematics, geography, and design behind the project. When it came time to engage children in this project, teachers made sure that these disciplinary principles were not forgotten. The success of this interdisciplinary project, as Rényi notes, resulted because "a watchful eye" was kept on the disciplinary learnings that supported the entire enterprise.

The same theme is amplified in the account of William Miller's classroom (chapter 1, in this volume). Miller's interdisciplinary unit on the Holocaust pays explicit attention to different ways of knowing in history and the social sciences, from how historians place a premium on locating events in time while building explanatory contexts, to how psychologists (such as Stanley Milgram, in his studies of obedience) sometimes isolate phenomena from their contexts in order to study and manipulate them experimentally. It was attention to these different forms of knowing that allowed Miller's students to develop a "meta-perspective" on the disciplines and to use that knowledge flexibly.

In both the Zia and Miller cases, topics were chosen that were amenable to interdisciplinary approaches: architecture is by definition an interdisciplinary enterprise, and the many dimensions of the Holocaust naturally give rise to multidisciplinary perspectives (cf., Friedlander, 1992). But as is clear from Roth's cautionary tale in chapter 6, the selection of the wrong topic or theme can serve as an impediment to student learning, even when teachers are keenly attuned to the disciplinary principles they want students to master. In Roth's interdisciplinary science-social studies unit on 1492, the themes of diversity and interdependence sounded good on paper. In practice, however, this meant that fifth-grade students were learning about North American plant life by jumping into the middle of the story, without first having understood principles of food chains or the cycling of matter in ecosystems. In the end, one discipline ended up as the handmaiden to the other, and Roth, a science educator, felt like she was teaching social studies. For students, the unit made as much sense as the "photosynthesis of Columbus." Yet it was precisely Roth's understanding of science and her understanding of the intellectual challenges that science presents to young children that allowed her to see what was being sacrificed in this unit. It is unlikely that a teacher without this disciplinary knowledge would have detected any great problem in student learning.

CONCLUSION

The chapters we have assembled here constitute neither a brief for nor an argument against interdisciplinary curriculum. They do not answer the question: Which kind of curriculum, traditional subject-based or interdisciplinary, is better? In fact, we think this is the wrong question: a trivialization of a complex issue that invites polarized rhetoric and simplistic response. Intellectual connectedness and integration go on in both traditional disciplinary classrooms and in innovative interdisciplinary ones. The larger problem for students is too often that they go on in neither.

What this collection does offer is a richer set of questions about a phenomenon that has spread rapidly across educational settings from coast to coast. For example, what do teachers need to know about their own discipline in order to work productively in interdisciplinary groups? What kinds of learning opportunities must teachers be provided with to create intellectually worthwhile learning experiences for children? How does the opportunity to work on interdisciplinary curricula allow teachers to understand similarities in disciplinary approaches as well as authentic points of divergence? Questions also arise regarding student learning. How can interdisciplinary approaches lead children to understand the complexity of human knowledge rather than to simplify this complexity into a formless mass of idealized "inquiry" or "research" skills? Such questions, we hope, will initiate a conversation about what happens when lofty educational aims are put into practice across diverse settings. We view this volume, and the questions it raises, as a modest attempt to start the conversation.

NOTE

The preparation of this book was supported by grants from the James S. McDonnell Foundation and the John D. and Catherine T. MacArthur Foundation/ Spencer Foundation Professional Development Research and Documentation

Program. We are grateful to both programs, while noting that the content of this book is solely the responsibility of the authors.

REFERENCES

Adler, M., & Flihan, S. (1997). *The interdisciplinary continuum: Reconciling theory, research and practice*. Albany, NY: National Research Center on English Learning and Achievement. (Report Series 2.36)

Aiken, W. M. (1942/1991). *The story of the eight-year study*. New York: Harper. (Republished by UMI, Ann Arbor)

Becher, T. (1989). *Academic tribes and territories: Intellectual enquiry and the cultures of disciplines*. Milton Keynes, England: Open University Press.

Black, S. (1997). Branches of knowledge. *American School Board Journal, 184*, 35–37.

Bloom, B. S. (1958). Ideas, problems, and methods of inquiry. In N. B. Henry (Ed.), *The integration of educational experiences* (pp. 84–104). The 57th Yearbook of the National Society for the Study of Education. Chicago: University of Chicago Press.

Brandt, R. (1991). On interdisciplinary curriculum: A Conversation with Heidi Hayes Jacobs. *Educational Leadership, 49*, 24–26.

Bruner, J. S. (1986). *Actual minds, possible worlds*. Cambridge, MA: Harvard University Press.

Capehart, B. E. (1958). Illustrative courses and programs in selected secondary schools. In N. B. Henry (Ed.), *The integration of educational experiences* (pp. 194–217). [The 57th Yearbook of the National Society for the Study of Education.] Chicago: University of Chicago Press.

Case, R. (1994). Our crude handling of educational reform: The case of curricular integration. *Canadian Journal of Education, 19*, 80–93.

Cawelti, G. (1994). *High school restructuring: A national study*. Arlington, VA: Educational Research Service.

Foucault, M. (1977). *Discipline and punish: The birth of the prison* (A. Sheridan, Trans.). New York: Pantheon Books.

Friedlander, S. (1992). *Probing the limits of representation: Nazism and the Final Solution*. Cambridge, MA: Harvard University Press.

Gardner, H. & Boix Mansilla, V. (1994). Teaching for understanding in the disciplines and beyond. *Teachers College Record, 96*, 198–218.

Goodlad, J. I. (1958). Illustrative programs and procedures in elementary schools. In N. B. Henry (Ed.), *The integration of educational experiences* (pp. 173–193). The 57th Yearbook of the National Society for the Study of Education. Chicago: University of Chicago Press.

Grossman, P. L., & Stodolsky, S. S. (1995). Content as context: The role of school subjects in secondary school teaching. *Educational Researcher, 24*, 5–11.

Henry, N. B. (1958). *The integration of educational experiences*. [The 57th Yearbook of the National Society for the Study of Education.] Chicago: University of Chicago Press.

Klein, J. T. (1990). *Interdisciplinarity: History, theory, practice.* Detroit: Wayne State University.

Little, J. W. (1997). *Collegial ties and interdisciplinary negotiations in the high school.* Paper presented at the annual meeting of the American Educational Research Association, Chicago.

Messer-Davidow, E., Shumway, D. R., & Sylvan, D. J. (Eds.). (1993). *Knowledges: Historical and critical studies in disciplinarity.* Charlottesville: University of Virginia Press.

Scholes, R. E. (1985). *Textual power: Literary theory and the teaching of English.* New Haven, CT: Yale University Press.

Tchudi, S. (1994). Interdisciplinary English and re-forming the schools. *English Journal, 7,* 54–61.

Tchudi, S., & Lafer, S. (1996). *The interdisciplinary teacher's handbook: Integrated teaching across the curriculum.* Portsmouth, NH: Boynton/Cook.

Tyack, D., & Tobin, W. (1994). The "grammar" of schooling: Why has it been so hard to change? *American Educational Research Journal, 31,* 453–479.

1

On Disciplinary Lenses and Interdisciplinary Work

VERONICA BOIX MANSILLA, WILLIAM C. MILLER, AND HOWARD GARDNER

THE DISCIPLINES IN QUESTION

A tension about the status of scholarly disciplines pervades the contemporary educational world. On the one hand, secondary schools are typically organized around disciplines, as they have been for many years. The newest national standards are set forth by disciplinary groups such as the National Council for the Teaching of Mathematics or the National Council for History in Schools; national and international comparisons are based on students' work in the disciplines. Yet, on the other hand, the disciplines seem to many an anachronistic arrangement of knowledge. Increasingly colleges and universities are organized around subdisciplines, specialties, and centers. Contemporary research is heavily problem-driven, drawing freely on a number of disciplines and subdisciplines. Postmodern critiques question the tenability of any rigid demarcation of knowledge.

Is this tension inevitable? Must one be for or against disciplinary knowledge? Or can one have the best of both—*disciplinary* and *interdisciplinary*—perspectives? In this chapter we argue that an education geared toward deep forms of understanding can make use of both perspectives. Such an education can help students integrate knowledge and modes of thinking from various disciplines to create products, solve problems, and offer explanations of the multiple worlds in which they live. In our formulation students demonstrate *disciplinary understanding* when they are able to use knowledge and ways of thinking in the disciplines appropriately in novel situations: Such usage should share at least some commonalties with expert practice in these disciplines (Gardner & Boix Mansilla, 1994). Proceeding along the same lines, students demonstrate *interdisciplinary understanding* when they integrate knowledge and modes of thinking from two or more disciplines in order to create products, solve problems, and offer explanations of the world around them.

In this chapter we argue that students should direct most of their energy toward mastering individual disciplines but that they should be ever mindful of gritty problems that are best approached by bringing disciplinary lenses together. We propose that disciplines like history or science are not collections of certified facts; rather, they are *lenses* through which we look at the world and interpret it. The disciplines raise healthy skepticism about what is known and provide concepts and modes of thinking that have been valued by knowledgeable experts over time. They orient our attention to specific questions about the world (e.g., universal and unique aspects of human behavior) and provide us with standards for what counts as viable answers to such questions (e.g., statistics, experimental designs, and historical source interpretation).

We propose that students may use various disciplines in multi- or interdisciplinary ways to address a particular problem in valuable ways. In multidisciplinary work, disciplines are juxtaposed with each other. Students move from one disciplinary perspective to the next without attempting to interrelate disciplinary perspectives. In truly interdisciplinary work, concepts and modes of thinking in more than one discipline are brought together synergistically to illuminate issues that cannot be adequately tested through one discipline. In this chapter, we claim that the path toward *interdisciplinary understanding* is filled with difficulties and unintended consequences (e.g., failure to move beyond common sense, failure to treat individual disciplines carefully, failure to integrate disciplinary perspectives).

To illustrate our argument, we examine a secondary level unit on Nazi Germany and the Holocaust taught by William Miller and James MacNeil in which students are tested in their understanding of history and science. Specifically, we portray students' attempts to intertwine history and psychology in order to explain obedience to malevolent authority on the part of ordinary people in Nazi Germany; and students' effort to bring together history and biology to explain how pseudoscientific theories of race were popularized during the period.

HISTORY AND SCIENCE: TWO DISTINCT LENSES

Historians ask: "How did things come to be the way they were in Nazi Germany?" "How did people experience the societal changes in Germany at that particular time?" Historical narratives organize events related to this period (e.g., incidents of discrimination, social policies, demographic shifts), proposing interpretations that confer a measure of coherence on the events. Knowledge in history emerges from careful interpretation of texts and documents, leveraged by interpretations proposed by knowledgeable disciplinarians. Such narratives explain events by scrutinizing people's worldviews and motivations (e.g., the different perspectives of the actors). Furthermore, historical narratives examine the broader social and economic conditions that shaped and constrained people's actions at the time.

When confronted with a phenomenon like Nazi totalitarianism, scientists ask: "Is race a tenable biological concept?" "What are the biological foundations of distinctions in the human species?" Scientific theories and laws purport to explain and predict natural patterns (e.g., patterns of trait inheritance). A central premise underlying the construction of scientific knowledge is that theories about such phenomena are constructed and stand in relation to bodies of empirical evidence. Scientific knowledge emerges through a process that entails generating hypotheses, testing them experimentally, and interpreting findings.

In the next section we visit a middle-school classroom where these disciplinary modes of thinking are being engaged. We examine how history and science inform each other as they shed light on the rise of Nazi totalitarianism. Then we examine our proposed definition of "interdisciplinary understanding" in light of obstacles and possibilities for such understanding in selected educational settings.

TWO CASES OF DISCIPLINARY CROSS-FERTILIZATION

William Miller teaches an eighth-grade social studies course in a public school in Concord, Massachusetts. Within a broader exploration of conditions that create a just society, Miller dedicates 10 weeks of the year to the study of Nazi Germany and the Holocaust using a Facing History and Ourselves curriculum (FHAO curricula seek students' understanding of the complexities of history—individuals and society over time). Students begin this portion of the course by examining the question, *How did the Nazis create a totalitarian state that failed to ensure conditions for justice?* Concepts like obedience to authority and Aryan supremacy are central to the creation of the Nazi totalitarian state. To help students understand how human beings come to accept and obey an evil bureaucratic authority, Miller uses both a historical and a psychological perspective. Students enrich their understanding of the period with an analysis of psychologist Stanley Milgram's obedience experiments. To understand how the notion of the superiority of the Aryan race became a "scientifically validated" popular belief among ordinary people, Miller draws on the disciplines of history and biology.

In collaboration with science colleague James MacNeil, Miller invites students to examine the eugenics movement in Germany both as a scientific program and a historical movement. In both cases of interdisciplinary work, students face the challenge of explaining the creation of totalitarianism under the Nazi regime in ways that go beyond common sense. Miller's experience prompts the following questions: How are history, psychology, and biology combined in these students' understanding? How do different disciplinary approaches inform one another while preserving their disciplinary integrity? How can students' performances go beyond simple common sense?

Case One: Obedience to Authority

Obedience to Authority Through a Historical Lens.   From a historical point of view, understanding obedience in early Nazi Germany requires an appreciation of the political, cultural, and economic conditions that allowed Hitler to consolidate power, and allowed the Nazi authoritarian ideology to take ground in the 1920s and early 1930s. Understanding this obedience also entails grasping the experiences and worldviews held by various historical actors (e.g., ordinary Germans, Jews, bureaucrats) at the time (Browning, 1992). Through interpretation of fragmented remnants of the past, historians seek to explain how the new moral and political order was progressively established in the collective psyche by the skillful use of propagandistic art, pageantlike Nazi rallies, and specific educational regimes.

Obedience to Authority Through a Psychological Lens.   Social psychologist Stanley Milgram explored the dynamics of obedience to authority with a sample of adult American men (Blass, 1991; Milgram, 1974/1997). Subjects were asked to administer progressively strong electrical shocks to "learners" (actors pretending to receive shocks) every time learners made a mistake in a memorization task. When ordered to do so by an experimenter who did not possess any coercive power to enforce his commands,

65% of the men in the sample proved willing to punish another person with increasingly higher voltages to the maximum (450 volts).

Far-reaching implications have been drawn from Milgram's research. Human beings show an unexpectedly high inclination to obey orders. This line of research strongly challenges the belief that only Germans or only sadists would willingly hurt a helpless victim. In addition, Milgram's research suggests a variety of situational factors that predict the extent of obedient behavior (Blass, 1991).

A psychological perspective provides us with reliable accounts of conditions that favor obedient behavior. It also allows us to generalize observed experimental findings to the broader populations from which samples are drawn. In addition, a psychological lens invites us to consider alternative variables such as subjects' character and prior experience with authority.

History and Psychology Intertwined. How might history and psychology work together to inform our understanding of obedience in the early years of Nazi totalitarianism? In *interdisciplinary understanding,* concepts or findings as well as specific modes of thinking in each discipline are woven together to shed new light on the problem. For example, Milgram's experiments inform our historical understanding by opening up the counterintuitive possibility that, given certain conditions, ordinary adults may obey evil orders in the absence of coercion. Furthermore, these experiments orient our attention to specific situational factors that might have contributed to fostering obedience in Nazi Germany (e.g., the symbolic power of the bureaucratic establishment, the anonymous suffering of targeted groups).

Another area of cross-fertilization lies in the efforts made by each discipline to probe the inner worlds of individuals. Milgram's experimental program calls for a reflection about alternative variables and competing explanations (e.g., inner dispositions toward authority, experience of abuse, character) to predict subjects' observed responses. By exploring a wide range of variables associated with obedience, psychologists aim at describing and explaining subjects' behavior—rather than judging their moral status. Milgram's subjects help counter the tendency to demonize ordinary Germans as inhabitants of an incomprehensible world. Instead they prepare us for a rational understanding of historical actors—one that seeks to consider their point of view, values, beliefs, and the options available to them at particular moments in time.

Finally, while Milgram's experiments shed light on various aspects of the German experience, they fail to provide a satisfying explanation of obedience as a historical phenomenon. As Browning (1992) points out, understanding the role that obedience played in the creation of the totalitarian state requires that we place human behavior in the midst of larger societal and cultural forces of the time. The economic and moral crisis following Germany's defeat in World War I and the Treaty of Versailles, the prevalent long-lasting anti-Semitism, the systematic Nazi indoctrination, and the use of sophisticated propaganda were historical conditions that shaped the German meaning of "authority" and "obedience" in the minds of specific actors at a particular time.

Obedience to Authority in Miller's Class. Miller's students examine "obedience to authority" as a psychological phenomenon, to inform their understanding of "obedience to authority" as a historical one. Early in the unit they watch a documentary of Milgram's experiments. After the video, they are challenged to interpret the observed results. Why do some people stop applying electrical shocks to their supposed victims? Why do some continue? What do we learn about human behavior from Milgram's experiment? The power of these questions lies in Miller's insistence that students "look deeply" before responding. He challenges students to probe their own initial explanations in search for deeper interpretations.

Simple answers such as "because they felt they had to follow orders" are unacceptable in Miller's class. He expects answers that identify situational variables affecting subjects' behavior (e.g., visibility of the suffering victims, scientific appearance of the setting) or propose competing hypotheses to explain Milgram's results. Challenging students to empathize with subjects and speculate about their inner worlds, Miller welcomes hypotheses about how subjects might have experienced authority during childhood, their stories of abuse, or the difficulty for isolated individuals to stand up against what they perceive to be empowered institutions. Ultimately, he expects that understanding Milgram's experiments will predispose students to understand the experience of the ordinary Germans who endorsed or at least did not resist the totalitarian regime.

"What does this have to do with Nazi Germany?" With this question Miller leads students into the uncertain interdisciplinary terrain. Their challenge is to capitalize on the fruitful cross-fertilization between psychology and history without succumbing to facile connections. Students who have not yet reached *interdisciplinary understanding* may give common-sensical opinions of how Germans came to obey an evil political regime. For example, they may express their outrage without any effort to consider complex patterns of obedient behavior nor the particular historical factors that might have influenced ordinary Germans' actions at the time.

In contrast, students go beyond common sense and demonstrate an *interdisciplinary understanding* of obedience when they use Milgram's findings to support the thesis that ordinary Germans *might have been willing* to attribute great authority to the German establishment. Such students' explanations do not draw on psychological aspects of human behavior alone. Instead they describe how broader societal forces such as the economic crisis following the Treaty of Versailles or the long-lasting anti-Semitism embodied in German culture provided ripe conditions for obedient behavior. Such explanations counter the common-sense tendency to reduce historical actors to cardboard heroes and villains.

Case Two: Eugenics

How did the notion of the superiority of the Aryan race become a "scientifically validated" belief among ordinary German people? Eugenics, the science concerned with the control of hereditary traits through selective mating, constituted the racist intellectual foundation of German totalitarianism. Understanding eugenics requires that we grasp (1) the scientific basis (and misconceptions) on which its theories were built, and (2) the historical contexts that influenced the development and popularity of this theory. In other words, we must understand the emergence of eugenics as a science and place it in the broader historical context of Germany after the First World War.

Eugenics Through a Scientific Lens.   Eugenicists were attracted by the explanatory power of "single gene determinants" as a characterization of human traits. Their research program sought to explain the heredity of human "traits" such as intellectual ability, physical strength, alcoholism, and criminality. They believed that such traits were genetically encoded and could be preserved or eliminated through rational human mating policies (Glass, 1997; Kevles, 1995; Müller-Hill, 1998).

In contrast to the sophisticated accounts of genetic coding provided by contemporary scientists, the "findings" reported by early 20th century eugenicists proved problematic in three major ways: (1) the measurement instruments used to determine "traits" such as intelligence or poverty lacked validity; (2) findings were rooted in the erroneous assumption that complex and heterogeneous phenomena such as poverty, success, crime, or insanity could be assigned to the actions of single genes; and most importantly; (3) eugenicists were typically more interested in *proving* that their hypotheses about genetically encoded "racial" differences were right rather than *testing* whether or not such hypotheses withstand systematic scrutiny (Hunt, 1995; Macrakis, 1993; Pearl, 1908).

Eugenics Through a Historical Lens.   As early as the 1920s, race became a focal point for scholars, including anatomists and psychiatrists, as well as professionals such as lawyers and public health officials. In Germany, officials were obsessed with rebuilding a genetically fit race, which had supposedly been decimated by the losses of the First World War (Glass, 1997; Kevles, 1995).   Hitler used the work of German eugenicists to support his theory of the supremacy of the Aryan race as well as his depiction of the Jews as a contaminating threat to the German genetic pool. By the early 1930s the eugenic policies that emphasized collective health gave way to one that focused on the dangers of blood pollution. In this unsettling context, Jews and other minorities became the scapegoats on whom to project collective frustration (Beyerchen, 1992).

Intertwining History and Science.   How can science and history be intertwined to explain the role of eugenics in the creation of the Nazi totalitarian state? An *interdisciplinary understanding* of eugenics draws on concepts, findings, and modes of thinking that are specific to history and science and brings them together synergistically. For example, by bringing together scientific concepts like "inheritance" and historical ones like "political change," performances of *interdisciplinary understanding* place eugenics findings in the broader context of post-World War I Germany.

Interdisciplinary understanding also illuminates how the sociohistorical conditions of Germany after World War I shaped the eugenics scientific research program to the point of compromising its scientific integrity. Biological science during this period was characterized by its absorption in politics; it came to share Nazi assumptions about race and inheritance, which resulted in generous economic government support for eugenics research. To understand the ways in which the scientific integrity of the research program was compromised, we must master general scientific processes, like hypothesis testing, as well as specific scientific claims such as the untenability of single gene explanations of complex sociocultural phenomena.

Finally, historical modes of thinking help us understand eugenics in its appropriate context (Gardiner, 1989). History alerts us to the temptation to produce oversimplified accounts of eugenicists and their work. For example, it challenges us to examine what eugenicists knew or did not know about genetic inheritance at the time rather than simply projecting current genetic knowledge onto their research programs. Furthermore, a historical view invites us to consider the motivations and constraints that these scientists experienced (e.g., honored scientific traditions, sociopolitical factors) and avoid a stereotypical portrayal of scientists as evil mercenaries of the Nazi regime (Gardiner, 1989).

Understanding Eugenics in Miller's Class. Miller's students examine eugenics as a scientific program and a social movement. They learn not only about the assumptions underlying such research but also about the methods used to reach conclusions (measurements used, populations selected, inferences made). Students take an intelligence test used by American eugenicists to inform immigration and sterilization decisions in the early 1910s and 1920s. Not surprisingly, many students in the class fail to perform at acceptable levels. In their journals they write about what it must have been like for people to have been declared "biologically unfit" and to undergo compulsory sterilization.

"What is the problem with these (eugenics) ideas? How could they have become so popular in Germany in the early 1930s?" With these questions, Miller and his science colleagues challenge students to produce coherent scientific and historical critiques of eugenics. Commonsensical answers such as "It's unfair" are considered insufficient because they fail to probe the scientific flaws underlying such ideas and the historical consequences that they brought about. In their discussion about eugenics, students are expected to go beyond their emotional reaction of anger to explain the broader sociopolitical conditions under which eugenicist ideas became popular. Miller values interventions that highlight eugenicists' dilemma of having to choose between being scientifically rigorous and losing political favor on the one hand, or engaging in pseudo-science to retain government support on the other. Students are challenged to critique the methods and assumptions underlying eugenicists' work. They are asked to explain how a biological view of social crisis rendered the so-called "Jewish problem" unsolvable, since one cannot change one's genes (Glass, 1997). Furthermore, students are challenged to examine how these biological ideas set the foundations for a widespread culture of eliminationist anti-Semitism completed with medical metaphors such as the necessary extirpations of tumors (Goldhagen, 1996).

DEFINING INTERDISCIPLINARY UNDERSTANDING

Our examples illustrate ways in which history and science are brought together in the service of a vital question: How did the Nazis create a totalitarian state which failed to preserve conditions for justice? Consistent with our definition, these cases illustrate how knowledge and modes of thinking from two or more disciplines can be integrated in ways that draw upon expert standards of practice in the disciplines involved. Three features are essential to our proposed definition of "interdisciplinary understanding": (1) an emphasis on knowledge use, (2) a careful treatment of each discipline involved, and (3) appropriate interaction between disciplines. In the following section, each criterion is illustrated with examples of Miller's students. We quote interview excerpts from four students—Shari, Jenine, Eron, and Sonia (all names are pseudonyms)—which illustrate more and less accomplished understandings.

Emphasizing Knowledge Use

Like disciplinary understanding, *interdisciplinary understanding* is more than recalling information or reasoning in uninformed intuitive ways. Students demonstrate *interdisciplinary understanding* when they are able to use what they have learned to solve problems, create products, or explain phenomena (Gardner, 1991; Perkins, Schwartz, West, & Wiske, 1995; Wiske, 1997). In their study of Nazi totalitarianism, some students may be tempted to list and memorize a series of events associated with the rise of Nazism but fail to draw on such information when they are challenged to explain how ordinary Germans came to endorse the Nazi regime.

Sonia illustrates a naïve approach, failing to incorporate historical or scientific knowledge in her explanations. In her reflection, eugenicist ideas are ill-defined. She explains the dissemination of such ideas using a naïve logic of friends and trust, failing to address broader social, cultural, and political enabling conditions:

> *Interviewer:* So, in your opinion—you tell me what you think—how was it possible that so many Germans participated in the killing of Jews and others?
>
> *Sonia:* I guess that Hitler somehow got this warped idea that Jews were not equals and he decided that they needed to be eliminated. He got a few people to work with him to get the message across that Jews were not equal and those people convinced more people—because I would trust what my friends say, maybe not exactly everything they say but they would certainly have a big influence on me.

In more successful examples of *interdisciplinary understanding*, students use what they have learned about the eugenics movement and Nazi Germany to interpret the role of eugenics in providing ordinary Germans with a "rationale" for genocide. They place such a "rationale" within the social, political, and economic context of totalitarian Germany.

> *Interviewer:* Why did you study eugenics in a unit where you were learning about how the Nazis created a totalitarian State?

Jenine: If I hadn't learned about eugenics I would really not quite understand why people in Germany took these ideas about the master race . . .

Interviewer: Can you tell me more?

Jenine: You really wouldn't know how people could even come to follow them. The scientists came to this conclusion that you could make the race better if you made sure that the Aryan people had children and all those who didn't fit the standards of the master race didn't [have children]. Scientists believed that they needed to improve the biology of the master race and that's why people couldn't mix with other races—they wanted to build a pure race. . . . Back then they thought it was true and people believed in it—therefore that gives sort of some excuse or whatever to see how these ideas were there and they influenced what people did. Eugenics ideas were spread all over the world. I think that people probably thought that scientists were these smart people so they trusted what they said. And this together with blind obedience, with inflation, with people being unhappy, and someone like Hitler. . . . It was not just eugenics but all together that lead to Nazism and the Holocaust.

Treating Each Discipline Carefully

Interdisciplinary understanding goes beyond its disciplinary counterpart in that it brings together two or more disciplinary approaches. Each disciplinary perspective contributes specific concepts or findings as well as specific disciplinary modes of thinking to shed light on a particular problem. To ensure careful treatment of the disciplines involved, educators must identify which specific concepts and modes of thinking (among the many available in each discipline) students will put into play, and ensure that they do so accurately. Consider the following examples of understanding in science (biology and psychology) and history.

Students tend to see scientific conclusions as unquestionable truths and experimental designs as geared *to obtaining desired results* rather than to *testing hypotheses* (Smith & Carey, 1995). Deeply rooted in early constructed theories about the world, such naïve beliefs need to be transformed according to currently held scientific standards.

The following interview fragment illustrates how successful students explore the experimental designs used by eugenicists to validate their findings. In it Shari and Jenine critique eugenicists' measurements, inferences, and hypothesis-testing procedures.

Laura: [explaining eugenicists' work in a critical tone] They [eugenicists] measured different characteristics. For example, they measured the skull and said: "The bigger the skull of a person, the bigger the brain, and the smarter the person."

Interviewer: It sounds like you think there is a problem with that.

Shari: The problem is that it's untrue. It's not true at all that the bigger the brain that means the more intelligent you are. They were just wrong. They really didn't have enough evidence. They did not do enough experiments to see if they were right.

Jenine: Yes, for many [eugenicists] their hypotheses became facts. . . . People actually started to accept these ideas. They were in the textbooks and people learned them as the right facts. The whole thing became like a new religion. People *had to* believe it [student's emphasis].

Shari: It would be like me making a hypothesis and saying it's true you have to believe it. Actually I would have to check to see *if* my beliefs are true, 'cause it could turn out to be completely wrong. The only evidence that they had to say this about skulls and intelligence was that they could see that little babies have small skulls and they know less or are less smart, and older people seem smarter. And that is maybe a good hypothesis if you don't understand much about it; but the truth is that it is too simple . . . you have to consider many other factors to say this about intelligence.

In the case of Milgram's psychological experiment, students demonstrate weak disciplinary thinking when they misinterpret scientific claims or fail to recognize their limitations. Eron illustrates this point when he interprets Milgram's conclusion as an unquestionable truth applicable to all human beings, regardless of context or internal disposition.

Interviewer: How was it possible that so many Germans participated in the killing of Jews and others?

Eron: The only way you can explain it is blind obedience. It is just human behavior that everybody follows orders no matter what, just without thinking . . . like that experiment.

Interviewer: *All* human beings? You mean . . .

Eron: Yeah, everybody. Blind obedience. It can happen to all of us.

In contrast, Shari and Jenine demonstrate careful disciplinary reasoning when they refer to problematic aspects in his experimental design, such as failure to control for specific variables. In Shari's view, Milgram could have collected data on subjects' prior experiences with obedience:

> The people in the Milgram experience they didn't just keep going [administering shocks] just because they were told to obey and that's it. They obeyed, I think, because of something in their past or something like how they were brought up or how they were taught. In the Milgram experiments they tried the experiment with different teachers [subjects] old and young, men and women, rich, poor, but they did not ask people: How were you raised? Did your parents teach you to stand for what you believe?

In a similar vein, students engage in careful historical thinking when they consider multiple causes of Nazi totalitarianism—for example long-lasting anti-Semitism, defeat in World War I, inflation. They do so when they explain how such forces shaped historical actors' actions without projecting present knowledge onto these actors' worldviews.

> *Jenine:* Another thing that I notice about steps [toward consolidating the totalitarian regime that led to the Holocaust] is that Hitler came really in after the war, the First World War. People were upset with what was going on with their country—you know, inflation, hunger, starvation—and this eugenics idea was like an excuse to blame a minority for all the crisis. . . . I think the Nazis were really subtle about these ideas. They made them seem like they were normal . . . with propaganda and exhibitions. People were getting these ideas against Jews subconsciously for a long, long time and that made it so that people slowly accepted these ideas and now they thought they were scientific.
>
> *Shari:* Also they didn't know where things were going, each step was moving them in one direction but they really didn't know where it was going to end up. . . .

Importance of Interaction Between Disciplines

Finally, and most importantly, in *interdisciplinary understanding,* disciplines are not simply juxtaposed. Rather, they are purposefully intertwined. Concepts and modes of thinking in one discipline enrich students' understanding in another discipline. In some cases, concepts that emerge as findings in one discipline contribute to generating hypotheses in another domain.

Successful students use the patterns of obedient behavior among Milgram's subjects to create plausible historical hypotheses about how ordinary Germans might have been willing to obey orders in the absence of coercion. Jenine's reflection illustrates this point.

> *Interviewer:* What would have happened if you had learned about how the Nazis created a totalitarian state, but you had not learned about Milgram's experiments?
>
> *Jenine:* To me the Holocaust before [this unit] was: "the Nazis—the bad people—killed the good people—the Jews—and there were six million of them." But when we learned that actually the common people, the mailman, the milkman, contributed in some way or another to so many people dying, it just makes it harder to understand. . . . When you see Milgram that was done here at Yale and you think about those people like the paper boy in Germany . . . it doesn't give people an excuse for what they did but it kind of gives you a reason. You can see kind of better that they might be able to obey. . . . If you did step A why not do step B? You did step B why not do step C? Just like the volts got higher and higher, the whole thing [in Germany] happened slowly in little steps. Just like the volt you could get to four hundred volts—like the Holocaust. The milkman probably went along with the program because he was in part blindly obedient. . . . But also he was under a lot of pressure with the economic problems the country was going through and propaganda. This is all after World War One.

In other cases, specific modes of thinking are applied across disciplinary boundaries. For example, entering the inner psychological world of Milgram's subjects prompted some students to look for historical actors' points of view when they studied Nazi Germany. In this case, the moves in one discipline served as entry points into the modes of thinking in another discipline. For example, Shari's speculation about ordinary Germans' progression toward the "Final Solution" was prompted by her efforts to empathize with Milgram's subjects and avoid stereotypical portraits. Adding to Jenine's explanation, Shari continues:

Also when they [Milgram's subjects] started they thought they were doing it for a good cause they thought that they were helping the scientists learn and everything. So when they did the shocks one by one it didn't seem like very much because the scientist had told them that they won't get hurt and nothing could go wrong. So they kept going and going thinking that the scientists know. . . . And I was relating that to the Holocaust and to the Nazis. Because maybe at the beginning some of them thought that they were doing the right thing helping out Hitler—because they had heard all of this about the Jews being a problem for the society and for the German genes and maybe they had agreed to it. They believed it, in the beginning, that helping Nazis was good and they did little by little. But then when it got to the point of the Holocaust, and the killing machines were there, then they couldn't stop it right there. . . . I think that the people who kept going with the volts weren't necessarily bad people they were just not strong enough to say "This is a problem"—and the same thing in Germany although in Germany they were really under so much pressure and they probably thought 'I better stand here and watch' because there was a lot of confusion; people didn't know where things were going to end, and maybe they were afraid.

In sum, as illustrated by these four students' claims, *interdisciplinary understanding* goes beyond its multidisciplinary counterpart—in which disciplines stand juxtaposed around a theme rather than intertwined. *Interdisciplinarity* becomes a prism through which students can interpret the natural, social, and cultural worlds in which they live and operate in them in informed ways. In this sense, *interdisciplinarity* is not an end in itself but a means of addressing problems or examining phenomena that are relevant to the societies in which we live. Supporting careful *interdisciplinary understanding* among youngsters is not an easy task. It requires close attention to the nature of knowledge and inquiry in specific disciplines, and to the ways in which aspects of each discipline can be combined to address an important problem or create a powerful performance of understanding (Wiske, 1997).

OBSTACLES TO INTERDISCIPLINARY UNDERSTANDING

Disciplines are both epistemological and social entities. As epistemological entities they involve bodies of knowledge, methods of inquiry, purposes, and forms of representation that are shaped by the types of problems that they explore (Boix Mansilla & Gardner, 1997). As social entities they involve departmental arrangements, organizational channels of communication, power relationships, patterns of socialization, values, and heroes (Becher, 1989; Siskin, 1994, 1997).

Interestingly, while teachers, researchers, and school administrators acknowledge the fragmentation of knowledge in schools, the remedies proposed are all too often limited to the social/organizational aspect of interdisciplinary work (Campbell, 1969; Siskin & Little, 1995). Advocates of interdisciplinary curricula propose various innovations in this regard. Some emphasize the importance of interdisciplinary teams where teachers of different subjects work with a single group of students and are encouraged to correlate at least some of their teaching (Five & Dionisio, 1996; George, 1996). Others propose a reorganization of time blocks and year plans to facilitate interaction between teachers in different departments (Brandt, 1991; Jacobs, 1991, 1997; Vars, 1991). Still others emphasize that interdisciplinary dialogue and communities of inquiry may help teachers reflect about their work and "let go of old models" centered in subject matters (Drake, 1991, p. 22).

Organizational questions often dominate. For example, much time is spent arranging schedules and yearly plans to ensure that specific themes are touched on by subject matter teachers simultaneously (Jacobs, 1997). Less time is devoted to questions regarding the nature and uses of disciplinary and interdisciplinary knowledge. *What can different disciplines contribute to a better understanding of important problems? How can multiple disciplinary perspectives compensate for the limitations of individual disciplines? What is the point of engaging in interdisciplinary work?* While coherent organizational arrangements of teachers and yearly plans are important enabling preconditions for interdisciplinary work, they are insufficient in themselves to foster *interdisciplinary understanding* among students. In fact, shorn of a careful reflection on the nature of *interdisciplinary understanding,* educational efforts have often resulted in curriculum integrations that have in various ways failed to contribute to students' understanding.

"Interdisciplinary" Work as Motivation

In some cases the proposed "interdisciplinary curricula" favor motivating activities over performances that elicit students' understanding. Student-centered activities such as designing a eugenics poster campaign typically engage students' interest and participation. Under closer scrutiny however, these motivating activities often fail to require that students use specific bodies of knowledge in two or more disciplines. As a result, students' posters may be creative but feature important biological or historical inaccuracies—for example, failing to include the biological rationale for rational human mating as part of their campaign.

"Interdisciplinary" Work as Common Sense

In other cases, "interdisciplinary curricula" lose sight of the contributions made by the specific disciplines involved. Because no attempt is made to challenge students' intuitive perceptions of concepts like "obedience to authority" or "human genetic inheritance," students' understanding of such themes amount to a collection of commonsensical opinions.

For example, in their initial analysis of Milgram's experiments, Miller's students' spontaneous descriptions of how subjects could obey experimenters' apparently inhumane orders were simplistic, emotionally driven, and filled with disbelief. Only after being challenged to examine intervening variables associated with these subjects' behavior and to contribute competing hypotheses to interpret Milgram's results were some students able to move beyond common sense.

"Interdisciplinary" Work as Algorithm

In some cases, so-called interdisciplinary curricula tend to combine disciplines algorithmically in an effort to "cover" a variety of topics. Students may learn about eugenic studies (in science), Nazism (in history), and German art (in art class), without a sense of how these three factors converged in the creation of Nazi totalitarianism. In these curriculum designs students move actively from one topic or approach to the next without a clear sense of the purpose of the enterprise as a whole. Ofttimes these designs are rooted on a conception—or, to be precise, a misconception—of disciplines as collections of certified facts to be transmitted to students. Rather than enhancing understanding, "interdisciplinary approaches" serve as efficient transmitters of facts.

Pros and Cons of Multidisciplinary Curricula

Many so-called interdisciplinary curricula are in fact *multi*disciplinary designs. A multidisciplinary approach can be very fruitful: it can provide students with rich perspectives around a particular topic or it can scaffold them toward further *interdisciplinary understanding*. What is lost in multidisciplinary understanding is the possibility of enriching each disciplinary perspective through fruitful exchange of concepts or modes of thinking across disciplines. For example, understanding the Milgram experiment from a purely psychological point of view does not demand that students consider the experiments' results against the background of Nazi Germany. By extrapolating what they have learned about Milgram's subjects' psyche to their analysis of ordinary Germans, students gain a new perspective on the historical actors' experiences. The fact that ordinary Germans were willing to obey inhumane orders even when under no particular threat becomes plausible in students' minds (Goldhagen, 1996).

NATURE OF KNOWLEDGE AND INTERDISCIPLINARITY

Fostering *interdisciplinary understanding* among students is an enterprise filled with hurdles. Even the most apparently congenial disciplines or subdisciplines (e.g., history and literature, or demographics and history) bring distinct emphases or foci to particular problems (Wineburg & Grossman, chapter 3, this volume). For example, a demographic analysis of Jewish exodus during the early years of totalitarianism contrasts with a narrative historical approach of Nazi Germany which foregrounds individuals' motivations and experiences. In each case claims are validated according to distinct criteria such as sound statistical analysis and professional interpretation of sources respectively.

While, sometimes, disciplinary emphases or frameworks are complementary, they are also often mutually exclusive. For example, in creating a work of art to depict the impact of eugenicist ideology in Nazi Germany, students often face a conundrum. As an artistic representation, the painting should typically elicit multiple interpretations—for example, by exploiting ambiguity in figurative visual languages. In doing so, it should focus viewers' attention on the aesthetic composition of the piece. As a historical account, the work should include accurate information about the steps toward radical human reproduction policies. It should lead viewers to reflect about the period portrayed—for example, its causes, development, or significance. In this case the ambiguity and purposeful multiplicity of meanings common in artistic expression may threaten the quality of the historical account.

Despite its sometimes problematic nature, the process of integrating less compatible disciplinary approaches may provide an opportunity to build deep understanding. For example, in choosing to depict specific historical scenes or eugenics beliefs in the painting, students are challenged to assess their significance and interrelation. In situations of this kind, educators may use students' reflections as additional evidence of *interdisciplinary understanding*.

Interestingly, the challenge that teachers (as well as experts) face in their attempts to develop fruitful interdisciplinary inquiries and products is one of developing a *meta-disciplinary* awareness (i.e., an awareness about how disciplines work). Only such awareness allows them to see the strengths and limitations of each discipline as well as the possibilities of interaction between them (Becher, 1989; Hunt, 1994; Klein, 1996; Kline, 1995; Sherif & Sherif, 1969). Such *metadisciplinary* language enables teachers to speak with one another about how their disciplines deal with the problems that they expect their students to understand.

Furthermore, teachers need to recognize that disciplines and subdisciplines favor distinct modes of thinking and knowledge representation (e.g., narrative, visual, numerical). Accordingly, combining appropriate lenses in the study of a particular topic opens the possibility that students with more diverse cognitive profiles will find a meaningful entry point to the problems under study (Gardner, 1999a, 1999b).

A CONCLUDING REMARK

Advocates of *interdisciplinary curricula* often propose it as a more appealing and engaging alternative to the "stagnant," "artificially compartmentalized," and "irrelevant" *disciplinary curriculum* (Anstead, 1993; George, 1996; Maurer, 1994; McCartan, 1990; Pate, 1996; Vars, 1991; Whitmer, 1990). This critique is often built on standard perceptions of disciplines in schools, as stable or even stagnant bodies of knowledge. In our view, disciplines are better thought of as dynamic sets of practices and beliefs, which are frequently influenced by other disciplines. As disciplinary practice evolves, it produces reformulations of the present body of knowledge as well as reformulation of its boundaries, preferred methods, and assumptions (Becher, 1989; Klein, 1996; Lyon, 1992).

A major aspect of a discipline's growth derives precisely from boundary crossings of the sort described in this chapter—that is, from the fruitful exchange of concepts or modes of thinking between and among disciplines. Such interdisciplinary exchange has become an intrinsic part of knowledge production (Kline, 1995; Mathews, 1988). The reconceptualization of disciplinary knowledge in schools in ways that emphasize its generativity and dynamism invites educators to see disciplinary and interdisciplinary work as mutually enhancing.

NOTE

This chapter was written with the generous support of Thomas H. Lee and the Louise and Claude Rosenberg Jr. Family Foundation. We would like to thank James MacNeil for thoughtful reflections on his teaching of eugenics and James MacNeil and William Miller's students for their energetic participation in interviews. Our special gratitude goes to Pamela Grossman and Sam Wineburg for their insightful comments on previous drafts; Alan Stoskopf for his careful advice regarding the treatment of eugenics in this piece; our research associate Wendy Fischman for her meticulous support; and our colleagues at Facing History and Ourselves for constantly reminding us of the challenges involved in teaching Nazi Germany and the Holocaust through multiple perspectives.

REFERENCES

Anstead, N. L. (1993). Hooking kids with humanities. *Educational Leadership, 51,* 84–87.

Becher, T. (1989). *Academic tribes and territories: Intellectual enquiry and the culture of disciplines.* Milton Keyness, UK: Open University Press.

Beyerchen, A. (1992). What we know about Nazism and science. *Social Research, 59,* 615–641.

Blass, T. (1991). Understanding behavior in the Milgram obedience experiment: The role of personality, situations and their interactions. *Journal of Personality and Social Psychology, 60,* 398–413.

Boix Mansilla, V., & Gardner, H. (1997). What are the qualities of disciplinary understanding? In M. S. Wiske (Ed.), *Teaching for understanding, a theory in practice.* San Francisco: Jossey Bass.

Brandt, R. (1991). On interdisciplinary curriculum: A conversation with Heidi Jacobs. *Educational Leadership, 49,* 24–26.

Browning, C. R. (1992). *Ordinary men.* New York: Harper Perennial.

Campbell, D. T. (1969). Ethnocentrism of disciplines and the fish-scale model of omniscience. In M. Sherif & C. Sherif (Eds.), *Interdisciplinary relationships in the Social Sciences.* Chicago: Aldine.

Drake, S. M. (1991). How our team dissolved the boundaries. *Educational Leadership, 49,* 20–23.

Five, C. L., & Dionisio, M. (1996). *Bridging the gap: Integrating the curriculum in upper elementary and middle schools.* Portsmouth, ME: Heinemann.

Gardiner, J. (1989). *What is history today?* London: MacMillan.

Gardner, H. (1991). *The unschooled mind: How children think and how schools should teach.* New York: Basic Books.

Gardner, H. (1999a). *An education for all human beings.* New York: Simon & Schuster.

Gardner, H. (1999b). Multiple approaches to understanding. In C. M. Reigeluth (Ed.), *Instructional-design theories and models, Vol. 2* (pp. 69–89). Mahwah, NJ: Lawrence Erlbaum.

Gardner, H., & Boix Mansilla, V. (1994). Teaching for understanding in the disciplines and beyond. *Teachers College Record, 96,* 198–218.

George, P. S. (1996). Arguing integrated curriculum. *Education Digest, 62,* 16–24.

Glass, J. M. (1997). *Life unworthy of life: Racial phobia and mass murder in Hitler's Germany.* New York: Basic Books.

Goldhagen, D. (1996). *Hitler's willing executioners: Ordinary Germans and the Holocaust.* New York: Knopf.

Hunt, L. (1994). The virtues of disciplinarity. *Eighteenth-century Studies, 28,* 1–8.

Hunt R. (1995, Autumn). Review of the book *Surviving the swastika: Scientfic research in Nazi Germany. The Journal of Interdisciplinary History, 26,* 313.

Jacobs, H. H. (1991). Planning for curriculum integration. *Educational Leadership, 49,* 27–29.

Jacobs, H. H. (1997). *Mapping the big picture: Integrating curriculum and assessment, K–12.* Alexandria, VA: Association for Supervision and Curriculum Development.

Kevles, D. J. (1995). *In the name of eugenics: Genetics and the uses of human heredity* (2nd ed.). Cambridge, MA: Harvard University Press.

Klein, J. T. (1996). *Crossing boundaries: Knowledge, disciplinarities, and interdisciplinarities.* London: University Press of Virginia.

Kline, S. J. (1995). *Conceptual foundations for multidisciplinary thinking.* Stanford, CA: Stanford University Press.

Lyon, A. (1992). Interdisciplinarity: Giving up territory. *College English, 54,* 681–693.

Macrakis, K. (1993). *Surviving the swastika: Scientific research in Nazi Germany.* New York: Oxford University Press.

Mathews, M. (1988). A role for history and philosophy in science teaching. *Educational Philosophy and Theory, 20,* 67–80.

Maurer, R. E. (1994). *Designing interdisciplinary curriculum in middle, junior and high schools.* Boston: Allyn & Bacon.

McCartan, M. A. (1990). Making the case for interdisciplinary programs. *Change, 22,* 28–36.

Milgram, S. (1974/1997). *Obedience to authority: An experimental view.* New York: HarperCollins.

Müller-Hill, B. (1998). *Murderous science: Elimination by scientific selection of Jews, Gypsies, and others in Germany, 1933–1945.* New York: Cold Spring Harbor Laboratory Press.

Pate, E. (1996). *Making integrated curriculum work: Teachers, students, and the quest for coherent curriculum.* New York: Teachers College Press.

Pearl, R. (1908). Breeding better men. *World's Work, 15,* 9818–9824.

Perkins, D., Schwartz, J. L., West, M. M., & Wiske, M. S. (1995). *Smart schools: Better thinking and learning for every child.* New York: Free Press.

Sherif, M., & Sherif, C. (1969). *Interdisciplinary relationships in the social sciences.* Chicago: Aldine.

Siskin, L. S. (1994). *Realms of knowledge: Academic departments in secondary schools.* Washington, DC: Falmer Press.

Siskin, L. S. (1997). *Restructuring knowledge: Mapping (inter)disciplinary change.* Paper presented at the annual meeting of the American Educational Research Association, Chicago, IL.

Siskin, L. S., & Little, J. W. (1995). *The subjects in question: Departmental organization and the high school.* New York: Teachers College Press.

Smith, C., & Carey, S. (1995). On understanding the nature of scientific knowledge. In D. N. Perkins et al. (Eds.), *Software goes to school*. New York: Oxford University Press.

Vars, G. F. (1991). Integrated curriculum in historical perspective. *Educational Leadership, 49*, 14–15.

Whitmer, B. D. (1990). The myopia of departmentalism: A social-studies teacher's response. *English Journal* (November), 68–70.

Wineburg, S., & Grossman, P. (1997). *Scenes from a marriage: Some theoretical and practical implications of interdisciplinary curricula in the comprehensive high school*. Paper presented at the annual meeting of the American Educational Research Association, Chicago, IL.

Wiske, M. S. (1997). *Teaching for understanding: A theory in practice*. San Francisco: Jossey-Bass.

2

Hunting the Quark

Interdisciplinary Curricula in Public Schools

JUDITH RÉNYI

DO DISCIPLINES EXIST IN K–12 SCHOOLS?

One of the finest lessons I ever witnessed was taught by a splendid teacher, Gloria Barnes, to 16-year-olds at the Franklin Learning Center in North Philadelphia in the late 1980s, which was at the time a school for underachievers and learning-disabled children. The lesson occurred early in the first unit of the world history course, "The Beginnings of Humankind," when students learned how to argue historically from evidence. Gloria divided the class of 33 inner-city students into groups of four or five, and gave each group a set of cardboard cutouts representing half a dozen different hominid skulls.

Each group was told to arrange the skulls in chronological order or relationship to human forbears and then to make a presentation to the whole class on their reasoning. They were to reference *evidence*—brow ridges, skull capacity, and other physical evidence, and they were to distinguish clearly *hypotheses* from *conjectures* and *conclusions*. After all the groups had made their various cases, the class as a whole voted on which group had made the most convincing case for the order of descent of the creatures represented by the skulls.

The students did an outstanding job. They discussed evidence and inference with judicious enthusiasm, they made excellent presentations, fought vigorously and convincingly for their positions, and yielded graciously (more so than many an academic) when proven wrong. It was an exhilarating class to observe, except for one thing: the students weren't learning history. They were learning archeology.

Should we fuss over whether it was history or archeology? Does it matter one whit to these young people? They all wanted the teacher to tell them "the real answer" after all the presentations were done—"which was 'the correct' order of the skulls?" This was the moment Gloria Barnes had been waiting for. "No one knows," she told them. "You have just repeated the controversies and arguments being offered by worldwide researchers with Ph.Ds; there are no better answers than the ones you have presented here today." The lesson was about the ongoing, ever-changing nature of research, the need to keep sifting through old evidence and adding new, in the dynamic that is scholarship.

The lesson's point was an important one to make at the start of a 2-year course designed to explore "how we know what we know," the overriding theme of the world history project. Is it important to know, however, whether you are using historical methods or archeological methods to know something? Is it possible to use both at once? Desirable? Who cares?

IS INTERDISCIPLINARY LEARNING POSSIBLE?

If the above story of Gloria Barnes's class is the sublime, I must also offer an example of the ridiculous. I was talking with a high school principal one day about increasing the interdisciplinary offerings of his school. "We're already doing that," he said. "My English and social studies department heads have lunch together at least once a week."

K–12 education administrators are probably issued the "we're already doing that" line for use whenever they spy education reformers looming down on them. But in all fairness, the principal could just as easily have pointed out, "We're already doing that—that's what 'social studies' *is*."

"Social studies," however, does not exist as a discipline at the higher education level. It does not have a recognized academic proving ground—a unified field from which it draws sustenance. It draws instead from a very wide array of such sources in both the humanities and social sciences. What gets taught and how it is learned in social studies classes can and does include everything from viewing fictional films to collecting opinion polls to analyzing skulls. More often, however, the social studies practiced by students in school involves learning the conclusions proffered by the writers (editors? collators?) of social studies textbooks, which tell the students what they should believe about historical events.

When Tom Holt, professor of history at the University of Chicago, was asked to reflect on the nature of history in U.S. schools, he pointed out that it was a form of disciplined creativity that had very specific defining features. In order to be doing history, one must create a narrative of human events with "some temporal order that is inherently causal" (Holt, 1990). All three elements—narrative, chronology, and causation—must be present. If any of these are absent, we are no longer doing history.

The students examining and seeking to postulate a chronology from the skulls were not, by this definition, engaged in doing history. They were, however, doing one of the social sciences (or an approximation, given that they were handling only two-dimensional cardboard models of skulls). Most well-formed social studies lessons do in fact focus on one single disciplinary approach, usually without that approach being specified by the teacher, and often, I suspect, without the teacher being particularly aware of which discipline he or she is using.

I suspect that it may not be possible to use more than one discipline at a time, while it is very possible to use multiple disciplines in succession. I also suspect that it is more valuable to articulate which discipline one is using than it is to rummage around unconsciously using one or another in an *un*disciplined manner. There is a simple reason for this suspicion: rocks and trees and poems and kingships differ. Their differences are what make life and study interesting and productive. Interdisciplinarity is, I suspect, a path to be taken when we are confronted with phenomena that *cannot* be understood from one or another discipline alone, and only yield their secrets and fascinations when approached with new tools and from new perspectives that derive their methods from more than one discipline.

The study of rocks gives rise to geology, geochemistry, and a host of related fields. Of trees to botany; of kingships to history and political science or political philosophy; of poems to . . . well, that *is* a problem in the field in which I received my Ph.D. What in the world *is* the discipline poems give rise to? And what is its equivalent in the public schools?

I have written before on the history of English Language Arts in the public schools (Rényi, 1993). Like modern history, it is a young, ill-defined discipline dating back less than a century, while mathematics and music and ancient history have deep roots in millennia of schooling. The disciplines are in constant flux in higher education, shifting ground and raiding borders at all times. In the early 1980s, for example, the chemistry department at New York University proposed a new course to the faculty senate on the "origins of life" to the outrage of the biology department. Similarly, the inroads of biochemists on one side and physicists on the other have squeezed chemistry itself to a fare-thee-well. K–12 educators just call it all "science," and if the new science standards take hold we will soon see more integrated teaching rather than isolated, year-long approaches to disciplines such as chemistry or biology.

To a very large extent, then, K–12 schools already have interdisciplinary, or more frequently, multidisciplinary, teaching. Social studies, English, and science teachers may use a succession of tools and methods to discuss kingships, poems, or trees, drawn from a succession of disciplines, but even when they are attempting to be interdisciplinary, they rarely are more than multidisciplinary.

The differences between these various ways of organizing curricula need to be defined. According to the National Commission on Teaching and America's Future, "[N]early one-fourth (23%) of all secondary teachers do not have even a college minor in their main teaching field. This is true for more than 30% of mathematics teachers. Among teachers who teach a second subject, 36% are unlicensed in the field and 50% lack a minor," (National Commission on Teaching and America's Future, 1996). Although the highest percentage of licensed teachers (83%) can be found in pre-K and elementary classrooms, few have studied academic disciplines of any kind, but have instead majored in elementary education, itself a multidisciplinary field largely comprised of teaching methods and developmental psychology. The National Goals Panel found that the number of secondary teachers with a degree related to their main teaching assignment *declined* from 66% to 63% between 1991 and 1994. Most teachers have had too little preparation in any discipline to be able to define one.

The distinction is important, because without discipline, we get mush, and too often an unexamined, inarticulate discipline is indeed mush in the classroom. The failure to distinguish clearly one approach from another means missing or confusing meaning, and just plain getting things wrong. Too often our classrooms—in English or even science or art—end up teaching bad sociology instead of good English or science or art, bad biography instead of good chemistry, confused anthropology instead of clear history. It matters a lot if we don't know which discipline we are actually using because our arguments will falter and we will reach dubious conclusions.

It matters a lot which discipline we choose, because over the millennia the disciplines have evolved as powerful tools for understanding rocks and trees and poems and kingships. It is those *tools* which we hope to leave permanently in students' hands when they leave school so that, should they encounter rocks or trees or poems or political systems in their lives, they will have ready at hand useful methods for understanding them. And, if they encounter in their lives treelike poems or rocklike kingships, they should be able to combine their toolkits in such a way as to understand those, too. *That* would be interdisciplinary.

The popularity of interdisciplinary curricula in the 1980s and 1990s arose out of two felt needs: a concern that there were phenomena in the world that would not reveal their secrets to the old disciplines alone, and a concern that the old disciplines kept us locked in old ways of seeing that either distorted or obscured the object of study. A few examples will suffice to show the validity of these concerns. The new "discipline" of "cognitive science" is an attempt to bring a wide array of researchers from psychology, philosophy, neuroscience, linguistics, artificial intelligence, and others together to take a crack at the mind-brain problem (among others). These tillers of parallel rows hope to rise up together to see if they are in a single field. "Cultural studies" has gained a toehold on fashionable campuses in recent years as academics who used to "do" English, sociology, languages, the arts, anthropology, and a host of other disciplines found themselves interested in a set of approaches to cultures that differed from the approaches of their old departments. And, of course, gender and ethnic studies take a fresh look at everything in the world from their various perspectives.

By "interdisciplinary" I mean studies that use the tools, arguments, and approaches of more than one discipline at once, such as analyzing a painting using art-historical and chemical analyses in combination to prove that a picture is both stylistically and chemically a work of a particular artist from a particular time and place. By "multidisciplinary" I mean studies that use tools, arguments, and approaches of more than one discipline *seriatim* to analyze different features and aspects of a work for different purposes. Almost all interdisciplinary curricula I have observed in schools fall into this latter category and are, in fact, multidisciplinary, using one discipline at a time. In essence, then, I propose that multidisciplinarity, or the use of a number of disciplines one after another, is both possible, and in certain settings desirable, but that interdisciplinarity, or using multiple approaches simultaneously, is usually neither possible nor particularly desirable.

WHAT GOES ON IN SCHOOLS?

What goes on in the schools in the name of subjects as well as the name of interdisciplinary teaching and learning is an odd assortment of lessons and topics that are more an accident of history than an articulated attempt to explicate the world that U.S. citizens need to prepare themselves to deal with.

Much of the English Language Arts curriculum, for example, derives from branches of study deemed appropriate for young Americans in the 1840s and 1850s when the Common Schools were established. These studies included clerical penmanship (for bookkeeping); moral sentiment (learning to read and write by copying out moral *sententiae* or sacred texts); patriotism (defining the nation through its literature); and rhetoric (for good salesmanship, and to prepare students to compose persuasive sermons for a clerical [religious] career). In an age when we expect both the bookkeeper and the boss to use computerized spreadsheets and Power Point demonstrations, when teachers still insist on teaching children the difference between a simile and a metaphor, but can't for the life of them explain *why* a child should know that, and when it is impossible to select a story for children to read without offending someone's moral sensibilities, it would seem high time to review what exactly ought to go on in English language arts classes.

Over the last decade, the movement to define subject standards and get them in place throughout the country has taken the wind out of interdisciplinary sails. The U.S. Office of Educational Research and Improvement (OERI) and most of the states that have forged ahead with state standards and frameworks have pursued their work along familiar school subject lines. No one has redefined literature in English as one of the arts; many have gone along with OERI's abandonment of social studies in favor of history and geography; and science and mathematics are left as enormous wholes. No one has yet provided any useful help to generalist K-8 teachers required to teach to all the standards, but who rarely have *any* disciplinary background of any use in preparing to do so. None of the standards explicitly recognizes project-based or problem-based learning that draws on a variety of subjects for their solution.

As the states take up the shift to standards-based requirements, they are moving away from inter- and multidisciplinary approaches. The standards, as developed by national subject matter associations, such as the National Council of Teachers of Mathematics (NCTM), the American Association for the Advancement of Science (AAAS), the National Council of Teachers of English (NCTE), and the International Reading Association (IRA), vary widely in their dealing with interdisciplinarity, but by and large do not address the definitional problem of discipline at all. Given the overwhelming pile of standards that generalist teachers are going to have to master (in fourth, fifth, and sixth grades, especially), they will inevitably try to do six impossible things before breakfast in every class they teach by attempting to amalgamate the standards across the disciplines. The teachers are pretty well doomed to fail, too. There is no existing "crosswalk" for the standards. Some districts are attempting to do this with their state standards, and also attempting to work technology in as well (most national standards only go so far as to exhort such activity or provide a handful of examples, but none have built the technologies in). Let's be very clear about exactly what is involved in the crosswalk: it is no less a task than taking most of the knowledge of the world, as defined by the standards, and trying to make sense of it for each grade or age group as a single, multidisciplinary whole. I don't think so. Not this year, and not next, and not by committee. The standards continue the old approach of subjects in silos. The kids' descriptions of their school day will forever remain "and then we had math and then we had English and then we had lunch." And much of what they will "have" for English will remain rather mushy; and in K-8 classes, science will continue to be neglected for lack of emphasis in their teachers' education; and much of what passes for "history" will be bad sociology; and no one will learn very much about the arts.

WHAT'S SUPPOSED TO GO ON IN SCHOOLS?

To the extent that the standards and the assessments that will be designed to test student achievement are put in place, these will become the actual curricula of the schools. I am not aware of states that promote interdisciplinary standards or new disciplines. The subjects survive, more or less in the configurations that have prevailed for some 80 years. There are major differences in approach and intensity of study, however. Some states adopting standards are specifying history and geography rather than social studies, and are hence moving away from interdisciplinarity and toward more specific disciplines in this area. In many cases, the approach of the committees that contributed to the OERI-funded subject standards was to put the tools of the discipline, rather than a long list of data, in students' hands. The impulse in most cases was to get students to think mathematically, or scientifically, or historically, rather than merely to specify a list of facts to memorize. All of this means that the teachers who forged the standards and the state policymakers who have adapted and adopted them are agreed that increased disciplinarity is the way to go in the new millennium.

The interdisciplinary lobby simply wasn't there when the governors met with George Bush in 1989, when OERI sent out their Requests for Proposals (RFPs), or in the states where Goals 2000 funds are being spent. Interestingly, in two fields with notable opportunities for interdisciplinary study, social studies and science, the standards were not crafted by the associations representing social studies or science teachers alone. Multiple, competing, and conflicting standards were produced in history, geography, economics, and social studies; by various groups of professors, teachers, and others, and there are three sets of science standards to choose from. The AAAS science standards attempt to deepen learning in science, as do the NCTM mathematics standards, by eliminating one-year high school courses in subjects such as biology and algebra. These new standards instead use the tools of these disciplines from K–2 along with the tools of other disciplines and topics.

At the K-8 levels, few classroom teachers have the depth of knowledge presupposed by each of the standards documents, and fewer will have such knowledge of more than one. Either each classroom generalist will be expected to prepare his or her students for testing in all the standards or districts will feature a smaller subset of standards in the elementary grades (reading and math) and continue to ignore science, history, and the rest. The entire push to define and teach to rigorous standards in other subjects will help somewhat to increase disciplinary knowledge, but the high stakes will remain what they have been since the 1840s: bare literacy and numeracy.

LET'S BE MULTIDISCIPLINARY!

There's just too much to learn, and more every day. How to choose what students must learn in 12 years of schooling is a vexing problem. There is certainly agreement on literacy and numeracy, disagreement on what those two mean, and difficulty in getting beyond them.

I believe there is an important place for disciplinarity and for interdisciplinarity in our schools after all, but we will have a very long way to go to establish it. First, rocks and trees and poems and kingships do differ in remarkable ways. Learning about each of them and learning to use tools that enable one to read any poem, understand any tree or rock, and deal with any political system would seem to be important and worthwhile ways of spending time in school. The disciplines as defined by Goals 2000 are as reasonable a collection of such disciplines as any, and some of the national standards documents (especially those published by NCTM, AAAS, and the National Center for History in the Schools) promise to be richly rewarding ways of approaching study in these fields.

If we are concerned, however, about increasing students' flexibility of mind and capacity to live and work in the world, then something is very definitely missing when all learning is rigidly isolated in parallel disciplines for 12 years of schooling.

Creative problem-solving and understanding of the messiness of the world and the human imagination requires something more than "and then we had science and then we had math and then we had lunch." There are two ways of getting to interdisciplinarity: the first is to learn as much as possible in parallel subjects for a number of years and then as a capstone to study a field that draws on learning from two or more of those subjects; and the second is to be confronted with complex problems or projects first, prompting a desire to pick up the pieces of information or tools of the disciplines specific to solving the problems at hand along the way. In a sense, we all use both methods to approach the complexities of the world all the time. The question is whether, and to what extent, either or both is desirable in the K–12 curriculum.

First we need to know what kinds of problems or fields of endeavor naturally require the finely honed tools of multiple disciplines for their solving. Engineering, design, and architecture are such fields. Each of these fields centers on objects that work in the world. As such, they differ markedly from the traditional fields of study in schools. While the *usefulness* of the traditional subjects of English, history, science, mathematics, and so on are clear, their usefulness is not object-centered in the way that I have defined it, nor is usefulness in the world the *only* reason for teaching them: English, history, science, and mathematics have historic, moral, patriotic, and theoretical applications of equal or greater importance to the policymakers who approve of their existence in public schools. Architecture, engineering, and design have been promoted at various times, particularly in the 19th century, as appropriate studies for the young citizens of an industrializing, expanding nation. In our own time, they have presented themselves to some teachers as a useful "hook" for engaging students, making sense of the parallel curricula of school, and preparing students both to sharpen their disciplinary skills and their ability to use those skills in combinations to demonstrate their competence to work and live in the world.

The British have built interdisciplinarity into their national curriculum standards, and have chosen to do so in fields that are in themselves interdisciplinary (design) as well as in the traditional school subjects. A recent publication (Davis, Hawley, McMullen, & Spilka, 1997) reviews the British experience in depth and presents a very strong case for the value of design in children's education. The study shows the value of design as a curriculum organizer that has proven to be of value in scores of programs in the United States as well as abroad for increasing overall student achievement.

The United States has gone down another route entirely, however, first by setting single subject standards, and even in some subjects that might give rise to interdisciplinarity (the arts), further splicing the subdisciplines and keeping them separate. The most interesting and impressive interdisciplinary curriculum developed in my experience of innovative curricula was the creation of eight teachers at the Zia Elementary School in Albuquerque, New Mexico. The result was *New Mexico's History*

Through Its Architecture: An Interdisciplinary Humanities Project of the Hispanic Culture Foundation, a title which doesn't begin to probe the depth or complexity of this work created in the early 1990s (Hafner, Lopez-Shiver, Reed, Sloan, Atkinson, Garner, Maize, & Gilder, n.d.).

The naturalness of the project derives partly from location: New Mexico boasts Paleolithic cave dwellings, the ruins of pre- and post-Colombian American Indians, several hundred years of mission architecture, contemporary pueblos, and varieties of Anglo architecture. At least three major cultures have inhabited New Mexico and coexisted for centuries, and several major different forms of farming, ranching, and other forms of food production have altered the landscape. Over a period of several years when the Zia teachers were creating the curriculum, they attended annual intensive summer institutes to deepen their knowledge of New Mexico's peoples, archeology, architecture, history, arts, and cultures. They consulted closely with many specialists in a variety of fields in addition to architectural historians. They met as a group for planning, review, and curriculum development daily and weekly throughout the school years. They had monthly seminars presented by specialists from the University of New Mexico, museums, and libraries. The core team did extensive research and summarized all they learned in a massive resource notebook they compiled for the rest of the school staff. They invested nearly all of their out-of-classroom hours in the work of creating and revising this whole-school work. In each of three successive years these teachers and resource people developed a different, year-long, comprehensive program of study for all of the children in the school. Some of the time spent doing this was supported by grant funds and some of it was provided by the school, but much of it was freely given by the teachers. Creating high-quality, interdisciplinary curricula from scratch is not a trivial exercise.

When I visited the school in the early 1990s the children had transformed the hallways of their typical one-story concrete block school (circa 1960s) into an astonishing replica of the major forms of New Mexico architectural history. Using miles of brown paper, older children had transformed a dull and ordinary doorway into the entrance to a 16th-century mission, while the kindergarten had constructed a model pueblo, complete with ladders made of pretzel sticks and roofs of Triscuits™!—to scale—out of graham crackers. The teachers always kept a careful eye on the disciplinary learning necessary to the work. For 5-year-olds to estimate the number of graham crackers needed to build a pueblo to scale, they needed ratios, as well as multiplication and division, and they also needed to know that the basic pueblo unit, the cube, has six sides.

As one of the teachers pointed out to me, usually that would be considered too hard a concept for such young children to understand, but it became a necessary concept for the children to succeed in building their model. They therefore learned it.

Even more impressive were the third graders, who papered a very long hallway with an immense diagram showing changes in climate, architecture, food production, flora and fauna, and cultural activities, by elevation. Rainfall, cultivars, homes, churches, domestic animals, and cultures were shown to depend very much on altitude. The disciplines feeding this fascinating wall chart are innumerable, and all came into play in its construction.

These are but two of the most dramatic projects the children worked on during the creation of the curriculum, whose riches almost defy such brief treatment here. Architecture was the unifying subject, the interdisciplinary topic that immediately connected history, mathematics, design, meteorology, anthropology, archeology, and a host of other subjects. Because the teachers were employing the whole school in day-long and year-long work, they were very careful to reference the state's requirements in the traditional subjects as they went. Reading, writing, and performing narratives sharpened students' skills in language throughout. No required skill or concept was neglected—on the contrary, the students' fascination with finding out how and why the built environment of New Mexico is the way it is, including the Anasazi cliff dwellings at Bandolier, the Spanish colonial life at Rancho de Las Golondrinas, and the culminating project that brought in the entire community, when the children decided to build an adobe wall at the school, create an outdoor classroom of native plants, and a mural depicting the life of the peoples of New Mexico. Surely state history—usually required in most states at fourth or fifth grade—never was this exciting before.

Interdisciplinarity worked in this project, perhaps ironically because the teachers took such care to assure that the required *disciplinary* topics were referenced throughout; it also worked because architecture is in and of itself interdisciplinary, taking cognizance of climate, terrain, physics, materials science, mathematics, design, and a deep understanding of the people who will inhabit and the purposes to which the structure will be put. Architectural history, in which New Mexico is particularly rich, affords children direct access to object-centered learning that immediately opens up questions concerning the practices and beliefs, migration patterns, and livelihoods of the people who built the structures. The mission and ranch architecture of the Spanish colonial period also led into a further exploration of how the Spanish Empire, and through it, the Mediterranean, Moorish, and European background the Spaniards brought with them were altered by the New Mexican landscape and native peoples they encountered.

The teachers at Zia Elementary also studied architecture in depth and prepared themselves in the myriad historical, scientific, and cultural subjects they needed to be wise guides for the children. Some of the work was uneven (there was a fair amount of food and imitation festival, and the language and literature learning tended to be weaker than the social sciences), but the faculty probed the riches of the subject matter far more deeply than ever before when they had focused only on the transmission of textbook-centered curriculum. The program also benefited from numerous field trips to archeological and historic sites, walking tours of the school neighborhood, guest presenters, and scholarly assistants.

At the heart of the Zia experience, I believe, was the teachers' own intensive learning in the arts and humanities. Month-long summer institutes for in-depth study with professors of arts and sciences, year-long support for at least 3 years for each school from a local resource institution, and year-long opportunities to network with colleagues from inside and outside of the school made the Zia experience possible. At Zia, the decision to create an interdisciplinary curriculum for children was partly the result of the way in which multiple disciplines were offered to the teachers in the adult learning sponsored by the Hispanic Culture Foundation (and the Rockefeller Foundation, which provided substantial support for such interdisciplinary multicultural programs throughout the country from 1984–1994). Another key to the success at Zia, ironically, is that at least half of the core team of eight teachers who worked most intensely on the project had received their undergraduate degrees in arts and science disciplines, not in education. Their liberal arts learning formed a solid foundation that enabled them to conduct research, combine disciplines into an integrated program, and offer a rigorous course of study for the children.

SHOULD EVERYONE HAVE A ZIA EXPERIENCE?

The results at Zia Elementary were impressive, but were they replicable? Should every child have an opportunity to study this way? Should curricula always be interdisciplinary, or just some of the time? What advantages and disadvantages are there to this approach?

To my mind, the Zia experience was a much deeper, more rigorous and more sensible curriculum than that normally used in elementary school. Student test scores went up; but more importantly, the students developed a passion for learning and a proven ability to demonstrate their learning through their work. I also understand that when they went on to middle school they were already well beyond the demands of the textbooks presented to them and some had difficulty adjusting to the slower pace of learning and dullness of the curriculum they found there.

So one lesson to be learned is that the unified, interdisciplinary curriculum as practiced at Zia needs to be followed up throughout schooling, or we risk student boredom and disengagement from schooling. A second problem is that the program did cost money: the field trips, the brown paper and graham crackers, the teachers' professional development, the participation of scholars and architects, poets and dancers, were all added by virtue of a grant. Developing new curricula is costly in terms of many hours of learning and planning by a host of teachers and resource people. The teachers subsequently received grants from the city that enabled them to continue the field trips for a while. Like many a grant-funded initiative, however, the program eventually dissipated. Several of the core teachers retired or left the school, and the remaining ones carry on as best they can in their isolated classrooms. As a whole-school effort, however, the Zia experience is no more.

Not every school can get grants. The energy and intellectual rigor of the liberally educated faculty was there to be tapped all along, yet the opportunity to participate in this grant program sparked something very special. Other schools throughout New Mexico were part of the grant–funded network of Rockefeller Foundation–funded projects—and none of them came anywhere close to the quality of the program at Zia.

I must end this excursion on an ambivalent note. Zia proves the art of the possible. For the teachers there, interdisciplinarity was disciplines, not just a mushing together of one thing with another whether it fit or not. Zia teachers kept their eyes firmly on long-term academic goals: what they wanted the children to know and be able to do. They chose a topic (architecture) that was naturally interdisciplinary. They studied hard and they had high expectations for the children's achievement. The resulting curriculum made sense from the child's point of view. Instead of a set of linear curricula without connectivity, where the goals are usually, "learn this now, you'll need it later," the children discovered their need to understand now in order to construct the next step of their learning (finding out that a room has six sides or the relation between altitude and tropical foods grown and eaten by different people). The children were given a focus (the built environment) to which they could relate the entire world they inhabit, both through time (history) and the natural environment. The curriculum truly had an organizing principle that was visible (and palpable) to the children.

That, ultimately, should be the goal rather than the theoretical question of which curriculum is better, disciplinary or interdisciplinary. The traditional curriculum just doesn't make as much sense, made up as it is of the ragtag bits of historically determined learning that we find in most schools. This lack of coherence is not being addressed by the standards movement, despite heroic efforts by states and districts to "do a crosswalk" to see what on earth they are requiring of fourth or eighth graders now that they have developed 5 or 10 linear subject standards.

The most important feature of what happened at Zia was its coherence, and it derived that from its seemingly narrow focus on the architecture to be found in New Mexico. I suspect that "the hook" could just as readily be almost any object or set of objects that could have the potential to radiate outwards to a host of other learning. The object at the center of study can be turned to view all its facets, studied in its setting, studied for the people who made it and used it, studied for its design, studied for its history, modeled and reconstructed, performed and produced, and so on. The trick is to identify, as the Zia teachers did, a set of objects that have the potential for such myriad, in-depth studies. We must remember that this was an elementary school program that focused for a year each on the Anasazi, the Spanish colonial period, and subsequent periods, and that for each historic era all the children were given opportunities to explore the same curriculum in different ways. It wasn't pueblos for the little ones and Spanish missions when they got older. It was *all* the children elaborating different and sophisticated responses to the same material.

One could raise concerns about this particular program: it used scant literature. I doubt that even the most comprehensive interdisciplinary program can cover every traditionally taught subject. All curriculum-making forces choices of what to include and what to leave out or underplay. I believe that it is more important to learn material from a teacher who is competent, confident, and enthusiastic in the field even if that means not learning another subject in which the teacher is ill-prepared. Conversely, I would also be content with a curriculum in English, for example, that was taught through only one poem, one play, one novel, and one biography, which were taught over and over by many different teachers for several years. Such a curriculum would teach children the many different ways of approaching the same texts, and therefore teach them how to approach *any* poem, play, novel, or biography.

Can a single interdisciplinary curriculum be sufficient? In the end, the teachers' desire for unity for Zia Elementary and its community paradoxically created a richness and depth rarely found anywhere in or out of education, and it produced inquiring young minds ready to tackle any and all manner of learning. That is a worthy goal for our schools, and I for one would be willing to junk any curriculum that can't get our children there.

EMERGENT DISCIPLINES AND SCHOOLING

A recent news item reported that when a group of Nobel Laureates offered to help shape California's science standards, they were rejected by the state's K–12 educators (Manzo, 1997). In setting national standards, few policymakers included significant numbers of academics in the process, and fewer academics still are in evidence at the state level. Academics, curators, and artists are the people paid by our society to shape disciplines, but their work is largely ignored by K–12 educators and policymakers when it comes to deciding what to teach in school.

What gets taught in school derives from a political process rather than an intellectual one. In the presence of political pressure, curricula change: for example, an interest group brings pressure on state legislatures for curricula portraying the interests of the group, and a new mandate to teach that subject or to teach an old one differently is issued as a result. In the absence of political pressure, nothing changes.

The academic disciplines are a moving target, whereas schooling is notoriously resistant to change, and this is probably as it should be. Academics are paid to experiment; children's basic education is an inappropriate venue for experiment. Parents and the public, meanwhile, are highly skeptical of change and devoted to "the basics." Brain research, for example, has not progressed to a point where definitive ideas relevant to teaching and learning can be derived, with a single exception. Linguists have shown that the ability to learn languages is at its height in the early years and disappears—becomes *physically* difficult if not impossible in the mid-teens—just the age when American public schools *begin* foreign language instruction. Despite all the talk about brain research, this country is not politically prepared to care a fig about second-language learning, and therefore ignores this one relevant piece of research.

Teachers are faced with far too much to do in too little time, with too few resources of any kind, and little help outside of the battered textbooks their district has seen fit to buy. Teachers' experience and instincts make them sympathetic to interdisciplinarity: when new requirements get added to the curriculum, but nothing is consequently removed, districts blithely tell teachers to "infuse" the new with the old. Teach them to read *by* reading about the new subject; teach them math *while* teaching them music, and so on. And when teachers search for ways of doing these things, they are not likely to look beyond a fairly superficial amalgamation of these subjects within the limits of their own knowledge and abilities. There's no time, and no one is being paid to help them.

Generally, then, interdisciplinarity in schools is the use of one discipline as handmaiden to another, none of which depends on how the makers of the disciplines (academics, curators, and artists) are shaping the disciplines in the first place. Should this picture change? If so, how?

The American Federation of Teachers' (AFT) most recent review of standards, *Making Standards Matter: An Annual Fifty-State Report on Efforts to Raise Academic Standards,* justifies the lack of interdisciplinarity in the standards movement by seeing it as "a pedagogical decision rather than a broad policy imperative." AFT believes that standards do "not dictate how . . . material should be taught. Those decisions are best left to the professionals in the schools." This is an interesting take on interdisciplinarity, which sees it not as *content* but as *method.* Yet AFT has taken a strong position on sharpening standards to be specific about exactly what and when students should attain knowledge. AFT's approach, then, is to name the books in English and name the specificities of how children should understand federalism and name the grade by which both should be learned, but leave whether these are combined in single assignments or not in the hands of the teachers.

The Zia Elementary example demonstrates that thoughtful, disciplined interdisciplinarity is both possible and desirable for creating a school with a clear academic purpose. Meanwhile, the standards movement is working in the opposite direction, to a firmer grasp of discrete disciplines *without benefit of reference to how these disciplines are being shaped by academics, curators, or artists.* Neither the standards nor the academic disciplines are in the business of creating vibrant *schools.* That is the job of the people in the schools, and the job that both states and academics have very little interest in or capacity to create.

The result, I fear, is the continuing separation of what the creators of disciplines are doing from what the politics of schooling demands, and *both* from what practicing teachers have demonstrated can work for children in school. Unity of purpose and community of learning, with careful reference to the knowledge and skill expected of children at various ages can work as it did at Zia Elementary, but Zia's success also depended on a vibrant link between teachers, academics, and artists. Teachers confronted with standards alone will not be motivated to create the unity of purpose that makes a great school, nor will they necessarily recognize their own need for deepening knowledge to carry it off. Meanwhile, postmodernism has come and gone in the academic world; and someone, somewhere is still teaching 14-year-olds the difference between a simile and a metaphor.

The voice of the people has been heard: stick to the basics, maintain order and discipline, and don't go haring after the fads and fancies of the academic and artistic worlds. The public is not convinced there's anything new in the world worth teaching anyway, except technology, which will bring salvation in some way yet to be defined. The voice of the teachers is rarely heard: How do I *motivate* these kids? How do I get through the overwhelming amount of what I'm expected to do? How can what I already do fit in with these new demands for standards? The voice of the makers of the disciplines old and new is not at all heard: K–12 educators tell them don't bother helping us with these standards, they have nothing at all to do with *you*.

Given these realities, the future of interdisciplinarity is dim. The best we should hope and work for is this: let's try to make the standards coherent by reconnecting teachers with their counterparts who spend their lives shaping the disciplines. As teachers receive the state and local standards, let's bring together school faculties with academics, curators, and artists, school by school, and let's give them a few years to design programs of study that try to make sense of the standards (and their presumed disciplines) from the *students'* point of view. Let's give these faculties the time to begin to work out how children will spend their days, weeks, and years in order to demonstrate their attainment of the standards. The result will, I believe, sometimes be interdisciplinary, as whole faculties puzzle out work for young people to undertake over a span of 12 years that will show growing evidence of clarity of thought and argument and grasp of principles, a developing ability to communicate and understand, and the power of persuasion.

REFERENCES

American Federation of Teachers. (1997). *Making standards matter: An annual fifty-state report on efforts to raise academic standards*. Washington, DC: Author.

The Consortium of National Arts Education Associations. (1994). *National standards for arts education*. Music Educators National Conference, Reston, VA.

Davis, M., Hawley, P., McMullen, B., & Spilka, G. (1997). *Design as a catalyst for learning*. Alexandria, VA: Association of Supervision and Curriculum Development.

Greenberg Research, Inc. (1996). *Keeping up with change: A survey on professional development growth conducted by the National Foundation for the Improvement of Education*. Washington, DC: The National Foundation for the Improvement of Education.

Hafner, L., Lopez-Shiver, L., Reed, S., Sloan, D., Atkinson, E., Garner, H., Maize, K. A., & Gilder, S. A. (n.d.), *New Mexico's history through its architecture: An interdisciplinary humanities project of the Hispanic Culture Foundation*. St. Louis, MO: CHART Network.

Holt, T. (1990). *Thinking historically: Narrative, imagination, and understanding*. New York: The College Entrance Examination Board.

LeMahieu, P. G., & Sterling, R. (1991). *CHARTing educational reform: An interim report of evaluations of The Collaboratives for Humanities and Arts Teaching (2 vols)*. Philadelphia: Collaboratives for Humanities and Arts Teaching.

Manzo, K. K. (1997). Scientists protest exclusion from standards writing. *Education Week, (November 21)* 5.

National Commission on Teaching and America's Future. (1996). *What matters most: Teaching and America's future*. New York: Author.

The National Endowment for the Humanities. (1998). *Overview of endowment programs*. Washington, DC: The National Endowment for the Humanities.

National Goals Panel. (1997). *The national education goals report*. Washington, DC: Author.

Public Agenda. (1995). *Public attitudes toward teachers' professional development: A focus group report by Public Agenda*. New York: Author.

Rényi, J. (1993). *Going public: Schooling for a diverse democracy*. New York: The New Press.

Rényi, J. (1994). The arts and humanities in American education. *Phi Delta Kappan, 75* (6), 438–445.

3

Scenes from a Courtship

Some Theoretical and Practical Implications of Interdisciplinary Humanities Curricula in the Comprehensive High School

SAM WINEBURG AND PAM GROSSMAN

They seem like perfect mates, so much in common. History and English, text-based disciplines that stress the careful examination of the written word, appear to offer each other many comforts. Who can argue with the notion that knowledge of literature makes history come alive, or that information about historical context opens up new literary vistas? But marriages that sound compelling in theory often turn out to be less charmed in practice.

Like many worthwhile educational ideas, the call to integrate curricula has become a "movement," with all of the attendant trappings. Eager staff developers find willing audiences among superintendents and principals intent on "staying current." In many instances, teachers from different disciplines are paired together with the charge to come up with "something interdisciplinary," often after an abbreviated workshop. The assumption guiding these calls, especially in the case of history and English, is that a natural attraction exists between the disciplines, a compatibility that instantly reveals itself once departmental barriers are dismantled.

Our position in this chapter differs considerably from this view. We do not see history and English as inevitable bedfellows, nor are we sanguine about hasty attempts to yoke them in matrimony. Both the academy and the school curriculum have maintained separate existences for these subjects for good reason: as disciplines (rather than as "themes" or "topics" or even subjects) English and history ask different questions, appeal to different kinds of evidence, and often place different values on forms of intellectual work done in and out of school. These differences at the school level often translate into distinctive subject matter cultures, each with its own set of folkways of reading, images of curriculum, and patterns of interaction around text (Grossman & Stodolsky, 1994). Such folkways are often not visible to the eye, but they are present nonetheless—exerting powerful influences over how their members communicate with one another and construe their points of agreement and difference. None of this is to say that integration of the two disciplines is a bad idea. Rather, our point is this: attempts to integrate curricula that disregard disciplinary cultures will, perforce, result in superficial programs that do justice to neither discipline. When this happens, kids lose out.

THE COMMUNITY OF LEARNERS PROJECT

We present an overview of a different approach to the creation of interdisciplinary curriculum than most of the inservices we have attended or about which we have read. We draw on data from a 3-year project among a group of history and English teachers at an urban Seattle high school. The foundations of this project were built on the notion that before teachers can plan solid curricula they must first come to know each other as fellow readers and thinkers. Teachers in this project (which was funded by the James S. McDonnell Foundation program for Cognitive Science in Education) came together in monthly meetings to read novels and historical monographs, to discuss these texts, and to reflect on the varied perspectives they brought to the discussion.

We wanted to use the process of reading together, and then hammering out a new curriculum, to forge a community of learners *among teachers*—a community that would include the full range of teachers from student interns through mid-career teachers to seasoned department chairs. The inspiration for our project came principally from two sources: our previous work with Lee Shulman on teachers' pedagogical content knowledge (e.g., Grossman, Wilson, & Shulman, 1989; Grossman, 1990; Wilson & Wineburg, 1988; Wineburg & Wilson, 1988) and the work of Brown and Campione (1994) on creating "communities of learners." We found the notion of a community of learners to be a compelling idea that leads to exciting classroom practices (Brown, 1992; Brown & Campione, 1994). But we also believed that a community of student learners is a fragile entity in a school where no parallel community exists among teachers.

The intellectual community we have tried to establish over the course of 3 years steers a middle course between the ambitious but difficult whole-school intervention and the tenuous and often short-lived approaches aimed at the individual teacher. The unit of change in this project is the organizational structure known as the *department*. While departments have long been part of the "grammar" of high school (Tyack & Tobin, 1994), they have been all but ignored in discussions of school change. Yet, if our interest is the intellectual core of secondary schools, the department constitutes a strategic intervention point, for it is often at the department level that key decisions about student learning are made—which courses are offered, who teaches them, and what gets tested. The department can also be viewed as an enactment of distributed cognition, where individuals with varied perspectives and backgrounds come together to deliberate on issues that directly influence student learning. It was our belief that if we wanted to change students' experience of literature and history as they travel through the high school curriculum, we needed to focus on changing the vision of the department rather than the vision of one or two teachers.

We recognized, however, that departments can also pose barriers to change. By sequestering teachers into communities bound together by shared subject matter commitments, some departments offer teachers few opportunities to share ideas with colleagues with different perspectives. Instead of providing opportunities for teachers to engage in distributed cognition, some departments may enforce a single view and censure those who deviate from it. Disciplinary communities are social as well as intellectual communities; they can constrain cognition just as they can expand it. The lack of interdepartmental communication may prevent new ideas and perspectives from infiltrating traditional departments, forestalling professional growth and thwarting reform efforts (e.g., Ladwig & King, 1992). For these reasons, our work deliberately crossed departmental boundaries.

The group of teachers in this project met regularly over 2 1/2 years. Some teachers came to our project having experienced a model of curriculum development in which they studied new material in the summer and quickly wrote lesson plans for the fall. But as we noted above, we elected a different route. Before rushing to engage each other over the substance of the curriculum, we first had to get to know each other as fellow learners. To do this, we borrowed the model of book clubs that meet in people's homes and imported it into an urban high school. As a group we selected pieces of fiction and history, often related to teachers' interests in curriculum development, and used these works to create a sense of shared intellectual community. Grant monies allowed us to release teachers for all-day meetings once a month (while substitute teachers staffed their classrooms), and after-school meetings were held in the intervening weeks.

It is not always smooth going when committed English and history teachers, joined by representatives from special education and English as a second language, come together and discuss books like Nathan McCall's *Makes Me Wanna Holler*, Bharati Mukerjee's *Jasmine*, or Christopher Browning's *Ordinary Men*. Day-long meetings and after-school follow-ups allowed our group to go beyond "polite disagreements" so that genuine disciplinary differences could emerge. Such differences, which rarely get surfaced in short-term projects, need to be part of the discussion. Otherwise, unrecognized and unspoken assumptions can become stumbling blocks that thwart group understanding (cf., Grossman, Wineburg, & Woolworth, 2000; Thomas, Wineburg, Grossman, Myhre, & Woolworth, 1998; Wineburg & Grossman, 1998).

For example, in an early meeting teachers debated the value of using the film *Disclosure* as a prelude to having students read a Supreme Court case on sexual harassment. Teachers disagreed vehemently about the value of this approach, with some teachers arguing for the need for students to connect the court opinion with something familiar and others arguing for the need for students to focus only on the text of the Court's opinion. The group initially interpreted this disagreement as an instance of interpersonal conflict among several well-spoken individuals. Now, after many similar disagreements, we understand this discussion as emblematic of dramatic differences in teachers' beliefs about how to read texts, about how kids make meaning from text, and about how and when to draw on students' personal experience in teaching the humanities.

Put differently, before we could have serious discussions about curriculum integration, we, as a community of readers, had to experience the give and take of discussion around important books: Do we trust the voice of the narrator when he is a white man speaking in the voice of a Vietnamese woman (Robert Olen Butler's *A Good Scent from a Strange Mountain*)? How can we judge the claim that Nazis administering "head shots" to innocent women and children on the Polish front were not barbarians, but rather "ordinary men," caught up in circumstances beyond their control (Christopher Browning's *Ordinary Men: Reserve Police Battalion 101 and the Final Solution in Poland*)? What can we learn about our own experiences with racism by examining the experiences of people from another continent (Rian Malan's *My Traitor's Heart*)? By reflecting on our own sometimes heated, sometimes lighthearted discussions, we forged a list of "guiding questions" that captured what *we* did as readers from two different disciplines. What do we pay attention to? What do we ignore? How does the past influence the present? Only after addressing such questions could we move to the next stage: planning the kinds of intellectual experiences we wanted for our students.

If we can say anything about what we have learned over the last 3 years, it is that the process of creating a shared understanding among teachers with different backgrounds is more circuitous than we ever imagined. This has certainly been the case when we reflect on the various opportunities a project like ours offers to teachers for learning to think about teaching, content, and students. So, for example, while we came together as a community of readers and can document improvements in the coherence and the quality of our group discussions, our collective progress in designing curriculum was halting, partial, and successful only in modest measure.

We offered teachers a model of professional development that promised to provide at least two different venues for learning—a chance to read interesting books with their colleagues and an opportunity to design new curricula for their students. Among the 22–25 participants, teachers varied in their reasons for joining the project, with some clearly preferring one or the other of these opportunities. For example, Barb, an experienced English teacher, was clear about her motives: "I'm in it for the community—the talk about books," she told us. At the other end of the spectrum was Grace, a 7-year veteran of the social studies classroom. After we had read our first book together, Grace, visibly upset, told the group that reading a book was "torture," particularly when it was not clear how the book related to her curriculum. Grace wanted the group to "roll up its sleeves and get down to business," which to her meant devoting large blocks of time to the design of curriculum. Our early meetings tried to achieve a balance between these two activities, alternating between discussions about common texts and small working groups brainstorming on curriculum. But as we quickly learned, harmony between teachers of English and history was more difficult to achieve than either of us had imagined.

READING WOLVES AND GETTING DEVOURED

To illustrate some of these difficulties we draw on a group discussion that took place 12 months into the project. Prior to this meeting, a recurrent theme in our discussions had been whether there were genuine differences in how we read history and English. The two primary contenders in these discussions were Charlie, an English teacher with 8 years of experience, and Lee, a social studies teacher, with 20 years of experience. In broad terms, Charlie maintained that all texts are literary, for they all "do things with language." To the extent that there were differences between the disciplines, Charlie claimed, they were more an issue of social convention than any fundamental difference. Lee, however, saw major differences between the subject matters, which he often cast dichotomously: literature's concern with "process," and history's with "content." Exchanges between Lee and Charlie became a familiar leitmotif during our first year.

As these issues recurred in our discussions, other participants would murmur "here we go again" or "oh, no, grinding the same old wheat." In individual interviews, participants often characterized the history-English debate as a "personality clash" between two strong-willed, argumentative individuals. Noticeably absent from these interviews was any reference to the epistemological issues that seemed to motivate the disagreement.

Approximately a year into our existence as a group, we created a specific exercise to focus on students' understanding of history. Our own role in these discussions tended to be ambiguous. We were explicitly not the teachers, and we cast ourselves—and indeed continue to see ourselves—as group members. We would often set the tone for the day by creating textual exercises for the group, but once the discussion was underway, our role was to contribute, not to guide or teach. However, our goal in planning this particular activity was more interventionist. We sought to introduce into the discussions about curriculum planning the role of student understanding, in this case, students' thinking about the nature of historical texts. For the last decade, one of us (Wineburg, 1991, 1998, 1999) has been engaged in trying to understand students' historical reasoning, often comparing high school students' ways of reading to those of working historians. Our goal with this activity was to introduce teachers to some of this work. We hoped that by displaying excerpts of student thinking (particularly student misconceptions about the nature of historical inquiry), we might spark a discussion on the beliefs that adolescents bring to the humanities. We hoped as well that the discussion would begin to inform the process of curriculum development.

We began by distributing a copy of a student's and a historian's response to a task that centered around the Battle of Lexington, the "shot heard 'round the world" on April 19, 1775 (cf., Wineburg, 1991). After reviewing a set of documents about the battle, both the student and the historian selected one of three pictures that best reflected "what happened on Lexington Green on April 19, 1775." Despite evidence to the contrary (and his own sizing up of the evidence during the reading), the student chose a picture that showed the colonists standing tall and returning fire; nowhere did the student make mention of the documents he had reviewed in the first part of the task. The historian, however, tied her remarks to the written documents, offering qualifications when her judgments were unsupported and showing doubt when she was guided by intuition alone.

We began the discussion with a broad question—"What do we notice?"—as a way to get started. But rather than focusing on problems in the student's historical reasoning, the discussion immediately turned to problems with the historian.

> *Sam:* What kinds of things do we notice?
>
> *Barb:* It seems like the student's, that the student one is so wonderfully, well it's almost personal in that the kid has placed himself in the shoes of the people, and [tries to] imagine how he might feel.
>
> *Rhonda:* Whereas the historian looks at the picture and says, "Well this seems to be more accurate because it corresponds to the various accounts that I read."
>
> *Barb:* [The historian's account] has that kind of cold, objective look versus this really emotional, "God, I could get shot." They invest in it emotionally—the kids do.
>
> *Olivia:* The historian can get outside of the evidence, though, and compare it to what he knows to current events. But again, it's the analytical approach rather than emotional one.
>
> *Sam:* The historian is a forty-five-year-old white woman who is a specialist in Japanese history. The student was a seventeen-year-old Asian American student in an AP class.
>
> *Olivia:* I thought it was interesting that the historian couldn't deal with the woman in the picture which would have made, maybe required more of an emotional involvement with the text, you know. "There was no evidence, so I don't know."
>
> *Heather:* It seems that the historian is trying to justify the position, or apologize for it.

This initial exchange (edited for brevity and readability) took us by surprise. To the group, it was the historian's reading that seemed problematic—cold, objective, analytical—as opposed to the "wonderfully personal" reading of the student. The historian, whose gender at that point had not been revealed, instantly become a "he." Even when we corrected this, the historian was still the one with problems: She couldn't "deal with the woman in the picture," perhaps because her analytical rigidity prevented her from considering a detail unsupported by written testimony. If there was any sense of a "good" reading of history embedded in this early exchange, it was one of deep emotional engagement with text, an ability to rouse one's own feelings and connect them to the past. Even the historian's attempt to qualify her conclusions, a feature that reflected the uncertainty of historical knowledge, was cast as an "apology" or a "justification," rather than a careful and sophisticated act of reasoning. In this initial exchange, English teachers set the tone.

For several minutes the discussion went back and forth with questions about how other students and historians reacted. Ten minutes into the discussion, Steven, the chair of the history department and a 31-year veteran of the classroom, made his first foray into the discussion when he pointed out that there "was no attempt by the student to draw on the written accounts" in coming to his conclusions. This comment was not taken up until one of us entered the conversation to ask how people regarded the student's comment that the colonists' "mentalities would be ludicrous" if they stood "ready to be shot." Lee, the social studies teacher, commented that the student was "applying contemporary standards" to these historical texts, a "presentist" reading. (He, however, did not use that word.)

In addition to sharing with the group the comments from the student and historian, we also distributed a primary document that shed light on the military culture of colonial New England. The document was a 1703 letter on the nature of Indian warfare that justified the Puritans' encircling of Indian settlements and burning them to the ground (cf., Hirsch, 1988). The author, Solomon Stoddard, claimed that such behavior would be inhumane if the Indians waged war as other people (cf., Wineburg, 1999). But they should be regarded as "thieves and murderers" because they "don't appear openly in the field to bid us battle." Because they "act like wolves," argued Stoddard, they are "to be dealt with as wolves."

Following Lee's concern that the student was applying contemporary standards to the task, we introduced the Stoddard letter (henceforth the "wolves document") comparing Indians to wolves. After some discussion about the problems students might have with the language and antiquated spelling, Lee observed that the wolves document and the student's justification for his picture selection made "exactly the opposite point" about the kind of behavior to be considered as "natural." Lee asked the group whether the wolves document was simply a "text," something to evoke a personal response, or whether it was something more: a piece of evidence that helped us see how people in the past construed their social reality. But as the following excerpt shows, Lee's question was interpreted by Barb and Karen, two English teachers, quite differently from how he had intended.

Lee: You can't read this text in a vacuum. Are you trying to have kids understand the differences in perceptions of Native Americans by the white people who came over here, or are you just trying to get them to analyze "text"? I mean I think it really depends on what your objective is.

Karen: I thought often about the interview that we had where we had to do that read aloud on the poem and everything. The one thing that struck me as I did it was the benefit my grammar education served me in how I read, that when I got stuck on what I was reading, I think, "Well wait, what's the subject, who's doing the action". . . . And as I think about, for example, my freshmen, who are about to launch into the *Odyssey*. There's some complex reading there. . . . Maybe I shouldn't choose something challenging.

Barb: Or choose a passage, just any passage. One thing I've done that works really well is I give the kids a poem but you give them one line at a time. Put the line on the board and say okay, I want you to write as much as you can—stream of consciousness—on that line, any and all—just free associate, any associations that come, words, images of what this reminds me of. And you go a line at a time, and it's something like "Nothing Gold Can Stay." . . . They're dying for that next line—they get such expectation. But that's a kind of a way to do this on paper, which I find very fruitful. Enormously fruitful, I think, just to read ahead, because when they read too fast they just don't get it.

Karen: I wonder if that's the problem. I mean it's just a society of television and commercials. You hear the name of a company six or seven times in one 10-second spot. And in football you never really have to pay attention the first time they play because there's always going to be an instant replay. And because everything comes at you so many times, to take time to creep through something—to really fight to understand—is more taxing than you feel like investing.

This exchange had many analogues in our early discussions. Lee's question—what is our objective in reading a particular text and what is the relationship of the text to a wider historical context—gets addressed obliquely, if at all, and in the process sheds its distinctive epistemological implications. For Lee, the central question is "How do we read *history*?" but in the very next turn, the question for Karen, and later for Barb (both

English teachers) becomes "How do we read?" In the space of a few short minutes, Lee's question boomerangs back to him, but it comes back refashioned as a recommendation to teach students to read difficult texts by presenting them a line at a time and having them "free associate." It was this suggestion—the notion of having kids free associate in response to text—that brought Lee to the boiling point.

"I mean, you write a line up on the board—this "Gold" one—that could mean anything you want it to mean," Lee objected. Shaking the wolves document in his hand, he declared, "This one can't!" The baldness of this statement, the claim that there is a restricted set of meanings that can be given to a historical text, was the signal for Charlie, Lee's counterpart in English, to enter the fray.

> *Charlie:* [challengingly] I think I could probably break this [wolves document] up into verse and make a poem out of it.
>
> *Lee:* Well, I'm sure you could, but that doesn't mean that it, that it is as ambiguous as a line of poetry.
>
> *Charlie:* Look, "They act like wolves and are dealt with all as wolves." That's poetry! In fact, I'll call the poem, "They act like wolves" [laughter].
>
> *Lee:* OK, you call that a poem, "They act like wolves." If you just wrote on your board, if you took this out of context and just wrote on your board: "They act like wolves," then we're talking about something completely different. But when you're taking the context of something that's talking about a specific action by a specific group of people, and you know that when you give them the assignments—
>
> *Charlie:* So did *they* act like wolves?
>
> *Lee:* But it's different than a line of poetry!
>
> *Charlie:* Well, but, the thing about poetry is—there's no specific definition. It's not a necessarily ambiguous—
>
> *Lee:* It's not necessarily ambiguous—in whose mind? In the person that wrote it?
>
> *Charlie:* Well, I would say, in terms of both, especially the person who—
>
> *Lee:* So when you read poems, you know what the poet wants to say?
>
> *Charlie:* Often you do—
>
> *Lee:* And how do you know that?
>
> *Charlie:* Because you understand language. I mean it depends on the poet. If you want to read T. S. Eliot, you might work a little

harder. If you read Carl Sandburg, you'd have maybe, more language like this. You know, so it sort of depends on who you are reading and what the intent is. The same thing in a piece of writing.

Lee: I think the "intent" of this is—

Charlie: —Is to convince people through poetic language that the Indians were cruel.

Lee: Or that one person perceived them as cruel.

Charlie: Oh, it's a perception, and trying to deliver a perception through writing.

Lee: Not necessarily, no.

Sam: Well, it seems like this is a pretty important argument, particularly if you think of integrating across history and literature as we form a curriculum.

Lee: Well, I think it is a fairly interesting distinction that we don't seem to get past—there's a big difference between historical text and some literary text. You can't get away from that! You can't make it into poetry.

Charlie: Is this historical text? Or is it literary [text]?

Lee: I think it is historical text!

There are many things to notice in this exchange. First, it is important to notice that we hear primarily the voices of English teachers—Charlie, and earlier Barb and Karen. Lee's voice, conversely, receives no echo from his departmental colleagues. His chair, Steven, who brings the broadest historical background to the group, was also one of the most reticent group members. Among the other members of the social studies department we found a range of educational backgrounds. One teacher had a background in physical education, while another held a bachelor's degree in education with a sampling of coursework in the social sciences. A third teacher studied sociology and physical education. Even Lee lacked a history major—ironically, he had majored in English! Among the social studies teachers present, only Steven, the department chair, studied history extensively at the university level. In this regard, our group mirrors national trends. Whereas English teachers typically major in English or drama in college and share a common knowledge of core texts, social studies teachers share the least common backgrounds among any department at the high school level (Grossman & Stodolsky, 1994). It is no wonder, then, that Lee's attempt to describe a historical way of reading goes unsupported by his departmental colleagues.

In the most heated exchange of the meeting, David, another English teacher, reported that his objective was to teach students how to "pay attention" when they read. He then tried to get Lee to agree to this as a worthy educational aim.

> *David:* I want them to pay attention. Pay attention. You want your students to pay attention to what they read? You do, don't you, Lee? That's an objective.
>
> *Lee:* That is not, that would not be the objective to giving them this [wolves document]. If I wanted them to pay attention to what they read, I'd give them something else to read.
>
> *David:* Why? Why?
>
> *Lee:* Something that would draw their attention. If that were my only objective.
>
> *David:* Oh, well it's easy to draw your, to get kids to pay attention with things that draw their attention. What about things they don't normally attend to? Isn't that part of our job?
>
> *Lee:* No. Not in the context of some—I don't think so, no.
>
> *Barb:* Lee, this is the place where we meet—we meet so completely in this text as history and language arts people. We meet in language.
>
> *Lee:* Doesn't sound like we're meeting very well—
>
> *Barb:* [emphatically] We *are*! We're meeting in language. And you're talking, Lee, you're talking objectives, and that's got nothing to do with what we're talking here. You're talking about language—deciphering language, understanding language.

As we see in Barb's comment, even the notion that there *is* a difference is denied. To Barb, David, Charlie, and several other English teachers at the table, disciplinary differences merge into a sea of common textuality, a position reminiscent of Wallace Stevens's claim that to a poet a tree is a symbol of a word. Lee, however, holds on to his belief that text points to rather than constitutes reality—and before it can be understood a text must be placed in historical context. In this sense, Lee argues, language does not transcend time and place. Without paying attention to factors outside of the text, Lee implies, the process of reading a document like "wolves" loses integrity.

Note, however, that these distinctions are made without recourse to explicit disciplinary markers. The entire exchange has a diffuse and scattered ring. When David invokes the injunction to "pay attention" to text, or Barb talks about the need to "have a dialogue back and forth with the self and the text," there is no explicit reference to traditions of reader response or aesthetic readings. In postmodern terms, this discussion is characterized by an absence of self-reflexivity and a lack of awareness of positionality. In its place is a concerted effort to convince Lee that there is a "way to read," a way that comes with a pedagogical strategy of focusing on text and encouraging student response.

Only near the end of this discussion does Lee receive collegial support. Steven, his senior colleague, raised the point that asking what "wolves mean to us" and the associations it stirs up of "Dances with Wolves" or "Never Cry Wolf" is a far different question from what wolves meant to Solomon Stoddard when he juxtaposed the categories Christians to Indians, civilized to beast, in a letter at the beginning of the 18th century. But even this statement elicited little comment. The discussion ended with the issue we hoped might be addressed—what beliefs do students bring to historical texts—never being broached.

EPISTEMOLOGY REVEALED AND NAMED

We turn now to a discussion 6 months later in the project of Robert Olen Butler's *A Good Scent from a Strange Mountain,* a collection of short stories told in the voice of different Vietnamese narrators. In the 6 months that passed between the wolves discussion and *Good Scent,* the themes of what it means to read—of text, context, etc.—were revisited several times. In the following excerpt, these issues become named, for the first time, as epistemological differences that inform a discussion of literature and history and help us understand where these disciplines intersect and where they depart. The following exchange took place in a discussion of whether or not people trusted Robert Olen Butler to represent his Vietnamese characters.

> *Lee:* I think what I hear from some people is that this, they question the validity of [Butler's] voice because he's not Vietnamese. It's not his point of view that's presented. And what I'm saying is that OK, you can question his voice, but you have more ammunition to question his voice if you have a frame of reference to question it with. And I might question his voice, but I won't question his voice about the story about the fall of Saigon because it feels real in relationship to other things that I've read about the fall of Saigon. So that's my point. On the other hand if you don't want, on the other hand it could stand alone, I guess. I mean if you're using [the book] to teach it to kids about the fall of Saigon, or teach kids about Vietnam or the

Vietnamese immigrant experience in America, then that's different than if you just look at it as literature. That's, that's what I think.

Heather: Do we use, it sounds, like what you're saying is that you use your evidence, the *historian's evidence* to decide whether it's a valid text or not. What you know about Saigon, does it match up with what's here?

Lee: I reason about it in the way that I think the expectations are for us to read it. If I'm just *reading it as literature,* then none of that matters.

Heather: Well, I would imagine that *as a historian* you bring that way of thinking to whatever you read. That one of the ways you decide if something is true, does it match up with the evidence that you have about the subject, about—

Lee: But if I read a book about something that I know nothing about then that doesn't come into play.

Heather: Right, then it doesn't come into play, of course.

Lee: And for a lot of people, they know nothing about Vietnam—

Heather: I'm wanting for us to develop a *guiding question* that we can all use. And I'm wondering *do language arts teachers* use the same evidence that *historians* are always talking about—questions of evidence. Do *we* do the same thing?

What we see in this snippet of dialogue is the explicit naming of difference: that the ways we read are not merely personal preferences or unpredictable idiosyncrasies, but reasoned and "disciplined" ways of thinking about questions to ask and evidence to seek. No magic intervention took place during these 6 months; we made no special presentation on Schwab's "syntactic structure" (Schwab, 1978) or Hirst's forms of knowledge (Hirst, 1974). Part of what has happened, as we see it, is the evolution of the group, the growth that comes when people read together, argue with one another, and work through the inevitable conflict that arises any time diverse perspectives gather around a table.

The teachers in our project are not particularly contentious or argumentative. If comparable disagreements do not echo in other venues where teachers assemble, odds are that there have not been the opportunities or the time for them to emerge. Indeed, the early meetings of our project, when teachers hardly knew each other, were marked by a polite but somewhat superficial cordiality. It was only when we started to read together, and started to listen to how we, as English and history teachers, reacted to varied texts, that we began to stumble upon a host of implicit theories about reading—theories that remain hidden in most venues of professional development. In fact, as we scanned the literature on inter-disciplinary curriculum—handbooks such as Tchudi and Lafer's *The In-terdisciplinary Teacher's Handbook*—we could find no sustained discussion of these issues.

Our suspicion is not that our group is exceptional or unrepresenta-tive; rather, our hunch is that other projects mask latent disciplinary dif-ferences and skirt conflict. In our review of the "how to" literature on curricular integration at the K–12 level, particularly as it pertained to his-tory and literature, we could find no parallel discussion of the issues of representation that reverberate in the disciplines, issues taken up when historians discuss the merits of Oliver Stone's *JFK,* or when novelists dis-sect Simon Schama's *Dead Certainties,* or when professors of English and history argue over the meaning of the Holocaust in Saul Friedlander's *Probing the Limits of Representation.*

In the first year of our project, the differences between members of the two departments were often cast as conflicts between individuals. "Why can't we all get along?" group members wondered. Impasses in discussions were understood as people's inability to "be nice." While it is true that we had to learn how to talk civilly with one another and to monitor nonverbal behaviors that broadcast disagreement or distrust, it is also true that our group profoundly misunderstood a continuing source of its own conflict. Only after the project was well on its way did this disagreement become named; only later did the name take on a set of coherent and stable meanings related to disciplinary differences. Once named, these differences could be discussed, analyzed, probed, and chal-lenged. This did not result in a happy marriage between English and social studies teachers. But it did result in a greater willingness to learn from each other as fellow readers and teachers.

All of this has taken time. But a second crucial factor has been that we were, first and foremost, a community of *readers,* and the texts we read loomed large in our collective history. So, for example, the questions raised about Vietnam in the above excerpt stemmed from a decision to read *A Good Scent from a Strange Mountain,* a book that raises questions about authorial intent, historical fiction, and authenticity of voice. Other texts we've read have placed disciplinary differences at the forefront. Tim O'Brien's *In the Lake of the Woods,* a novel that pretends to be a piece of history (replete with footnotes, some of them fabricated) forced us to confront implicit assumptions about textual forms and their relationship to truth. And Doris Kearns Goodwin's *No Ordinary Time,* a history that reads like a novel, allowed us to see where the craft of the historian over-laps with that of the novelist and, particularly in the use of detail, where it diverges.

The act of reading together in a community of learners helped make epistemology visible, and the act of surfacing and naming assumptions created the conditions for self-awareness and intersubjectivity. We did not necessarily agree any more than we did before, but our disagreements were richer and more productive. Instead of being treated as instances of individual intransigence, our debates about different ways of reading came to be understood as reasoned and legitimate differences from which we could all learn.

We contend that such discussions are a necessary prerequisite to the design of interdisciplinary curriculum. In the rush to innovate, it is all too easy to forestall such difficult conversations. In the rush to implement, it is all too easy to appropriate ways of knowing from one discipline and claim that they hold across another. Yet, for curriculum integration to occur with integrity, the kinds of discussions we engaged in are, in the words of Charlie, "painfully necessary."

REFERENCES

Brown, A. L. (1992). Design experiments: Theoretical and methodological challenges in creating complex interventions in classroom settings. *Journal of the Learning Sciences, 2,* 141–178.

Brown, A. L., & Campione, J. C. (1994). Guided discovery in a community of learners. In K. McGilly (Ed.), *Classroom lessons: Integrating cognitive theory and classroom practice* (pp. 229–270). Cambridge, MA: MIT Press.

Browning, C. (1992). *Ordinary men: Reserve police battalion 101 and the final solution in Poland.* New York: HarperCollins.

Butler, R. O. (1992). *A good scent from a strange mountain.* New York: Penguin Books.

Friedlander, S. (1992). *Probing the limits of representation: Nazism and the "final solution."* Cambridge, MA: Harvard University Press.

Goodwin, D. K. (1994). *No ordinary time.* New York: Simon & Schuster.

Grossman, P. L. (1990). *The making of a teacher: Teacher knowledge and teacher education.* New York: Teachers College Press.

Grossman, P. L., & Stodolsky, S. S. (1994). Considerations of content and the circumstances of secondary school teaching. In L. Darling-Hammond (Ed.), *Review of Research in Education, Vol. 20* (pp. 179–221). Washington, DC: American Educational Research Association.

Grossman, P. L., Wilson, S. M., & Shulman, L. S. (1989). Teachers of substance: Subject matter knowledge for teaching. In M. Reynolds (Ed.), *Knowledge base of beginning teachers* (pp. 23–36). London: Pergamon Press.

Grossman, P., Wineburg, S., & Woolworth, S. (2000). *In pursuit of teacher community.* Paper presented at the annual meeting of the American Educational Research Association, New Orleans.

Hirsch, A. (1988). The collision of military cultures in seventeenth-century New England. *Journal of American History, 74*, 1187–1212.

Hirst, P. H. (1974). *Knowledge and the curriculum: A collection of philosophical papers.* London: Routledge.

Ladwig, J. G., & King, M. B. (1992). Restructuring secondary social studies: The association of organizational features and classroom thoughtfulness. *American Educational Research Journal, 29*, 695–714.

Malan, R. (1990). *My traitor's heart.* New York: Atlantic Monthly Press.

McCall, N. (1994). *Makes me wanna holler: A young black man in America.* New York: Vintage Books.

Mukerjee, B. (1989). *Jasmine.* New York: Fawcett Crest.

O'Brien, T. (1995). *In the lake of the woods.* New York: Penguin.

Schama, S. (1991). *Dead certainties: Unwarranted speculations.* New York: Knopf.

Schwab, J. J. (1978). Education and the structure of the disciplines. In I. Westbury & N.J. Wilkof (Eds.), *Science, curriculum, and liberal education: Selected essays* (pp. 229–274). Chicago: University of Chicago Press.

Tchudi, S., & Lafer, S. (1996). *The interdisciplinary teacher's handbook: Integrated teaching across the curriculum.* Portsmouth, NH: Boynton Cook.

Thomas, G., Wineburg, S., Grossman, P., Myhre, O., & Woolworth, S. (1998). In the company of teachers: An interim report on the development of a community of teacher learners. *Teaching and Teacher Education, 14*, 180–195.

Tyack, D., & Tobin, W. (1994). The "grammar" of schooling: Why has it been so hard to change? *American Educational Research Journal, 31*, 453–479.

Wilson, S. M., & Wineburg, S. S. (1988). Peering at history through different lenses: The role of disciplinary perspectives in teaching history. *Teachers College Record, 89*, 525–539.

Wilson, S. M., & Wineburg, S. S. (1993). Wrinkles in time and place: Using performance exercises to assess the knowledge of history teachers. *American Educational Research Journal, 30*, 729–769.

Wineburg, S. S. (1991). On the reading of historical texts: Notes on the breach between school and academy. *American Educational Research Journal, 28*, 495–519.

Wineburg, S. (1998). Reading Abraham Lincoln: An expert/expert study in historical cognition. *Cognitive Science, 22*, 319–346.

Wineburg, S. (1999). Historical thinking & other unnatural acts. *Phi Delta Kappan, 80*(7), 488–499.

Wineburg, S., & Grossman, P. (1998). Creating a community of learners among high school teachers. *Phi Delta Kappan, 79*(5), 350–353.

Wineburg, S. S., & Wilson, S. M. (1988). Models of wisdom in the teaching of history. *Phi Delta Kappan, 70*, 50–58.

4

Disciplinary Landscapes, Interdisciplinary Collaboration

A Case Study

FREDERICK L. HAMEL

A HEALTHY DISAGREEMENT?

We meet Lee and Barb, two secondary school teachers, in the middle of a professional development meeting. They have just watched, with a dozen other social studies and English colleagues, a videotape of 11th graders discussing a chapter from *Huckleberry Finn* in an English class. As the conversation progresses, Lee and Barb begin to disagree about a student comment:

> *Lee:* Somehow there is something personal. . . . It's not just about his analysis of the text.
>
> *Barb:* And Lee, that's exactly what making meaning out of a text is all about.
>
> *Lee:* But is that making meaning out of a text, or is it trying to relate their lives to the text? I mean this is where—
>
> *Barb:* It's all part and parcel of the same thing.
>
> *Lee:* Yeah, and that's the question that you have to ask yourself: Exactly what do you want out of this text? Do you want them to find meaning that's personal in the text? Or do you want them to actually analyze what is stated in the text?

Call it a healthy disagreement. The two teachers express a difference about how students should be encouraged to read literature. For Lee, students should focus on what's "in the text" rather than something "personal." For Barb, knowing a text involves "making meaning," a process that incorporates the personal. In a departure from common teacher discourse, which skirts fundamental disagreement (cf., Huberman, 1993; Little, 1982, 1990), both teachers feel confident enough to challenge the other's point of view. Both think through their own pedagogical positions, listen attentively, and articulate a public response. In other words, at this moment, we may have located—in the thick of open argument—an exceptional moment for teacher learning (Habermas, 1984; McLaughlin, 1993).

In terms of cross-disciplinary collaboration, however, the disagreement may be more aggravating than educative. In follow-up interviews, Barb, an experienced English teacher, and Lee, an experienced social studies teacher, express frustration rather than mutual enlightenment. Both feel misunderstood. The misunderstanding, each believes, involves disciplinary knowledge and subject matter boundaries:

> *Barb:* My sense is that Lee has some real fears, or some misconceptions, about what it is you do in an English class. He has a perception that there's pertinent and impertinent things, when you're with kids and literature.
>
> *Lee:* And maybe this is where a lot of people are just having a hard time understanding what I'm saying. I just think there's a big difference in what it is that I am teaching, you know?

Barb and Lee hold each other's teaching in high regard. Yet each is disconcerted by the other's conceptual road map for their two disciplines—and more inclined to critique, than learn from, the other's sense of subject matter.

How do teachers think about their own and others' ways of knowing in a cross-disciplinary setting? What disciplinary road maps, if any, do teachers employ for interdisciplinary work? How do they work through the subject matter differences that have, in fact, brought them together? This chapter reports on the thinking and interactions of Barb and Lee, participants in a 3-year school-university collaboration (Wineburg & Grossman, 1998). Their intellectual disagreements over a number of professional development meetings were the starting points for my investigation. I hoped to probe their publically articulated differences and understand those differences as an interdisciplinary phenomenon—that is, in the context of an English-history exchange. Surfacing Barb and Lee's explicit and implicit notions of the disciplines, I hoped, would be a valuable step toward understanding their interdisciplinary relationship and its potential to generate new thinking about practice.

METHOD

Barb, a 12th-grade English teacher, and Lee, a 12th-grade social studies teacher, had participated actively in the "community of learners" setting described more fully in chapter 3 of this volume. In group discussions of books and various teaching episodes, and in small group curriculum conversations, both exhibited a relatively high degree of subject matter knowledge, interest in teaching, and positive collegial rapport. Barb taught several sections of an advanced writing course for seniors, for which students at the high school receive college credit. She also was teaching literature to sophomores. Lee's teaching load consisted of civics courses, primarily Advanced Placement American Government and Constitutional Law—and occasionally U.S. history. Lee, in addition, holds an English degree, and taught English briefly in his early career.

As project participants, Barb and Lee found themselves on the opposite ends of a recurring intellectual disagreement about how students should be encouraged to read texts. To explore the disciplinary conceptions embedded in the conflict, I held a series of "recursive" interviews. First, I reviewed transcripts from project meetings and selected excerpts where Barb and Lee had explicitly differed in open discussion. In separate interviews, using these excerpts, I asked each teacher to reread what they had said, to clarify what they had meant, summarize what they heard their colleague saying, and comment on the nature of the difference, if any, they saw expressed. I followed these interviews with a second interview where Barb and Lee together conversed about specific excerpts from the first interviews. My goal was to provide an extended opportunity for Barb and Lee to clarify, revise, or extend their thinking—more than that afforded by the project meetings alone.

EPISTEMOLOGICAL OPPOSITION

My first finding was no surprise to observers of this group. Barb and Lee hold divergent epistemologies. In other words, they orient themselves differently toward the nature of knowing and learning. Their views often surfaced in polar opposition, as if Lee found his views compromised and threatened by Barb's, and vice versa. In addition, these general orientations had no clear disciplinary referent. That is, they could exist, in some version, within a variety of disciplines. For Lee, students must get beyond, as best they can, their narrow circle of experience. A text must be received, as far as possible, on its own terms. During one project meeting, for example, Lee shared a teaching lesson that involved a Supreme Court document. He opened his presentation in this way:

> Let me tell you what this is not, okay? This is not a discussion about *how they feel* about sexual harassment. This is also not a discussion about what kinds of sexual harassment they have had to deal with. What this is is a discussion of this text, okay? That's what it is. It's using the text as the center of the discussion.

For Lee, a text holds a kind of autonomy. Texts dictate carefully the meanings that students can extract. Hartman (1995) calls this a "logocentric" stance, where readers "systematically work toward understanding a passage through a deference to and desire for constructing meaning circumscribed by the author" (p. 548). Personal opinion and experience, while always present, tend to act as distorting and anachronistic influences, to be overcome in the act of reading.

Lee elaborated upon these concerns during our interviews. He raised questions, for instance, about the approach some English teachers take toward literature. Too often, he believed, teachers misplace their focus on student experiences rather than on the text itself:

> In some classrooms the analysis of literature becomes more about students' own thoughts or their own experience, and it's not about the literature. It's not about what happened in the book. . . . It's not about, you know, what Mark Twain's intent might be, or what exactly is being stated by Mark Twain.

Textual interpretation, for Lee, is about "what happened in the book," understood as "what [the writer's] intent might be" or "what exactly is being stated" by the writer. Students' own preconceptions, in short, too often come to interfere with a reader's reception.

For Barb, however, textual meaning does not exist independently of a reader, nor does it await analysis. Authors do not circumscribe meanings for their readers. Rather, texts *depend* on what readers bring (for more about reader-response theory, see Iser, 1978; Rosenblatt, 1938/1976, 1978). Barb stresses personal connection, calling forth one's history and experience to involve the reader with a text. She commented:

> Perhaps the first real lesson in reading is to make a connection and then you can build on that. . . . It is what education is all about—

the ability to use your own mind in connection with the text, to have a dialogue back and forth with yourself and the text.

For Barb, readers cannot help but bring their own life experiences to what they read. Good teaching calls personal experience to the fore, so that students might consider such experience openly. Texts, in this view, are less predictable. They do not invite any and all interpretations. As Barb says, "I wrestle with kids all the time about this—the text has to stay in focus." However, students must explore their own unique relationship to a text—a relationship that relies on active engagement with the self. In contrast to Lee, Barb comments: "I say it like a broken record to kids that you're not analyzing literature, you're analyzing your own response to literature."

EPISTEMOLOGY AND DISCIPLINARY THINKING

The disagreement between Lee and Barb, then, involves contrasting hermeneutic assumptions—text-centered versus reader-centered, or objectivist versus constructivist—assumptions about reality, the nature of the human self, and interpretation that extend through the disciplines. What about the disciplines? Are such general epistemological orientations related to disciplinary thinking at all? To what extent is Barb and Lee's interaction, in fact, an "interdisciplinary" event? One might view Lee and Barb's differences as "philosophical," or related to personality type or gender. In their review of research on epistemological theories related to learning, Hofer and Pintrich (1997) note several studies that are grounded in "general processing" models. These models suggest that epistemological assumptions move across disciplinary boundaries and may be strongly affected by factors such as age, gender, ethnicity, and education level. Barb and Lee's differences about knowing and learning could be understood by analyzing any of these life factors.

However, Hofer and Pintrich identify a growing body of research that suggests that "epistemological beliefs might vary as a function of disciplines and domains" (p. 126). In this view, which I adopt here, disciplinary thinking and more generalized orientations toward knowledge may coexist "in an interconnected network of ideas" (Hofer & Pintrich, 1997, p. 126). The relationship between general epistemology ("domain-generality") and disciplinary thinking ("domain-specificity") may operate in complementary and interactive fashion—a dialectical relationship where each informs and influences the other. Given such an intersecting relationship, teasing out specifically "disciplinary" thinking remains difficult, especially since teachers, like Lee, may have backgrounds in more than one subject area. Yet interpreting disciplinary conceptions may be critical to understanding the intellectual relationship of teachers such as Barb and Lee. To build my interpretation below, I analyzed moments in the transcripts where Lee and Barb referred explicitly to their subject area teaching, to historical or literary texts, or to the processes of historical or literary thinking.

DISCIPLINARY LANDSCAPES

Lee: Separating the Subjects

Knowing history, for Lee, is clearly distinct from knowing literature. For Lee, teaching history is passing on a cultural body of knowledge, critical events, issues, and principles, in ways that help students reflect on the implications of such events and their interconnection with other events. His notion is not reducible to "conveying facts," a stereotype that Lee resists. Rather, he thinks in terms of grasping the configuration of a chain of events in its complexity. He is, in other words, interested in "what happened," but not in a narrow or decontextualized sense. Lee commented during one interview:

> History is not facts. . . . It's not about facts. . . . I don't *quiz* them on the facts—but if they know that the 22nd amendment is what limits the amount of terms that the president has, it's not because I made them learn it. It's because they . . . learned it in the context of something else.

For Lee, historical texts contain generalized meanings that students can comprehend without need for fine-grained, word by word, or theoretical, analysis. Comparing historical reading to reading literature, he said, "interpreting historically . . . is more general." He added: "For me, the reading doesn't have to be as close, OK? . . . I mean, I think it's pretty obvious." Lee's students are taught to be careful readers. In a lesson he presented to his colleagues, Lee pursued a detailed reading of a Supreme Court decision. Thus, "close" reflects *what* students look for and why— in this case, linguistic details rather than an overall sense of what happened. The gist of a historical text for Lee is fixed, transparent, and accessible to attentive readers. In this spirit, Lee claims that a historical reading is "about a general sense of what exactly is being stated" in a text.

Lee was less inclined to cultivate in students the critical distrust that professional historians bring to their reading (Wineburg, 1991). The task for Lee's students is to understand an event as recorded. In the second interview, he talked about teaching the Sixth Amendment:

> I talk about Gideon versus Wainwright, which is about a guy who robbed a pool hall. . . . But it's not about reading some interpretation of that person's life. It's about what the Supreme Court decided and why, and what impact it has on our judicial system and on their own lives.

In teaching this text, Lee is concerned about its given content, rather than its construction, or the processes students go through in making meaning from it. To read a text historically is to understand its author's intention, to take away the facts of "what happened," and to find connections to other events.

My interviews with Lee revealed, however, that this perspective was not monolithic. Lee saw other learning objectives for students as well. I asked him, given his trusting approach to texts, how students would assess the historical validity of a film he has used on Franklin D. Roosevelt for his American Government class—a film Lee clearly understood to be sympathetic to, if not romanticizing, the president. Lee replied:

> OK, for one thing, this is an American government class, which I think is different than a history class. . . . If the objective of watching the video is to find out what action FDR took to try to remedy the situation caused by the Depression, then that in itself is an objective, OK? But if the objective is . . . OK, you have a list of presidents, and FDR is usually second or third: Was FDR a great president and why . . . and try to analyze different voices in order to figure out if he was or if he wasn't. I mean, you'd watch that video and you'd think he was. But then you might watch something else and you think he wasn't. Because we do this thing on Japanese internment, and the kids have a hard time trying to kind of conciliate those two things.

In this response, Lee first distinguishes American government class from history class, suggesting that in American government, assessing the validity of texts cannot always be his objective. In other words, Lee may perceive more opportunity for interpretive historical thinking in nongovernment classes or in history classes per se. Second, Lee suggests that social studies teachers work off a menu of objectives. He indicates that he, in fact, has a pedagogical repertoire for engaging students in historical questioning and interpretation, for instance by bringing differing accounts of FDR into juxtaposition. Such critical thinking, however, represents one way he can elect to approach a text, rather than something central to the event of historical understanding itself.

While Lee values students' critical interpretation, he wants students first and primarily to understand a text's intentional message or point of view. The relationship between "what happened" and that intentional message, of course, is a key problem for any historian. Lee's trust in historical texts, on this point, seems related to his general epistemology but may also be shaped in part by his extensive practical experiences in teaching American Government—a task that he takes to involve certain, non-negotiable content.

What about literature? Lee understands literary texts, like historical texts, as self-contained. Their meanings are to be received rather than constructed by readers.

> I think even if you taught literature that at some point you have to be able to separate your own life from what's being read . . . not that it can't be personal, but that you somehow analyze the literature in [and] of itself.

While Lee's logocentric concerns remain, he drew on his experiences as an English teacher and English major to frame specific expectations for teaching literature. Lee believes, for example, that classic literary texts hold universal themes—ideas not tied to particular contexts, ideologies, or cultures. In defending his view to Barb, he referred to a paper he had written in college on *Gulliver's Travels*. "But what about these kind of universal things?" he told Barb. "I mean [when] people read *Gulliver's Travels* for example, there's some universal things happening in that text." For Lee, not only do such themes exist, but specifying such ideas for students is an appropriate way to focus a literary discussion. During a project meeting, after a wide-ranging discussion of the novel *Jasmine*, Lee made a pedagogic point:

> This exercise that we just had was great, but I think students might get frustrated because it's so open-ended, and it almost makes it seem like if you look close enough you can find almost anything in some book. And I think we would have to have a better idea of what exactly we are looking for, or what we wanted them to see in the book.

Despite this logocentric approach with both historical and literary texts, Lee perceives strict delineations between the objectives of English and those of history. Rather than "general meanings," literature classes appropriately focus on specific language—the techniques of language, as fashioned by a writer. He says: "In language arts there may be more interest in . . . what language is used, what metaphors, similes, whatever, what descriptive words are used." Lee, in fact, used the construct of "language" throughout our interviews as a way to differentiate English and history:

> "I think what might be done in language arts class is to dissect the language more closely . . . to be as interested in the language as the message."
> "But what is paramount in your activity is not what was said finally, but what language was used to say it."

Lee perceives language as a utensil that an author employs to achieve a particular effect. A reader's goal in English, for Lee, is to understand the rhetorical tools used to create such an effect. Lee, for example, contrasts this disciplinary task with that of history:

> [History] is not as nitpicky. You know, we're not looking at the words, what word did they use to describe this that made it different. The specific language is not as important.

On the one hand, then, Lee carves out a defined role for English in relation to common texts in an interdisciplinary setting. But on the other hand, Lee voices subtle impatience here with the specific disciplinary concerns of English. Literary study itself is here designated as "nitpicky" in comparison with history—in other words, overly focused on detail.

Lee, in fact, had difficulty articulating a version of English with which he seemed completely comfortable. He acknowledged, initially, that connecting with students' emotions may be a legitimate goal in English class.

> I think [Barb] has a different type of objective than I do. And I think both are important for kids. I mean I think it's important for kids to have that kind of emotional education, but they shouldn't have it in social studies class.

Later in the same interview, Lee's approval of emotional education receded further:

I think kids need that, but I'm not sure it's education. I mean, what are they learning, you know? And I think, I don't have the luxury of doing that in a social studies class. I mean, it's a whole different kind of thing.

In rejecting emotional education, Lee draws a dividing line between the disciplines, suggesting that English may indulge itself in questionable content. In other words, Lee implicitly creates an intellectual hierarchy—with learning in social studies considerably more rigorous and objective than in English/language arts. In fact, Lee told Barb at the end of our interviews, regarding teachers changing to new subject areas: "I think it's easier to go from social studies to language arts than vice versa. The amount of subject knowledge."

Lee, in the end, perceives English as something of a conflicted discipline—a discipline that attends to the emotional lives of students, only to obscure the process of learning from texts. Literature study legitimately focuses on an author's use of language, yet Lee himself finds the effort "nitpicky." These observations frame Lee's comments about the entire course of interdisciplinary conversation at McDonnell Project meetings:

I think the frustration for me is just the whole concept of analyzing literature. . . . I'm at a place intellectually where I'm tired of analyzing literature. I've done it a lot in my life, and so I'm not really interested in it . . . and I'm not sure what exactly it is, so for me it's just not very satisfying.

Lee's dissatisfaction with the literature discussions stems in some measure from his unresolved version of English—a discipline with which he has yet to come to terms. While he has "done it a lot" in his life, he also admits "I'm not sure exactly what it is." He perceives little to gain from interpreting novels with colleagues. In the same conversation, Lee said: "But to sit around and talk about *Jasmine* . . . you know, I've done it so much in the past that I'm not—I don't know what it is I could learn."

Barb: Integrating Literature and History

In her initial interview, Barb commented that her M.A.T. program in English education had shaped and affirmed her views about teaching English. Barb says she gained theoretical validation for her instincts—for valuing student response and for not always grading. She says of her own approach to narrative, "I'm not analyzing literature anymore, I'm analyzing my response to literature." For Barb, interpreting literary texts presumes an open field of meaning. The personal and the textual are interrelated. She criticizes, for example, Lee's belief that "the personal" may be irrelevant to reading:

> My sense is that Lee has some real fears, or some misconceptions about what it is you do in an English class. . . . He has a perception that there's pertinent and impertinent things, when you're with kids and literature. And my feeling is . . . anything goes and you sort it out.

Barb's views reflect an overall constructivist orientation, yet she frames her comment in terms of disciplinary perceptions. Lee's "misconception" is a particular affront to what goes on in English class, for example. Although Barb is aware of other disciplinary approaches to literature in her department, she defends her views as central to literary understanding.

> When you deal with literature . . . you encourage kids to make any and all responses, and that's why the response journal is so important. What's on your mind here? . . . Let's talk about what you've read, and everything gets dredged up, brought to the surface in language, either in writing or in talking. . . . And then the things that get said and read get looked at. . . . So many kids . . . have kind of buried hostilities and strange reactions to literature that they've never been allowed to voice before. . . . If you get those out in the open, sometimes they are very valuable.

For Barb, literature allows students to voice things "that they've never been allowed to voice before." Literature encourages a unique mode of thought, an explicit attention to, and reflection upon, the self in the processes of reading, something other than the "reading for content" that students often carry over from other subject areas.

Barb's views strongly echo the reader-response tradition in contemporary literary theory, a view of literary understanding with growing influence in secondary schools (Marshall & Smith, 1997). In fact, she resists any approach to interpreting literature that would short-circuit student response or personal meaning-making. She struggled, for example, with the thematic focus of her curriculum group during project meetings. Planning around broad themes represents a popular strategy for integrating curriculum, yet Barb described her discomfort with this approach, a discomfort related to her vision for literature:

> I get a real strong sense that they are theme-driven, and I'm not.

It's never the literature for the literature's sake, but it's trying to find literature that works for the theme, and that always seems a little, oh, not misguided, but it wouldn't be my first way to organize. I've tried thematic approaches before, and they don't work for me. I like the quirkiness of individual works of literature.

Brainstorming literature "to fit the theme" sabotages the process of literary understanding for Barb. Formulating themes *for* students diminishes the interaction between reader and literature—limiting possibilities for meaning and the chance for the unexpected. The thematic approach, in other words, gives too much control to the teacher and too much power to the text itself when it comes to literary understanding.

However, Barb rejects the idea that her discipline is untethered and emotional, a misconception she believes Lee holds: "Well, Lee seems to think that 'I'm here as a representative of the factual bastion, and you guys are over there mucking around in your emotions.'" In the same interview, Barb said, "Well, I guess, he seems to be worried that we're not doing what's important; that somehow we're out there just doing, letting kids spew their opinions out." In contrast, Barb sees herself keeping text and reader in balance. In our first interview she recalled Lee's surprise during one project meeting at his English colleagues' rigorous reading of a novel:

> His sense is that it was all free floating. [But] we were all expecting each other to go find the text, in the text, nose ground[ed] to the text to get where—I mean there was a real strong sense that you had to point to a place. And he was very surprised at that, and that felt very, I think, respectable to him, that we were grounded in our discussion.

A grounded reading of literature is no surprise for Barb. In her interview with Lee, she balanced her emphasis on student response with a focus on the text: "I wrestle with kids all the time about this. The text has to stay in focus. You can't go off on a tangent." Barb offered an example of a student who began writing about *Waiting for Godot*:

> I said I want to know what's on your mind about this, and [one student] wrote a paper about swimming. And she started talking about *Waiting for Godot* and then she went on for two pages on herself. And she sort of thought she could get away with it. . . . Let's get back to the text. Whatever's on your mind has got to be seen through the text. You've got to be quoting.

Teaching history, for Barb, is a matter of helping students construct meanings from texts and documents whose meanings cannot be predetermined. Such readings, as with literature, should be both response-oriented and text-based. While Barb would direct students toward "What happened?" in a historical text, the answer to that question would not necessarily be under the teacher's control. I asked Barb in the first interview if her ideas for literary reading would fit a history classroom. She replied:

> Oh, I would hope so—that kind of open-ended, up for grabs, connecting to history and the writing texts about history. It's . . . almost heresy being given documents about Lexington and then saying "you go make some meaning here." And it's like, we're not going to tell you what to think, you've got to make meaning out of all these documents.

Barb seems aware that students do not usually learn history in this way. Yet she believes that encouraging students to employ their imaginations with historical texts will help them make sense of history in personally relevant ways. In our first interview, she referred to excerpts from a study of student historical understanding, which teachers had read at a project meeting. In that study (Wineburg, 1991), a student trying to make sense of different accounts of the Battle of Lexington had imagined himself on Lexington Green. Barb told me:

> And somebody—like the high school kid who in fact could actually set himself into the scenario and understand fear . . . I mean that's so wonderfully personal as a way of making meaning. How often does that ever happen in a history situation? That's what I was really impressed with.

Barb values the student's process of setting himself "into the scenario" of a historical text—to feel the events for himself. Reading texts in this fashion makes the process "wonderfully personal." These comments echo Barb's thoughts on teaching the novel *Things Fall Apart*:

> The author is so particularly good at drawing you into the novel. I don't think anyone could read that book and not feel the emotional education. . . . Oh yeah, I can learn about Nigeria and what happened in Nigeria and not feel a damn thing. [But] that book seems to me to be such a wonderful education about feeling what happened and thereby understanding it.

Barb specifies a way of knowing that she believes is appropriate to the stories of both history and literature: namely, "feeling what happened and thereby understanding it." She seeks above all an empathic reader, a reader willing imaginatively to "live through" other situations and times in order to make sense of them. Barb, in fact, became animated by the thought that history classrooms would begin to support students "placing themselves" within narratives:

> What's so interesting to me is that here are alternative ways of presenting history as almost a mystery and a puzzle and points of view that really put the responsibility on the kid for dealing with the information. . . . Who would have ever imagined placing themselves in [Lexington] Green and imagining where you would be. That strikes me as being an interesting way to learn history.

Barb made few explicit distinctions, throughout our interviews, between ways of reading literature and ways of reading history. What she saw as distinctly historical understanding remained unclear; in fact, she resisted somewhat any separating of the disciplines. Asked to identify the objectives of each discipline in relation to specific texts, Barb replied: "Let's just talk about these as texts, and how we as readers are reading these, regardless of what our specialties are." In Barb's initial project interview she remarked that she would teach social studies much like she teaches English. In our first interview, she speculated about "incorporating" social studies into her own classroom:

> I suppose I've considered to what extent I can incorporate more social studies activities. . . . I guess I've even thought, you know, that historical documents are so oriented to language [they] seem like fair game for an English classroom. There shouldn't be any kind of problem. . . . I certainly don't have to stick to literature in working with documents.

Barb has realized, over the course of the project meetings, that historical texts can serve as rich interpretive events. She is willing to move beyond short stories, novels, and poems with her students. For Barb, this was a new idea, and one she felt she might be able to pursue in the classroom. Barb's views on historical understanding itself, however, remained unclear.

INTERDISCIPLINARY IMPASSE

In the end, Lee's vision for interdisciplinary collaboration involved parallel teaching. He carefully delineated the tasks of social studies:

> Okay, let's just hypothetically say that we're reading a book about a woman that had an abortion, and in the language arts class they're talking about that book. Well, in my class we could talk about Roe versus Wade, and we could talk about what states had abortions before Roe versus Wade, and we could talk about Webster versus Reproductive Health Services, and we could talk about [how] President Clinton just vetoed the law. We could talk about the Fourteenth, Ninth, Fourth Amendment, whatever! And then . . . I would be doing my job.

Lee enumerates a list of specific content objectives that would define his role. He leaves little room for disciplinary cross-over. Lee's job, in this imagined collaboration, involves conveying the information of his own curricular niche—namely, content knowledge in American Government and Constitutional Law.

Barb, on the contrary, looked to bring the disciplines together. As Barb's comments suggest, she perceives both literary and historical texts as language events requiring human response and interpretation. In some ways, Barb's practical picture of interdisciplinary work resembles Lee's. That is, she hopes to apply her *own* orientation to texts—irrespective of what her colleague is doing. The structure of the profession may play a significant role here, as Lee and Barb both fashion interdisciplinary visions that are self-contained and promote intellectual autonomy. That is, as they imagine teaching across disciplines, neither Barb nor Lee creates a scenario in which they rely much on another colleague's input or knowledge for their own teaching.

But the forces are not only organizational. Barb's rejection of themes as a way to organize literature instruction contrasts conspicuously with Lee's reliance on themes as a compass for thinking about literature. Lee's belief that the analysis of "language" (rhetorical devices, words) belongs to English conflicts with Barb's view that historical texts are "so oriented to language." Lee holds onto a version of English with which he has not come to terms completely. Barb has difficulty articulating a distinct view for historical understanding. Barb's and Lee's differing epistemological orientations shape relatively incompatible road maps for literature and history. However, their unique disciplinary constructions may also serve to keep their respective epistemologies in place. Rather than "borrowing" disciplinary perspectives, Lee and Barb tend to project one "way of know-ing," a way each assumes extensively within his or her own discipline, across both subject areas.

Not surprisingly, Lee and Barb perceived themselves to be at a kind of impasse. Reflecting on the first transcripts, Lee questioned Barb's un-derstanding of the disciplines: "I think I understand more than she does . . . the differences in the content areas—the difference in what our objec-tives are." Barb offered the following, by contrast: "Lee may need to con-nect with us more than we need to connect with him. . . . He hasn't con-nected in language arts in any way for so long. . . . He really needs to understand more about what we're doing."

CONCLUSION: INTERDISCIPLINARY POSSIBILITIES

It may be, as Beane (1995) suggests, that life itself does not know the compartments we call the disciplines. Neither, the argument goes, should our curricular designs and activities. Yet, while "life itself" may not know such subject divisions, Lee and Barb know them, experience them, and regularly employ them as part of the intellectual context of their work. As the opening excerpt shows, Barb and Lee were willing project partici-pants, openly debating literary and historical texts during large group meetings. However, their potential for "combining and synthesizing" dis-ciplinary perspectives for teaching remains problematic. Such potential collaboration seems to falter in part on divergent disciplinary landscapes for history and literature and on contrasting ideas on how to bring these subject areas into relationship.

Lee and Barb's differing conceptions for history and literature should not surprise us. Yet their case illustrates issues that typically go undis-cussed as teachers and districts adopt interdisciplinary models. For ex-ample, teachers' own disciplinary assumptions often operate largely be-neath the surface, rather than explicitly (Applebee, 1995). Making such subject matter thinking visible, for oneself and for colleagues, may be a critical step in better understanding learning contexts for secondary teachers and in creating possibilities for interdisciplinary reform. If any-thing, the case of Lee and Barb should awaken us from a complacent belief that interdisciplinary arrangements can revive our schools without profiling the nuanced disciplinary thinking of teachers themselves.

Research on subject matter contexts for secondary teachers has yet to consider the way in which teachers think about disciplines *other* than their own—and the implications this may hold for interdisciplinary re-form. Neither Barb nor Lee, as we have seen, is a blank slate with respect to each other's discipline, waiting to "receive" the disciplinary tools and perspectives of one's colleague. Rather, each brings express views on how the other's discipline should operate, and on what it means for students to understand in the other's subject area.

Barb believes, for example, that history classrooms can accommodate her vision of reader response. Yet the role of "imaginative empathy" in relation to historical understanding raises pivotal questions. Despite the motivating connections students make when they draw on personal experience, this kind of empathic understanding may unwittingly confine a contemporary reader's historical perspective. Seixas (1996), for example, specifies "historical empathy" as a common but potentially misleading approach to historical texts. Reading texts in this way "specifies no safeguards against thoroughly ahistorical 'imaginative reconstructions' based on insufficient evidence from traces of the past" (p. 20). In other words, the approach may fail to cultivate in readers an understanding of the nature of historical evidence. Students may fail to appreciate the role psychological distance and detachment must play if historical readings are not simply to become exercises in anachronism—defining the past in terms of one's own personal experiences (Wineburg, 1999). Barb, in blurring the subject matter lines of history and English, may in fact encroach upon the disciplinary nuances that distinguish historical reading *as* historical and which provide it power as a distinct way of knowing.

For Lee, literature classrooms should focus more clearly on the text in itself and on the intentional use of language by an author. This text-based stance reflects a New Critical approach to literary texts, a school of criticism that may have governed Lee's university work in English. On the one hand, this exclusive view of literary understanding reduces a wide horizon of approaches to literary understanding to a single view. On the other hand, a "text-based stance" begs the question: What exactly makes a reading uniquely literary? Langer (1995), for example, conceives literary understanding as a process of "envisionment"—imagining new worlds, exploring possible horizons, trying out roles that one might otherwise be excluded from, or fear, in everyday life. Literary discourse is not about gathering or sharing information (both text-based activities), but about "living through a situation in a subjective manner" (p. 25). For Langer, a common misconception in teaching and learning literature is to understand the process as "analysis"—in other words, as making and defending points. By contrast, students who "understand" literature must learn to evoke, and temporarily live through, "secondary worlds" (Benton, 1992), so that these worlds can then work back upon them, loosening, reshaping and enlarging readers' present conceptions of reality. Rosenblatt (1938/1976) thus argues that through understanding literature one acquires not so much additional information as additional *experience* (p. 47). As Barb suspects, Lee's vision for reading literature may close off uniquely "literary" aspects of students' engagement with literature.

Supporting teachers' interdisciplinary efforts may first involve help-ing teachers interpret their own disciplinary assumptions, both about their own and about other disciplines. Interdisciplinary teaming, efforts that bring different ways of knowing into dialogue, must include more than designing lessons and units for students. Teachers need time to sur-face their own beliefs and to define the unique questions of their disci-plines. Successful interdisciplinary work will require, paradoxically, a strengthening of interactions *within* departments. The department itself may be the most productive location for teachers to hash out their com-peting versions of subject matter, become more conscious of their own disciplinary assumptions, and develop a vocabulary for making such assumptions explicit for cross-departmental colleagues (see Newell & Holt, 1997).

Disciplinary assumptions are woven into the landscape of secondary teaching, so much so that they are often difficult to locate and disen-tangle. Yet such assumptions represent powerful inner networks for teacher thinking and ultimately set the conditions for interdisciplinary cooperation. A close examination of Barb and Lee's interaction may help illuminate the complexities of that process—and may encourage more informed thinking about those teacher interactions that will have decisive implications for student learning.

REFERENCES

Applebee, A. N. (1995). *Curriculum as conversation: Transforming traditions of teach-ing and learning*. Chicago: University of Chicago Press.

Beane, J. A. (1995). Curriculum integration and the disciplines of knowledge. *Phi Delta Kappan, 76*(8), 616–622.

Benton, M. (1992). *Secondary worlds: Literature teaching and the visual arts*. Bucking-ham, England: Open University Press.

Habermas, J. (1984). *The theory of communicative action, Vol. 1, Reason and the ratio-nalization of society* (T. McCarthy, Trans.). Boston: Beacon Press.

Hartman, D. K. (1995). Eight readers reading: The intertextual links of proficient readers reading multiple passages. *Reading Research Quarterly, 30*(3), 520–561.

Hofer, B. K., & Pintrich, P. R. (1997). The development of epistemological theories: Beliefs about knowledge and knowing and their relation to learning. *Review of Educational Research, 67*(1), 88–140.

Huberman, M. (1993). The model of the independent artisan in teachers' profes-sional relations. In J. W. Little & M. W. McLaughlin (Eds.), *Teachers' work:*

Individuals, colleagues, and contexts (pp. 11–50). New York: Teachers College Press.

Iser, W. (1978). *The act of reading*. Baltimore: John Hopkins University Press.

Langer, J. A. (1995). *Envisioning literature: Literary understanding and literature instruction*. New York: Teachers College Press.

Little, J. W. (1982). Norms of collegiality and experimentation: Workplace conditions for school success. *American Educational Research Journal, 19*(3), 325–340.

Little, J. W. (1990). The persistence of privacy: Autonomy and initiative in teachers' professional relations. *Teachers College Record, 91*, 509–536.

Marshall, J., & Smith, J. (1997). Teaching as we're taught: The university's role in the education of English teachers. *English Education, 29*(4), 246–268.

McLaughlin, M. W. (1993). What matters most in teachers' workplace context? In J. W. Little & M. W. McLaughlin (Eds.), *Teachers' work: Individuals, colleagues, and contexts* (pp. 79–103). New York: Teachers College Press.

Newell, G. E., & Holt, R. A. (1997). Autonomy and obligation in the teaching of literature: Teachers' classroom curriculum and departmental consensus. *English Education, 29*(1), 18–37.

Rosenblatt, L. (1938/1976). *Literature as exploration*. New York: Noble & Noble.

Rosenblatt, L. (1978). *The reader, the text, the poem*. Carbondale, IL: Southern Illinois University Press.

Seixas, P. (1996). Conceptualizing the growth of historical understanding. In D. R. Olsen & N. Torrance (Eds.), *Handbook of education and human development* (pp. 765–783). Oxford, England: Blackwell Publishers.

Wineburg, S. S. (1991). Historical problem solving: A study of the cognitive processes used in the evaluation of documentary and pictorial evidence. *Journal of Educational Psychology, 83*, 73–87.

Wineburg, S. S. (1999). Historical thinking and other unnatural acts. *Phi Delta Kappan, 80*(7), 488–499.

Wineburg, S. S., & Grossman, P. L. (1998). Building a community of learners among high school teachers. *Phi Delta Kappan, 79*(5), 350–353.

5

Curricular Conversations in Elementary School Classrooms
Case Studies of Interdisciplinary Instruction

ARTHUR N. APPLEBEE, ROBERT BURROUGHS,
AND GLADYS CRUZ

In this chapter, we will examine issues of interdisciplinary instruction from a perspective that treats curriculum as creating domains for conversation, and instruction as the ways in which we help students enter into those domains. In approaching curriculum as domains for conversation, we are interested in particular in the kinds of conversations that the curriculum is designed to foster and support. (We construe contributions to the conversation broadly to include contemporary and classic texts in a variety of media, as well as the contributions of the teacher and students.) These conversations are the vehicle through which a student learns to enter into the various universes of discourse that our society values—to read, write, and talk about current and ongoing issues in history, literature, science, or the arts, for example. Effective entry into such conversations requires knowledge of content as well as knowledge of appropriate ways of knowing and doing within each domain: The facts must be right, and the arguments and evidence must be appropriate, bridging the dualism of "knowing how" and "knowing that." From this perspective, the teacher plays a crucial role not only in organizing the curricular domain within which the conversations will occur, but also in mediating between the language of the classroom and that of the larger conversations to which the classroom domain is related (Applebee, 1996)—typically, the conversations that take place within the academic disciplines.

In earlier studies, we have examined the features that create continuity and coherence within the curricular domains within discipline-based classrooms (Applebee, 1996; Applebee, Burroughs, & Stevens, 2000; Burroughs, 1999; Stevens, 1999). We found that two mechanisms were important. One had to do with the overall structure of the conversational domain—the extent to which issues and topics were related to one another, allowing new understandings to be developed and enriched over time. The second had to do with the conventions for participating in the conversation: Curricular conversations gained coherence from a stable set of expectations about the roles of the participants, the issues that were considered discussable, and the kinds of argument and evidence that would be accepted as convincing. These underlying domain conventions vary greatly from discipline to discipline, and even within subareas within the same school subject—they define genres of speech and writing (Bakhtin, 1986) that govern all aspects of participation. (See also Berkenkotter & Huckin, 1995; Grossman & Stodolsky, 1995; Herrington, 1985; Langer, 1992; McCarthy, 1987.)

THE INTERDISCIPLINARY CONTINUUM

What happens, however, when traditional discipline-based activities are replaced by integrated or interdisciplinary approaches to instruction? Such approaches have been widely advocated in recent years (Beane, 1997; Jacobs, 1997; Tchudi & Lafer, 1996) but have been difficult to evaluate, in part because they include a wide variety of different configurations of curriculum and instruction. At one extreme an interdisciplinary team may be used simply to describe an organizational approach in which a set of subject area specialists (usually math, science, language arts, and social studies) share pastoral responsibility for the same group of students but develop and teach their disciplinary curricula independently. In such cases, the curricular conversations that are developed remain firmly within the traditional subject areas. At the other extreme, an interdisciplinary team may develop and plan a totally new curricular domain that draws on concepts and addresses issues that span or even go beyond those of any of the contributing subject areas. Entirely new conversations may result, as, for example, in environmental studies.

At the Center on English Learning and Achievement, we have defined an interdisciplinary continuum that highlights some important variations from one program to the next (Adler & Flihan, 1997). As depicted in Figure 5.1, at one end of the continuum are curricular domains that simply correlate related subjects: Literature may be correlated with history, for example, by teaching both chronologically. In these cases the

FIGURE 5.1: The Interdisciplinary Continuum

Correlated Knowledge	Shared Knowledge	Reconstructed Knowledge
Represented as: Multidisciplinary Complementary Juxtaposed Parallel, sequenced Thematic (passive) Webbed	*Represented as:* Thematic (active) Interdisciplinary Integrated Broad-field curriculum	*Represented as:* Synthesized Blended, fused Core curriculum Problem-centered Integrated/ive

Characterized by:
Related Concepts
	Characterized by:
	Preserving
	  disciplinary
	  boundaries
	Overlapping concepts
	Emergent patterns
	Disciplines mutually
	  supported
		Characterized by:
		Eliminating disciplinary
		  boundaries

Disciplines most distinct ➤ Disciplines most blended

curricular conversations that take place in each subject will proceed quite independently of one another, each illuminating different facets of the shared superstructure (the history, arts, and literature of the Middle Ages, for example). In the middle of the continuum are curricular domains in which important concepts are shared across disciplinary fields, though discussions continue to be located within one or another of the independent disciplines. Social studies and English classes, for example, might both explore concepts of justice during the Middle Ages. At the other end of the continuum are reconstructed curricular domains that merge concepts and understandings across disciplines in order to create curricular conversations that go beyond disciplinary boundaries (as in the New Historicism, which would merge the discourse of history and literature in the Middle Ages in a way that moves beyond the meanings typically constructed in either field).

The interdisciplinary continuum as presented in Figure 5.1 is an abstraction that can be helpful in program planning and evaluation, though we are finding that in practice different parts of a curriculum—and different participants in an ongoing course—may fall at different points along the continuum. In some of our case studies, the curricular domain has shifted over the year from correlated toward reconstructed—and sometimes sharply back again toward the end of the course when external examinations (almost always disciplinary in focus) begin to loom.

The present chapter draws on one extended and several shorter examples of interdisciplinary curricula drawn from our studies. Using case study methodologies, we have studied individual classrooms over extended periods of time, exploring through interviews with teachers and students, classroom observations, and analysis of classroom work the ways in which curricular conversations were defined and enacted within each classroom (see Applebee, 1996; Applebee, Burroughs, & Stevens, 2000; Burroughs, 1999; Stevens, 1999).

In the examples that follow, all of the teachers involved felt that they had successfully aligned a variety of disciplines to create a more coherent environment for teaching and learning. As we will see, however, in each case there are significant questions about how successful these curricular domains were in fostering coherent and cumulative conversations.

INTERDISCIPLINARY CONVERSATIONS
IN A FIFTH-GRADE TEAM

Our first example is a fifth-grade team working to create a curricular domain that would represent shared knowledge on our continuum. Matt Grey and Ernie Green worked as a team with about 50 students at White School in Riverhill, New Jersey. (All names and places are pseudonyms.) Grey was the language arts and social studies teacher; Green was the science and math teacher. Typically, the students had 2 hours of language arts/social studies per day and 2 hours of science/math per day, although that varied depending on how each teacher had structured a particular unit. In addition to creating separate language arts/social studies and science/math curricula, Grey and Green also created "team units" where students integrated all four subjects. Within these units, the curriculum was organized to highlight shared concepts across the subject areas.

Conversational Domains in Language Arts and Social Studies

In Grey's language arts/social studies curriculum, social studies drove the conversations, perhaps because Grey was trained as a high school history teacher. In an early interview, Grey was explicit about his intent to let social studies drive the curriculum:

I just want them to develop [a] kind of process. I'm also using language arts to build understanding in science and social studies. The students are reading historical novels . . . [and] gain insight into the characters . . . and they are also understanding the time period more than just reading the textbook. (Interview, October 6)

Though Grey had a language arts curriculum apart from social studies, the study of novels was embedded within historical conversations, rather than literary ones, raising issues of what is lost as well as gained in such combinations.

There were two major conversational domains in Grey's social studies curriculum. The first concerned colonization, the second, the Revolutionary War. We will use colonization to illustrate how this classroom worked.

Colonization.   From September to March, Grey's students talked about colonization and colonial life in various ways. As a backdrop to colonization, they began by studying various Native American tribes and tribal life, discussing such topics as what makes a society, divisions of labor, living conditions, gender roles, and "discovery" as a relative term. From Native American societies, students moved to talk about different regional colonies. They compared the English and Spanish colonies; they studied the "lost colony" of Roanoke, Virginia; they studied the southern colonies; they studied the Puritans. As they talked about each different region, they applied many of the concepts they had discussed in relation to Native Americans.

The whole conversational domain was framed by a fairly elaborate software package entitled "Decisions, Decisions: Colonization" (Tom Snyder Productions, 1996). Using video, print, and computer software, this simulation guides students through some of the decisions involved in founding a colony. During the course of the simulation, they run into a native population, they don't find energy sources, and they struggle with the pressures exerted by return-hungry investors.

Students played this simulation about halfway through the fall semester after they had studied Native American tribes, but before they had studied colonization. The "decisions" format became a way of focusing conversations about colonization. Grey explained his approach as:

We will speculate about what happened at Roanoke where a colony disappeared. We will talk about the theories of what happened and then we will take our criteria from "Decisions" and apply them to Roanoke and other colonies. (Interview, December 21)

At the end of March, when Grey moved away from topics of colonization, he had his students run the "Decisions, Decisions: Colonization" simulation again. His intent was to see how their notions of colonization had changed with the benefit of real historical data to reference:

> [Students] gain a bit of a historical perspective from the book that comes with the software. . . . Then we are going to go into the textbook and cover all the topics we talk about in "Decisions," using them as criteria for judging the decisions the other colonists made. . . . At the end of the program they evaluate student decision-making and give certain scores. We will save the scores and then two months later see how we do with the historical perspective. It is one of those few times when you can actually show the kids how a historical perspective can help make decisions. (Interview, December 7)

It is important to note here that the simulation was not a substitute for the study of history. Rather, it was a place to begin the study of history by providing students a frame for their conversations about history, though admittedly a frame that stresses using history for other purposes.

Language Arts.   Grey often integrated the language arts part of his curriculum with the social studies curriculum. For example, almost all of the novels that students read through the year were tied to themes developed in the social studies curriculum. Novels like *Squanto, The Double Life of Pocohontas,* and *Constance,* for example, were read during the early units on Native Americans.

Grey did think of himself as having a separate language arts curriculum, however, and here he focused on what we have called "domain conventions": These are the strategies and ways of knowing that are appropriate within a given conversational domain. As he explained in an early interview:

> The main thing I want to stress this year is active reading strategies, where students are really thinking about what they are doing, thinking about the reading process. Doing some predicting and previewing before they read, developing guidelines or deciding what they want to know, and using that as a guide throughout the reading so they are not just reading words but they are searching for something. (Interview, October 6)

Strategies like predicting, making inferences, and drawing conclusions were highlighted for the students to help them become more expert participants—in their reading, writing, and discussion. Grey tied this focus on process to the social studies curriculum as well. He was most interested in getting his students to see "processes" involved in studying history:

> I'm getting them used to the way to study history and historiography basically. What types of materials are primary and secondary sources and how to look at things and debate them. . . . My main concern is that they look at historical fiction as a source to gain insight into characters' views but also look at things like the electronic encyclopedia, biographies and straight textbooks and really be able to draw their own conclusions. (Interview, March 31)

As with the simulations, Grey used the novels as an aspect of his social studies curriculum, not as a substitute. For example, in the colonization conversation students read a letter from Columbus to a Spanish friend. Grey framed the conversation to focus upon the issue of reconciling an author's perspective in interpreting documents.

Though the novels were integrated with the social studies conversation, they were also dominated by the conversation and limited by it. The focus was almost entirely upon the novels as settings for historical events and as contexts for imaginative insights into past lives as they were represented in fictional characters. Grey also often paired the reading, writing, spelling, and grammar activities of the language arts curriculum with the social studies unit.

Conversational Domains in Science and Math

Green's integration of the science and math curricula mirrored Grey's approach to social studies and language arts: One subject, in this case science, drove the curricular conversations, but throughout, Green maintained a consistent emphasis on the conventions that govern scientific conversation, emphasizing what he called "learning how to be a scientist." In fact, this emphasis on the processes of science and mathematics provided the underlying coherence within his curriculum.

In the wrap-up interview at the end of the year, Green addressed specifically the problem of content and process. He emphasized the critical thinking and problem solving that his curriculum was intended to foster:

Yes, there are certain fundamental truths, certain fundamental for-
mulas in math, especially in the elementary level, that are very important. . . . [But] at our level we either get them very excited about
continuing with science or we turn them completely off to it. So being able to act like a scientist, first of all they learn better and sec-
ondly it builds an excitement for learning. . . . Knowing where to
find the answers is more important in science now. So we are doing
less things now but we are doing them better. (Interview, June 14)

It is worth noting here that Green, like Grey, construes his subject matter
more broadly than science or mathematics. As Grey seemed to stress a
more generic group of thinking skills than "historical thinking," Green
here also stresses a more general kind of critical thinking or problem
solving than a specific form of disciplinary thinking. Given their goals, it
is not surprising that neither Grey nor Green were conducting disciplinary conversations in their fullest sense.

Integrating Conversational Domains

Grey and Green further integrated their curricula in special units that
they created in tandem. A unit on exploration is a good example. The
unit lasted about 3 months, focusing on 3 different explorers, one each
month. The first month focused on Columbus; the second on Matthew
Henson, an African American colleague of Perry's; and the third on astro-
naut Sally Ride. The exploration unit as a whole had strong ties to the
social studies conversations about colonization. Topics such as "exploration," "discovery," and "clash of cultures" were often discussed within
the colonization domain.

The integration that they achieved is evident in the projects and activities created for the Columbus unit. In one project, the students created
"boats" out of a 6-inch-square piece of aluminum. They were told to create the best flotation device to hold a "treasure" of pennies. The boat that
held the most pennies was the winner. The project was based on the idea
that Columbus's ships had limited space and that bringing back treasure
to Spain was a primary goal of exploration. Green commented that this
was also a good lesson in surface tension. He also had students compute
the range, median, mode, and mean number of pennies in each class. As
Green explained,

The range, mode, and median became meaningful because they began to realize things like, the average [mean], wasn't just a term. It
meant something to them because now, "I fell below the average."

Also the range. If they saw they were in the low range, who brought the average down, who brought it up. (Interview, October 7)

In terms of our interdisciplinary continuum, Grey's and Green's curricula are a good example of an emphasis on shared knowledge, where the disciplines are distinct yet mutually supportive. In this case, the strongest connections had to do with the conventions underlying the curricular domain—the shared concern with appropriate strategies and processes. Other parts of the curriculum reflected what we have called correlated knowledge, as when Grey used stories by and about Native Americans in conjunction with the study of the period of colonization.

SOME OTHER EXAMPLES OF INTEGRATION

Grey's and Green's emphasis on processes of understanding created a context in which the work going on in four separate disciplines reinforced some conversations but neglected others. In this section we will discuss three additional examples: An integrated kindergarten curriculum where the disciplines did not play a significant role; a correlated first-grade curriculum where the interdisciplinary ties sometimes interrupted rather than reinforced the curricular conversation; and a correlated fourth-grade curriculum in which the connections among subjects were evident to the teacher but went largely unnoticed by the students.

All of these classes were part of the Rockville (New York) Academy of Arts, a magnet school with a curriculum that focused on art, music, and the study of languages. The school served a multicultural student body: 48% of the students were classified as white, 44% as African American, 6% as Hispanic, and the remainder as Asian.

Extending Everyday Concepts

Elba Gomez taught a full-day kindergarten class of 21 students, basing her curriculum on the language arts series adopted by the district. This was organized around themes drawn from children's everyday knowledge and experiences, including such topics as "All about Me" (focusing on self-awareness, names, feelings), "Family" (families, relationships), "Color is Everywhere" (color awareness), and "In the Barnyard" (barnyard animals, rural areas).

Gomez introduced 16 of these themes over the course of the school year, using them as the focus for conversational domains that integrated work in all subject areas. As Gomez described it,

If the theme is "Family" or "Pumpkins" or so forth, all the books will be based on that theme, and then I'll try to extend that to the other areas such as math and science. For math . . . we could graph how many members are in a family, where the child falls in that family, if they be youngest, the oldest, and so forth, and we try to make it more natural for them to learn. (Interview, October 26)

Focusing on everyday, familiar experiences, the kindergarten themes elaborated upon these experiences by generating as wide a variety of connections as possible. Gomez talked about how she planned her activities for the theme "Color is Everywhere":

Our theme right now is colors, so during literature . . . we'll do color books, color poems, color songs. During art, we'll do color mixing. During social studies, we can read about an artist, and talk about the colors they use, and so forth, so what I'll try to do is use that same theme throughout the curriculum and integrate it so everything we do kind of ties together. (Interview, November 6)

Gomez organized her classroom around learning centers (e.g., writing, housekeeping, blocks, art, math and science, reading, listening, and the rug—six at a time, with the topics changing somewhat over the year). Students were broken up into six different groups, and each group would get to spend 15 or 20 minutes at each center and then be rotated. Activities at each center were tied to the theme. During a theme on pets in April, for example, we observed the math and science center set up to make pets with paper towel rolls and other materials (feathers, straws, paper). The reading center had books about animals; the writing center had posters about animals, divided into land, air, water, and underground animals—students cut pictures from magazines to complete the posters, or drew their own pictures and wrote about them. There was also a pet shop where students role-played buying and selling as shopkeepers and shoppers.

Integration of this sort adds depth to children's everyday knowledge and provides a context for many separate reading, writing, and discussion activities. It provides a sense of coherence to these activities, but does little to promote conversations with any continuity over time. Instead, the curriculum remains a collection of relatively isolated conversations and activities, each related to the common topic but not related in any fundamental way to each other. Jacob, a student in Ms. Gomez's class, provides a good example of how students might experience these loosely related activities tied to a theme. Describing what he had learned in the last theme of the year, Jacob said he: "Learn[ed] stuff about bears. . . . Like we made a bear. And yesterday we got to bring home the Three Little Bears thing. And we got to do all different kinds of stuff . . . " (Interview, June 7)

Although the teacher labeled the various activities in her classroom with traditional content-area labels (math, art, reading, social studies), the focus remained on familiar concepts drawn from the everyday world—"stuff about bears." Many of the subject area associations the teacher made were arbitrary, as when she associated reading about an artist with social studies. Because such curricula do not reflect any systematic approach to subject area knowledge, it seems best to follow Gardner and Boix-Mansilla (1994) in treating them and the conversations they foster as predisciplinary rather than interdisciplinary in emphasis. Such curricula may provide an appropriate transition from the conversations of the home to those of the school, but they seem different in kind from curricula that reflect systematic understandings. Indeed, framing such a curriculum as interdisciplinary confuses rather than clarifies what is happening. It leads, for example, to questionable associations between particular activities and their supposed disciplinary roots (reading about an artist as a social studies activity, for example).

Correlations that Interrupt Conversation

Although cross-disciplinary connections are designed to enrich and strengthen students' understanding, this only happens when they are planned in a way that supports rather than interrupts the curricular conversation. Martha Holmes's first-grade class of 25 provides an example of the difficulties that sometimes arise.

Holmes saw literature as the foundation of the curriculum, "the main thing that has to be discussed and taught in school. Literature does not stop or start with language arts. Again it is across the board" (Interview, November 30). Holmes used the themes in the literature series provided by the district to define her conversational domains, and rearranged the units in her science and social studies materials to correlate with those in literature. This meant, for example, that Holmes ignored the internal order of a social studies curriculum that began with the self and worked its way out to the world, placing the various units instead where they worked best with the sequence of themes in the language arts series.

The kinds of relationships that resulted were evident in the activities and discussion surrounding Judy Delton's *Two Good Friends*. Holmes correlated this language arts selection with social studies work on "friendships, chores, responsibilities, environment . . . ," science on "food, day/

night, weather, environment . . . ," math on writing "cookie/friendship recipes, fractions, measurement," and writing "Write about a good friend. Make cookies or something you like to share with your friend and bring it to class."

By using the language arts stories for the entire year as the frame, she was able to juggle the units and concepts to be covered in the other curriculum areas so that by the end of the year, she could feel confident she had covered all of the curriculum in all of the subject areas (Interview, June 7).

This approach, while covering the various curricula in a relatively systematic way, created problems of its own. The first stemmed from the somewhat tenuous connections that sometimes resulted from rearranging curricula that had originally been developed and organized with quite different concepts in mind. The stretch from friends to food to environment around "Two Good Friends" is typical of the kinds of extrapolations that were necessary, producing conversational domains in which some of the between-subject connections were strained at best. In the classroom, this created real discontinuities and distortions in the conversations that resulted. For example, in another series of lessons, the curriculum was correlated with "Beatrice Doesn't Want To," a story about a girl who doesn't like to read and is unhappy about going to the library with her brother. The social studies activities that were linked to this story had to do with "Buildings, historical sites, businesses, services offered. . . . " The following excerpts from our field notes describe the lesson that resulted.

> [After some preliminary vocabulary and spelling work, Holmes began just after 9 a.m.] to talk about the story and the library and how the library is the place that everyone can go and use. Then she asked the children about other buildings a town or city has for people and wrote them down on the board. She then shows them a sheet of a town with streets and different buildings and tells them they will do that sheet later on. . . . She then asks what is important for Ms. Holmes to ride around on the streets. Students reply:
> S1: A stop
> S2: A light
> S3: A sign
> She then tells the students they were right about signs. She then continues to talk about signs and says that a stop is like a period, a yield is like a comma: "You have to slow down." She then draws a No Smoking sign on the board. [The No Smoking sign is the beginning of an activity in which the students draw and write about

their own "don't wants."] Ms. Holmes says they are doing this activity because they are reading the story, "Beatrice Doesn't Like To."

At 11:15 she sums up the activity and relates it to the story they are reading and to signs. She then talks about signs. (Cruz, Classroom observation, March 14)

Although the teacher was clever in constructing transitions as she moved from one part of this lesson to another over a 2-hour period, the materials she was covering from the social studies curriculum were not related in any fundamental way to the story the class was reading or the writing they were doing. The continuity Holmes created was an artificial one that did not help the students enter into the conversation; indeed, the resulting class discussion was largely monologic (Nystrand, 1997), with students limited to giving brief answers at the points that Holmes had scripted.

This kind of correlation also resulted in some confusion on the students' part about what they were studying and how it related to anything else. In interviews, they had a clear sense of what they were doing for reading and writing, but had trouble talking about science or social studies. Danny told us that they spent the most time on science, social studies, and math because:

Danny: Ms. Holmes mixes science, social studies, and math all up. . . .
Cruz: How do you know she mixes them all up?
Danny: Because she told us. . . .
Cruz: What is mixing it up and how does she mix it up?
Danny: I don't know how she mixes it up she just mixes it up. (Interview, June 8)

Danny's "mixes it up" is an ironically accurate description of how Holmes constructed her curriculum, as she struggled to find connections among curricula originally written with very different curricular conversations in mind. Although it is clear that Holmes intended her interdisciplinary curriculum to enrich the concepts and understandings of the individual disciplines by building on connections among them, the gap was too large and the resulting conversations were sometimes simply "mixed up."

Correlations that Get Lost

In any classroom, curricular conversations operate at several different levels: as a formal plan for what will be discussed, as a set of activities and experiences that are negotiated among teacher and students, and as a set of understandings that students come away with. Although ideally there will be an obvious and natural connection among these versions of the curricular conversation, that is not always the case: conversations that frame the teacher's planning may not be enacted in the classroom, and things that seem obvious to the teacher may go unnoticed by the students. (Conversely, students may make connections and create conversations of which the teacher had not thought.) Intended conversations across disciplines are as liable to these kinds of slippages as are other aspects of the curriculum. Victoria Winters's fourth-grade class at Rockville Academy of the Arts illustrates this kind of problem.

Winters was responsible for teaching language arts, social studies, science, and math to her 25 fourth-graders; they had other teachers for a variety of other subjects. Winters sought to correlate the various subjects she taught around five themes that were explored in turn during the school year: Learning about Nature; the Iroquois; Children Respond to Adult Problems; Special Abilities; and Reading Books for Skill and Pleasure. As the titles suggest, the subjects that could be integrated easily varied from theme to theme. The curricular domain for the study of the Iroquois, for example, drew primarily on social studies and language arts. Planned activities included readings on early America and the Iroquois from the social studies text, Indian legends and tales (collected from the library) that students read and retold to the class, a visit from an Iroquois storyteller, vocabulary lessons around words drawn from the theme, activities in which students made birch bark baskets and their own dioramas of Iroquois life, and a culminating presentation to parents.

Winters was aware that connections could be strained, and saw no reason to force them:

> I just feel like it's quite enough that I can bring the language arts and the social studies together—and from things I've read—I mean the way they would bring the math in is to say you know there were seven Iroquois braves and three you know how . . . [laughs]. I feel I can make better use of my time than to recreate math problems using those vocabulary words. (Interview, December 8)

With other themes, other subject areas became part of the domain. In planning "Learning about Nature," for example, Winters included science activities on green plants, social studies lessons on land and climate, and math activities collecting information from graphs. Instruction in subjects that did not fit well with the theme of the moment continued, but (unlike

Martha Holmes) Winters did not stretch to make connections when they did not occur easily and naturally in the material to be covered.

Yet in spite of the careful correlations between subjects that Winters laid out in her planning, the conversation broke down into separate subjects in the classroom itself. Although activities within the separate subjects were linked by topic to the overall theme, in the classroom there was little writing or discussion across subject boundaries. Separate textbooks (or sometimes trade books) were used for each subject, in separate time periods, and discussions remained focused on the activity at hand. Winters clearly saw her curriculum as cumulative and reinforcing, but the conversations that were enacted undercut her larger goals.

In interviews, the students in this class saw little connection among the subjects, responding to a question about what they were studying with a list—science, social studies, math, reading—and an elaboration of the current activities within each subject. The correlations that Winters carefully built in were rarely articulated as the curriculum was enacted, and thus never became part of the conversations in which the students were involved. After talking with Kathy about the different activities she had been doing in Ms. Winters's class, for example, we asked her if any of them were related:

> *Kathy:* Well in Spanish and music you can sing songs in Spanish. I think that is it.
> *Cruz:* Do you think reading and writing are related?
> *Kathy:* Well you have to know how to read to write and you need to know the alphabet to write words and sentences. (Interview, December 19)

In a similar interview, Alvin was less willing to be led:

> *Cruz:* Have you noticed any connections or relationships between the activities?
> *Alvin:* No.
> *Cruz:* Like is reading related to social studies or is reading related to writing?
> *Alvin:* No. (Interview, March 27)

In this case, between-subject correlations that provided some sense of coherence to the curricular domain during the teacher's planning did not carry over into the curricular conversations that the students experienced. Presumably the benefits that are claimed for interdisciplinary curriculum did not carry over either.

CONCLUSION

In these examples, we have used the concept of curricular conversations to sort out some of the complexities that arise in interdisciplinary curricula. By one set of criteria, all of these curricula could be considered to be interdisciplinary, and in the casual vocabulary of the classroom (in which school subjects and their disciplinary roots are rarely disentangled) all of the teachers certainly considered them to be so. Subject areas were aligned in a variety of ways in the teachers' plan books and activities, and related concepts, processes, or themes were introduced in parallel across the subject areas. Yet if we judge interdisciplinarity in terms of the conversations supported by the curricula, the picture looks very different. As Matt Grey and Ernie Green worked to develop shared knowledge across disciplines with their fifth graders, the conversations that they generated tended to use one subject to support and enrich the other (language arts to support history; math to support science). Martha Holmes and Elba Gomez, in their attempts at correlated curriculum, similarly used the framework from one subject (in their cases, literature) to structure the curricular domain, subordinating other subjects to it. The particular choices made by these teachers may have resulted from their own interests and academic majors, but the subordination of one discipline to another is a frequent complaint in such combinations (for reviews, see Adler & Flihan, 1997; Applebee, 1974).

In contrast, Matt Grey and Ernie Green were quite successful in engaging their students in conversations about parallel processes of understanding within the four subjects they taught, helping students enter into meaningful conversations in a variety of domains. The development of these conversations was supported by a shared emphasis on the domain conventions appropriate to each subject, in particular the ways of making sense in social studies, science, language arts, and mathematics, as well as on broader processes of problem solving that the teachers saw as holding in common across these domains.

Focusing on curriculum as a domain for conversation, rather than on curriculum as a body of knowledge or content, also highlighted some of the ways in which well-intentioned efforts to make connections among subject areas can sometimes work against coherent curricula, disrupting conversations or serving to organize material for the teacher without making the connections evident to the students. Thus, Martha Holmes reorganized all of the content from her language arts, science, and social studies curricula into thematically related units, but because she was focusing on curriculum as content she was unaware of the extent to which her rearrangement worked against coherent conversations within and across the contributing disciplines. As a creative and energetic teacher, she carried her class with her, but it took immense effort because she was working against the very structures she had created to make teaching and learning easier.

Other issues raised by these case studies have to do with the notion of disciplinarity itself, its relationship to subject areas, and the ways in which disciplinary knowledge evolves over time. School and college subjects are at best loose amalgams of disciplines: science, math, English, and social studies have many contributing disciplines with different histories, vocabularies, and ways of gathering evidence and validating claims. In elementary school classrooms such as those discussed here, much of the effort is directed toward developing broadly based literacy and language skills that provide students with the resources to enter into new conversations that go beyond the knowledge they bring from home and community, but the alignment with disciplines is very general. Even in the fifth-grade example, where the subject area frames are most distinct and even taught by separate teachers, the underlying emphasis on general strategies of language and learning is very evident.

One way to view the development of disciplinary understanding across the school and college years is to see it as the elaboration and differentiation of increasingly specialized genres of language use (Bakhtin, 1986), genres which carry with them a wide range of expectations about appropriate content, use, and organization. These genres ("discourses" in James Gee's [1996] sense) evolve out of the genres of home and community as students learn to participate appropriately in the conversations of ever more specialized academic domains (Applebee, 1996). From this perspective, the simple explorations of elementary school science, math, social studies, and language arts can be seen as legitimate precursors of the highly specialized disciplinary and interdisciplinary explorations of the graduate school and university, in a developmental process in which, for example, the genres of elementary school science will evolve into those of high school biology, physics, and chemistry, and those in turn into the highly specialized genres of such areas as spectroscopy (Vande Kopple, 1998). It is possible to superimpose interdisciplinary connections at any point in this development, but we need to be sure that we do so in ways that will strengthen students' abilities to participate in an increasingly broad range of conversations, clarifying rather than muddying their knowledge of the conventions of language, content, and argument appropriate to the relevant genres.

In looking at these cases, we have raised more questions than we have answered, and these questions in turn remain to be considered as we examine other efforts at interdisciplinary work in elementary and secondary schools. In constructing interdisciplinary domains for conversation, it is clear that many frames for such curricula privilege one subject, and reduce the others to "enrichments" that may indeed enrich students' understandings of the superordinate discipline but that do not necessarily help them enter into the diversity of disciplinary conversations. However, given the variety of courses and teachers that students will encounter over time, such emphases may balance out, and the distortions may be more than compensated for by the motivation and enthusiasm that interdisciplinary curricula often seem to engender.

More importantly, perhaps, these cases illuminate the variety of levels on which interdisciplinary curricula function and make it clear that if such curricula are to begin to achieve the benefits that are claimed for them, they will have to be conceived from the start in terms of the conversations that they are designed to foster.

NOTE

This report is based on research supported in part under the Research and Development Center Program (award numbers R305A60005 and R117G10015) as administered by the Office of Educational Research and Improvement, U.S. Department of Education. The findings and opinions expressed here do not necessarily reflect the positions or policies of the funding agency.

REFERENCES

Adler, M., & Flihan, S. (1997). *The interdisciplinary continuum: Reconciling theory, research, and practice* (Report Series 2.36). Albany, NY: Center on English Learning and Achievement.

Applebee, A. N. (1974). *Tradition and reform in the teaching of English: A history.* Urbana, IL: National Council of Teachers of English.

Applebee, A. N. (1996). *Curriculum as conversation: Transforming traditions of teaching and learning.* Chicago: University of Chicago Press.

Applebee, A. N., Burroughs, R., & Stevens, A. S. (2000). Creating continuity and coherence in high school literature curricula, *Research in the Teaching of English, 34*(3), 382–415.

Bakhtin, M. M. (1986). *Speech genres and other late essays* (Vern W. McGee, Trans.). Austin: University of Texas Press.

Beane, J. (1997). *Curriculum integration: Designing the core of democratic education.* New York: Teachers College Press.

Berkenkotter, C., & Huckin, T. N. (1995). *Genre knowledge in disciplinary communication.* Hillsdale, NJ: Lawrence Erlbaum.

Burroughs, R. (1999). From the margins to the center: Integrating multicultural literature into the secondary English curriculum. *Journal of Curriculum and Supervision, 14*(2), 136–155.

Gardner, H., & Boix-Mansilla, V. (1994). Teaching for understanding in the disciplines—and beyond. *Teachers College Record, 96*(2), 198–218.

Gee, J. P. (1996). *Social linguistics and literacies: Ideology in discourses.* (2nd ed.). Bristol, PA: Taylor & Francis.

Grossman, P. L., & Stodolsky, S. S. (1995). Content as context: The role of school subjects in secondary school teaching. *Educational Researcher, 24*(8), 5–11, 23.

Herrington, A. (1985). Writing in academic settings: A study of the contexts for writing in two college chemical engineering courses. *Research in the Teaching of English, 19* (4), 331–361.

Jacobs, H. H. (1997). *Integrating curriculum and assessment K–12.* Alexandria, VA: Association for Supervision and Curriculum Development.

Kain, D. L. (1993). Cabbages—and kings: Research directions in integrated/interdisciplinary curriculum. *Journal of Educational Thought, 27*(3), 312–331.

Langer, J. A. (1992). Speaking of knowing: Conceptions of knowing in the academic disciplines. In A. Herrington & C. Moran (Eds.), *Writing, teaching, and learning in the disciplines* (pp. 69–85). New York: Modern Language Association.

McCarthy, L. P. (1987). A stranger in strange lands: A college student writing across the curriculum. *Research in the Teaching of English, 21*(3), 233–265.

Nystrand, M. (1997). *Opening dialogue: Understanding the dynamics of language and learning in the English classroom.* New York: Teachers College Press.

Stevens, A. (1999). *Tracking, curriculum differentiation, and the student experience in English.* Unpublished doctoral dissertation, State University of New York at Albany.

Tchudi, S., & Lafer, S. (1996). *The interdisciplinary teacher's handbook: Integrated teaching across the curriculum.* Portsmouth, NH: Boynton Cook/Heinemann.

Tom Snyder Productions. (1996). *Decisions, decisions: Colonization* [computer software]. Cambridge, MA: Tom Snyder Productions.

Vande Kopple, W. J. (1998). Relative clauses in spectroscopic articles in the Physical Review, Beginnings and 1980: Some changes in patterns of modification and a connection to a possible shift in style. *Written Communication, 15*(2), 170–202.

6

The Photosynthesis of Columbus
Exploring Interdisciplinary Curriculum from the Students' Perspectives

KATHLEEN J. ROTH

But History should be our Cautionary Science.

—Boorstin, 1987, p. ix

As a science educator, I often take on a teacher-researcher role to gain insights about how to help students understand science in rich and meaningful ways. I first took on this role while teaching fifth-grade science and social studies in an urban elementary school. I worked to create a conceptually rich, inquiry-focused curriculum in science. Similarly, I strove to make the social studies curriculum disciplinary-based, representing history in ways that would go beyond facts and chronology to focus instead on big ideas, issues, concepts, and modes of inquiry. When I talked to colleagues about what I was doing, the first question almost always reflected an assumption of interdisciplinary teaching: "So how are you integrating science and history?" Why is everyone assuming that I would integrate the two subjects when it is taking so much energy just to make the curriculum integrated and conceptually focused *within* each of these two disciplines?

After reading more about interdisciplinary integration, I became concerned about how readily the idea of interdisciplinary curriculum was being enthusiastically supported. I did not hear the hard questions being asked: What does it mean to understand something in an interdisciplinary way? What would this interdisciplinary understanding look like in elementary-aged students? Where is the evidence that interdisciplinary teaching promotes meaningful, integrated learning? What kinds of interdisciplinary teaching and learning are compelling, powerful, and meaningful for students? Does one discipline become subservient to another—or to a "theme"—and thus get misrepresented or diminished?

I begin by describing two examples of integrated teaching and learning. In both cases, my coteachers and I taught fifth-grade science and social studies. In the first case, the two subjects were taught separately, although the science and social studies teachers engaged in a weekly 2-hour study group to support each other's efforts. The students experienced science and social studies/history as two distinct subjects, but end-of-year interviews with students revealed evidence of interesting integrated learning (both within and across the two subject matters). The second case took place 1 year later, with the same set of teachers. In this case the teachers jointly planned and taught an interdisciplinary science and social studies/history curriculum. This second case raises interesting issues about the challenges of creating an interdisciplinary curriculum that makes sense from the students' perspectives without sacrificing the richness of the respective disciplines. Together, the cases challenge us to focus on the curriculum from the students' perspectives and to rethink the kinds of integrated learning that are most important for students to learn and the kinds of teaching that best support students in making powerful connections.

THE CONTEXT

A Professional Development School Setting

As part of a larger school-university collaborative effort, I participated with three teachers, another university professor, and three doctoral students in the Literacy in Science and Social Studies Project. The project explored ways to teach for understanding in science and social studies, with an emphasis on the role of discourse and writing in promoting understanding. After 2 years of weekly study group meetings and other activities, the group decided to conduct a careful study of student learning in science and social studies/history during the 1990–91 school year (Case 1). During 1992–93 a similar study was planned that focused on interdisciplinary teaching and learning (Case 2).

In Case 1, I taught fifth-grade science, while Elaine Hoekwater and an MSU doctoral student, Corinna Hasbach, taught social studies/history to the same group of students. We each participated in research activities, including data collection, analysis, and report writing. In Case 2, I co-planned and cotaught an integrated science and social studies/history curriculum, with Hoekwater and Hasbach as my teaching partners.

The Teacher-Researcher Study Group

Our work as teacher-researchers centered around our ongoing study group meetings, where we met together all morning one day a week. We brought a wide range of subject matter interests. The science interest and background came from the university members of the group—myself and two doctoral students. Elaine Hoekwater, a fifth-grade teacher, came from a musical background but enjoyed teaching social studies. The other members of the group held primary interests and expertise in language arts teaching; they joined the project because of their interest in learning how to enhance students' experiences with writing and discourse in science and social studies.

Teaching for Understanding.   After an extensive process of reading, discussion, and research, we developed a shared goal to teach for understanding in each of the subject matter areas. In the case of science, the school subject matched its parent discipline in larger society, and our definition of the understandings we wanted students to develop were clearer than in social studies. In social studies, the focus slipped back and forth between broad social studies goals and historical understanding. History goals focused on historical inquiry, interpretation, use of primary sources, and the examination of historical events from multiple perspectives. The social studies goals were always embedded in the history but engaged students in thinking about issues that came out of their historical inquiry, such as racism, power, conflict—in present-day contexts that moved the discussion out of history and into areas more connected to the social science disciplines such as sociology and political science. In the end, the curriculum we developed represented an integration of history and the social science disciplines.

Defining Disciplinary Understanding.   Based on our reading and research, the group defined several aspects of scientific and historical understanding that we wanted students to develop. We included our broader social studies goals under the umbrella of historical understanding.

We wanted students to develop scientific and historical understandings that were:

1. *Connected, well-structured, centered around "big ideas."* Historians and scientists view their disciplines as organized around "big ideas,"

or concepts, which are used to structure the disciplines and to make clear the many connections among ideas, concepts, and "facts."

2. *Useful in science* for describing, predicting, explaining, designing, and appreciating real-world, natural phenomena. *Useful in history* for describing historical persons and events, interpreting historical episodes, identifying historical patterns, making decisions based on historical patterns, appreciating the rich and varied history of humankind, and developing empathy for events and persons from the past. *Useful in students' lives* for decision making, for social action and responsibility, for understanding and celebrating differences among people, and for describing their place in the world in a historical sense.

3. *Viewed as tentative, constantly changing, building, deepening over time as new ideas and evidence emerge.* Both science and history are never "finished." Historians and scientists share a disposition to inquire, but the two disciplines have different ways of growing—different sources of evidence, different research methods, and different norms of argumentation.

4. *Developed in a community* that cooperatively constructs new knowledge, using agreed-upon modes of inquiry and ways of knowing that generate knowledge based upon evidence and reasoning.

CASE 1: DISCIPLINARY TEACHING . . . INTERDISCIPLINARY LEARNING?

Case 1: The Curriculum

Interdisciplinary integration was not an intended goal; instead, we focused on developing integrated understandings within a *disciplinary* perspective. For example, we wanted students to develop connected networks of concepts in each subject area, not just to memorize terms and dates. We hoped students would learn to use organizing concepts to describe the connections among the various topics, activities, and issues we explored during the year. We also wanted students to integrate their study of science and history with their personal lives, experiences, and ideas. By making such personal links, students might find the concepts and ideas more meaningful and useful. And we wanted students to understand how processes of inquiry in science or history are inseparable from conceptual knowledge development within each discipline. We wanted students to appreciate the power of scientific and historical modes of inquiry by coming to understand how these ways of knowing could help them develop deeper, more exciting understandings of important ideas in science, history, and social studies.

But the students taught us about integrated *learning* across subjects even though such integrated *teaching* was not planned. Each of us conducted in-depth disciplinary-based interviews with a subset of the fifth graders at the end of the school year. Each student had a science interview, a social studies/history interview, or both. The interviews were designed to explore the aspects of students' historical/social studies and scientific understandings described above.

There were no questions designed to explore students' interdisciplinary understandings. However, students' interview responses reflected their efforts to make such interdisciplinary connections. In the science interviews, for example, students used ideas taught in their social studies/history class in meaningful and interesting ways. Similarly, in history/social studies interviews, students used concepts that were taught in science. Such data prompted us to reexamine interdisciplinary integration from the students' perspectives.

Case 1: The Students' Perspectives

Interdisciplinary Ideas about Perspectives.   An example of students' cross-subject matter connections was their frequent use in the science interviews of their learning about "perspectives" in history/social studies class. Although the concept of perspective was never explicitly used in science class (nor mentioned by the interviewer), over half of the students interviewed about science used the idea of "perspectives" in response to questions about science.

Perspective had been explicitly taught as a way of interpreting history as well as a tool for examining issues in our lives today. Each unit of study in history included an examination of the time period from the perspectives of underrepresented groups (women, African Americans, Native Americans, Hispanics), so the notion of perspectives was one that students had explored in many contexts. The term was also used in social studies/history class as students examined and compared a variety of sources, including the textbook, other print references, art and photographic representations, video resources, and interviews with family, neighbors, and visiting experts. Recurring questions that students explored when using these sources were: Whose perspective is being told here? What perspectives are missing?

As we hoped, students often used the idea of perspective in their social studies/history interviews, but we were surprised that they transferred this understanding about perspectives into science without explicit interdisciplinary instruction. The following excerpts from the year-end science interviews illustrate the variety of ways that Lucas, Michelle, and Nathan wove the idea of perspectives into their responses to questions about science. In some cases the students explicitly acknowledge that this idea came from social studies/history class, yet they seem comfortable using the idea in a science context.

In the first excerpt, Lucas, a student who had received resource room help in reading since kindergarten and had repeated a grade in school, uses the concept of perspective in the context of talking about books as a way to learn about things:

Roth: What questions do you have about early humans?

Lucas: How they looked, how their culture was.

Roth: How would you find out about their culture?

Lucas: Books, but books are not always true. . . .

Roth: Books are not always true?

Lucas: Some books, you don't really know what you'll find out until you read it. Books could say different things. If you're a scientist, you could make a book with your perspective and different peoples'.

Roth: Scientists have different perspectives?

Lucas: Yeah.

Roth: Is that good or bad?

Lucas: That's good because if you have different perspectives on something, you can pick the one you like the most.

Of course, Lucas's notion of picking the perspective you like best fails to reflect the disposition to consider multiple perspectives in coming to a reasoned historical or scientific perspective. Despite regular efforts on the teachers' part to emphasize drawing upon multiple perspectives rather than picking a favorite, the notion of an either/or choice is difficult for students to give up.

Michelle made a more personal connection between "perspectives" and science class. A quiet member of the class who was considered by her peers and teachers to be academically weak, Michelle clearly valued the idea that her own perspectives were important in science:

Roth: Why is it important for people to do science?

Michelle: To find out different things, so they aren't going with just one point of view. Like when we did the bean plant, we weren't just looking at the book.

Roth: Why is it important not to go with just one point of view?

Michelle: Cause you'd be getting your *own* ideas, too. Like when we were reading books on plants, we weren't just going by that *perspective*, we were going by *our perspectives*, too. Like doing different experiments with beans.

Nathan is a shy, quiet boy who typically keeps to himself. Science class was a setting where he gradually built confidence and became an active participant in small group and whole class discussions. Previous teachers describe him as a C student. In his science interview, he uses "perspectives" to define the work of scientists:

Roth: What kinds of things do scientists do?

Nathan: They have to research stuff. They have to look at different scientists' *perspectives* and see what they think. Then they try to see if they thought it was any different, maybe find that scientist and talk about it.

Roth: Can you say more about perspectives?

Nathan: Like if they're in a book, they might read it, and get some ideas, and they might say, "Well, I don't think this is right." They might change their idea.

Roth: Was that idea new to you?

Nathan: I didn't know that they looked at different scientists' *perspectives.* I thought they just said what they thought it was.

Interdisciplinary Ideas about Stereotypes. The idea of "stereotype" was introduced to students in science class at the beginning of the year in the context of talking about stereotypes of scientists. In September, all the students drew pictures of males when asked to draw a picture of a scientist. In a spring unit about the history of life on earth, students were again asked to draw a picture of a scientist and all of the girls drew female scientists. The concept of stereotype was explicitly discussed with the students in these science activities and throughout the year as it came up in our work in science.

The explicit teaching of the idea of stereotype in the science curriculum represented an unconscious example of interdisciplinary teaching. The stereotype idea comes from the social sciences, and we had taken that idea and given it a central role in science. To me, the idea was crucial in helping students feel welcomed into science; the stereotypical view of a scientist was explicitly challenged.

Although not explicitly taught in social studies/history class, the students brought the stereotype idea to label some of their observations about the history of the Mexican War. When they realized that the Americans wanted to have slaves in Texas and that the Mexicans had abolished slavery, they were surprised. The students then introduced the idea of a stereotype ("It's like we learned in science!") that the American cowboys are the good guys and the Mexicans are the bad guys. But they also took this idea of stereotype out of history and into their own lives, using it to label behaviors they observed in their own classrooms and communities. In the context of talking about the Mexican War and stereotypes of Americans and Mexicans, one of the teachers asked: "What does it mean to be a Mexican American?" Gary laughed and blurted out, "A Mexican burrito." This led to a serious class discussion about the ways that Mexican Americans are discriminated against in our society. The students made explicit reference during this class discussion to their exploration of stereotypes in science.

In the year-end interviews about science, most students used the idea of stereotype to describe images of scientists as males (with crazy hair!) working alone with chemicals in a laboratory. But many also used the stereotype concept in the social studies/history interviews. In this context, a few students used the concept of stereotype to talk about events and issues in U.S. history; most often these students mentioned stereotypes in relationship to women in history. But students more often linked the idea to broader social studies-learning goals than to history-learning goals. Although stereotype was taught in a science context, students integrated this knowledge about stereotypes in quite personal ways, often using it to think about their own interactions with members of the opposite sex—a topic of great interest for these soon-to-be middle schoolers.

For example, Nan used the idea of stereotype to think about her own interactions with boys and girls in her class. She struggled for many months to work effectively in her small group of all girls, but Nan was especially intrigued with her success in having her ideas heard and valued by boys when she started working in mixed groups. She used the idea of stereotype to make sense of her personal social interactions:

Roth: Were your ideas heard as well when you switched to groups with both girls and boys?

Nan: Yeah, cause I'm surprised that the boys listened to me. The boys got a lot of ideas, but I mean they listened to my ideas.

Roth: Did the boys listen more to you than the girls?

Nan: About the same but most boys, this is one of those words that starts with an "s," that most boys never listen to girls cause they don't like them. [Nan's speech disability made stereotype a challenging word to pronounce.]

Roth: So your stereotype of boys changed?
Nan: Yeah.

In a year-end small group interview, Nan used the idea of stereotypes to continue her thinking about these issues in a conversation with
Heidi, Michelle, and Tiffany (the girls who Nan had such difficulty working with at the beginning of the year). Notice how the girls brought up
issues that are personal and important to them. The girls integrated ideas
studied in science (stereotype) and social studies (perspectives) with personally important concerns and experiences. The question they considered is whether teachers should put boys and girls together in small
groups:

> *I:* If you were with boys and boys were with girls, what do you
>   think you can learn from each other?
> *Michelle:* That you can work with different people.
> *Heidi:* And that boys have good things to say just as well as girls
>   and you can, you can, if you do have boys and girls *you can
>   learn different perspectives by working with different people.* . . . If it's
>   all girls in the group, all we would end up doing is fooling
>   around talking about bras and junk like that.
> *Nan:* I take my thing that I said back. *I changed my mind.* I think
>   there should be a girl and a boy . . . in a group. Cause, see,
>   boys, you don't really get into a conversation with.
> *I:* Why not?
> *Nan:* Cause, I don't know. But they are very, they like say stuff
>   about sports and the girls, they just wanna talk about sports.
> *Heidi: That's a stereotype! It's a stereotype I tell you, it's a stereotype!*
> *I:* Do you think so, Nan?
> *Nan:* Well, boys, well, boys like to talk about different things than
>   we do. And they, they'll start giving up with different subjects
>   than what we want to talk about.
> *Heidi:* Well, like we want to talk about our hair and our, and our
>   training bras and stuff like that. . . . *Yeah, that's a stereotype. Those
>   are stereotypes, I think.*

Case 1: A Hopeful Tale—Interdisciplinary Connections

These examples (as well as other interdisciplinary connections described
in Hasbach, Hazelwood, Hoekwater, Roth, & Michell, 1992; and Rosa-
en, Lindquist, Peasley, & Hazelwood, 1992) of students making interest-

ing connections from science class to social studies/history class and vice versa stimulated much analysis and discussion in our teacher-researcher study group. Both the literature and our own teaching experience told us not to expect students to make even the most basic cross-disciplinary connections without a lot of explicit instruction. But when we allowed students to tell us about ways they were putting ideas together, we found evidence of meaningful connections across disciplines and to their personal lives.

We have identified four shared understandings that we think enabled us to create learning settings that supported students in seeing the science and social studies/history classes (and subject areas) as extensions of the other. The shared features of our pedagogies included:

1. *Epistemological Orientations.* The features of our learning communities were built upon shared understandings about the disciplines that we are teaching. For example, collaboration was central in our classrooms not only to engage students actively in their learning, but also because it is a basic aspect of knowledge construction in science and history. This emphasis on collective cognition is consistent with a social constructivist epistemology of science or history in which knowledge is located in the discourse community. We encouraged students to view their texts (including textbooks, other books, videotapes, visitors, statements by students and teachers, experiments, etc.) as authored, as tentative statements of knowledge, as open to change and question. Students were supported in critical reading of multiple texts and in understanding the rules of evidence used to create historical interpretations or scientific explanations.

2. *Views of a Learning Community.* In our study group sessions, we conceptualized the kind of learning community we were trying to create in each of our classrooms. We drew on Hermine Marshall's (1990) distinction between the metaphor of a classroom as a workplace compared to a classroom as a learning place. In a learning-oriented classroom, students still complete work, but there is an emphasis on how and why the work is being done. Thinking, questioning, discussing, making mistakes, trying and sharing new ideas, and so forth are valued and rewarded as much as the workplace emphasis on completing a finished, correct product.

3. *Curricular Centrality of Students' Personal Lives and Experiences.* In both science and social studies/history, curricular planning and teaching centered around students' thinking and experiences. We thought about the content from the students' perspectives in planning and altered our

teaching as we learned more about the students' ideas and experiences. We encouraged students to make connections with their personal lives and to share their experiences with the class.

4. *Studying a Few Concepts in Depth and in Multiple Contexts.* In both science and social studies, a few big ideas were developed in depth, and the ideas were revisited in multiple contexts across the school year. U.S. history, for example, was presented not as chronology, but as themes that cut across time. In Case 1, only the following episodes from U.S. history were examined: history of our school, colonization, westward expansion, the Civil War, and the Civil Rights movement.

This curricular practice supported students in developing deeper understandings of the concepts by helping them learn to use the concepts in different contexts over time. The practice also encouraged students to make connections among ideas and topics. Nathan, when showed a timeline of topics studied in science, immediately recognized how concepts and ideas studied in science across the year connected to each other:

Nathan: Oh, it's stuff that we studied. . . .
I: This year in science.
Nathan: Well, *all of them sort of connect.*
I: Oh? Tell me about that.
Nathan: Cause we learned about *stereotypes of scientists,* and then there are scientists who found out about food for plants. And then, *The Power Cell* [title of student text about the use of food and oxygen in body cells]—what's food for humans? And *that sort of connects in.* And then we were trying to figure out how dinosaurs breathed, and *that sort of connects, too!*

Case 1: A Cautionary Tale—Was This Interdisciplinary Understanding?

Although the students made significant connections across the two subject areas and to their personal lives, these connections fall short of representing rich interdisciplinary understandings. For example, many students in this case used the concept of *perspective* from their study of history to describe how scientists collaborate to put ideas together. But their use of the perspective idea in historical contexts, where the idea had been explicitly taught, was limited in important ways. Most strikingly, the students often used perspective as an either/or or good/bad choice, as if history is a matter of choosing which perspective you like best. In this same vein, students often treated perspectives synonymously with opinions. Thus, I suggest that one important feature of interdisciplinary understanding is that the learner's use of a concept across disciplines reflects a rich understanding of the concept in its discipline of origin.

The students' use of the stereotype idea raises another question about interdisciplinary understanding. Students used the *stereotype* idea effectively in talking about scientists and in talking about their personal experiences with stereotypes (especially stereotypes of girls and boys). However, they did not use the stereotype idea in the interviews to talk about their understandings of events and patterns in American history. Because they could use the concept in both science and personal contexts, I could argue that there was an interdisciplinary science and social studies understanding. But I would not argue that there is a history-science interdisciplinary understanding until they could use stereotype in ways that reflect both scientific and historical ways of knowing. For example, students might challenge the stereotype of a scientist by describing what scientific work is all about and providing examples of different ways that scientific work can be approached. In history, students might use the idea of stereotype to interpret a historical event.

This work is helping me begin to define what I would use as evidence of interdisciplinary understanding: (1) Does the idea being integrated across the disciplines represent a central organizing idea of the discipline(s)? (2) Do students hold rich understandings of the concept/idea in its discipline of origin? (3) Can students use the idea across disciplines in ways that reflect the particular ways of knowing in each discipline?

CASE 2: INTERDISCIPLINARY TEACHING . . . AND LEARNING?

Case 2: Initial Concerns

Excited about the kinds of interdisciplinary connections the students in Case 1 were making, we wondered if we could improve the power of those connections by explicitly teaching in an interdisciplinary way. This led to interdisciplinary planning and teaching in our second year of coplanning, teaching, and research.

We entered this venture with concerns about interdisciplinary teaching. Analyzing the content and organization of interdisciplinary theme units that had been tried by teachers in our group as well as by other teachers in our school and by teachers in the literature we had read, we found that the content of theme units often does not focus on the powerful ideas or organizing concepts from the disciplines. For example, while the American Association for the Advancement of Science (1989, 1993) recommends interdisciplinary themes such as systems, models, patterns of change, and interactions, the theme units we studied focused around such things as a color (black), teddy bears, bubbles, and apples. Missing were considerations of the importance and usefulness of the ideas within the various disciplines, the potential power of the ideas for students, the connection of the ideas with children's knowledge and experience, and the possibilities of representing the ideas in meaningful ways to children (an appropriate pedagogy).

Case 2: The 1492 Curriculum

With such concerns in mind, we chose the quincentennial celebration of Columbus's arrival in America as the starting point for a 1492 interdisciplinary theme curriculum. In our curriculum, the 1492 theme was organized into a sequence of integrated science/social studies/history units, with each unit having its own central guiding questions. But we also had a set of guiding questions that overarched all units across the year, and these questions were displayed prominently on classroom bulletin boards: What was the land like 500 years ago in different parts of North America? What were the people like 500 years ago in different parts of North America? How has the land changed over the past 500 years? How have the people changed?

In working on these ideas, we wanted students to develop understandings of the different ways of knowing and ways of doing inquiry that characterize science and history. For example, the science strand would begin with an exploration of species in different ecosystems, organized around central questions such as: How are different species adapted to survive in their environment (ecosystem)? How do these species interact? How have these species/ecosystems changed since 1492? Why should we in Michigan care if species or ecosystems are endangered?

In parallel with this study of species diversity, adaptations, and ecosystems, the students' historical inquiry focused on the diversity of Native American cultures in each of these major types of ecosystems in America in 1492: How did different Native American cultures adapt to their environment? How did they interact with their ecosystems in 1492? How did they interact with each other and with the settlers? How have cultures changed since 1492?

The science explorations would then continue along the 1492 theme in subsequent interdisciplinary units. Beginning with a science-focused central question—"How do plants get their food?"—subsequent questions would engage students in applying science concepts to history. They would examine the colonial period from the perspective of food and plants: What happened in the colonial period when plants from the two worlds began to be exchanged? We had grand visions of exploring the close links between sugar and slavery. Thus, students would explore U.S. history in the context of plants and study plants in the context of history and social conflicts. The connections fascinated us as adults.

But we abandoned the 1492 theme after immersion in it across the fall. The story of our experience suggests why.

Case 2: Starting with Science

We began with explorations of what it means to be a scientist. Students drew pictures of scientists, and we discussed how their stereotypes of scientists differed from "true" characteristics of scientists. A "hands-on" activity then challenged students' conceptions that scientists always work with chemicals. Each small group was given three different species of plants to observe. A student handout included an introduction that emphasized the focus on "Becoming Scientists."

> We have been talking about stereotypes of scientists . . . But what is true of all scientists? To explore this question, we are going to become scientists ourselves. . . . Today we are going to look at three different species, or kinds, of plants. The first thing we will do with the plants is to observe and describe them and to ask questions about them.

This activity also provided a stepping stone toward the introduction of the big framing question: How have living things changed over the last 500 years? How might they change in the next 500 years? Students continued a series of activities with plants; these activities supported students' learning about concepts of structure, function, and adaptation, which would be key concepts we would expect them to use in analyzing life on earth in 1492 and beyond.

Case 2: Bringing in History

The 1492 theme and central questions could not get into full swing until we brought in the history. To do this, we introduced the idea of "perspective" using a children's picture book called *The True Story of the Three Little Pigs* (Scieszka, 1989). The book tells the story of the three little pigs from the wolf's perspective. We then presented a simplified description of how both scientists and historians use the idea of perspectives in different

FIGURE 6.1: Overhead Transparency of How Scientists and Historians Use the Idea of Perspective

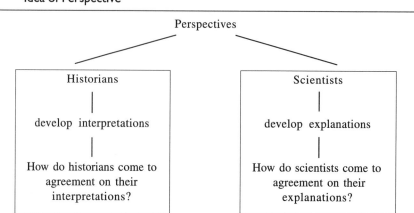

ways. This idea was represented on an overhead transparency to the students (see Figure 6.1):

The students were then divided into two groups. One group reread the story as historians, considering what they would want to do before deciding on the best interpretation of the story. The other group approached the rereading as scientists, thinking about ways to prove or disprove the wolf's story and to develop an explanation of what really happened. Whole group sharing afterwards enabled the teachers to scaffold and shape students' descriptions of what it means to be a historian or a scientist.

The next series of lessons gave students the chance to learn more about being historians and about what life in America was like in 1492. Students were divided into small groups, with each group being assigned a different Native American culture to study. The cultures were selected to represent distinct geographical differences, which would enable our science study to include contrasting ecosystems and a wide diversity of organisms to study. Each group was given four sources to study; the sources included the textbook and others that presented conflicting information or additional information. Teachers supported groups and helped them analyze the differences and similarities among the sources. Lessons typically ended with a whole class discussion in which groups shared findings about conflicting or incomplete reports in sources.

Case 2: Interdisciplinary Time!

Working in their small groups, students were now given the task of furthering their explorations of their Native American groups. From a historical perspective, they were challenged to find out how the lives of these Native Americans had changed since 1492, and what their lives are like now in 1992. From a science perspective, students were to research and describe as many different species as possible of plants and animals that lived in their Native American group's geographical area. What structures/functions enabled these plants and animals to be well adapted to their particular ecosystem? How much diversity of plant and animal life was there? How were these living things interdependent? How have these ecosystems changed since 1492? Why?

This introductory unit of the 1492 interdisciplinary curriculum theme ended with students giving oral presentations in which they shared spoke map drawings and explained what they had found out. Students were encouraged to highlight gaps in their research and to report on conflicting reports they found in their sources. However, it was apparent from the students' presentations that in this last (and most interdisciplinary) phase of the research, they had focused on finding information and were not questioning their sources or considering that their sources might be limited or incomplete.

Case 2: 1492 from the Students' Perspectives

In planning this interdisciplinary curriculum we were fascinated by the many connections we were making between history and science. But such connections were not as fascinating and clear to our students. By late November we found that the theme was not helping students connect with these important concepts—especially the science concepts—in the powerful ways we had hoped. Instead of understanding the critical importance of structure/function relationships and adaptations in plants and animals, the students were learning, at best, the names of plants and animals that lived in the ecosystem that their small group was studying. Instead of thinking and inquiry, the students focused on naming and cataloging plants and animals in a particular kind of ecosystem. And their descriptions of ecosystem changes over the 500 years since Columbus were superficial and vague. The following end-of-unit interview segment with Chad is illustrative of the kinds of student responses to questions related to the science concepts:

I: And what did you learn about the Iroquois environment?

Chad: They lived in the woods, lots of trees and animals to hunt.

I: What were you trying to find out about their environment?

Chad: What kinds of things lived there, different kinds of plants and trees and different kinds of animals.

I: Can you tell me about some of the plants?

Chad: Well, it was mostly trees—like oak trees and pine trees. Oh yeah, and there were bushes with berries on them like black-berries and strawberries, I think.

I: Has the Iroquois environment in 1492 changed much since then?

Chad: Oh, yeah. They've cut down lots of trees since then. Like this happened in Michigan, too. They cut down trees to make farms. And well, in some places there are cities. And there weren't cities in 1492.

Most students understood that there was a connection between the Native American culture their group was studying and the ecosystem the group was exploring. They could describe ways in which "their" Native Americans' way of life (historically) was shaped by the environment in which they lived. As Sharelle explained:

The Sioux had teepees for homes because they were easy to fold up and carry to a new place and the Sioux were moving around a lot because they were hunters and had to follow their food—like the buffalo. In the grasslands, they didn't have like lots of bushes with berries to pick or big trees with nuts or something like that.

Whole class lessons about the Columbus "discovery" and about changes in Native American life since 1492 helped them begin to develop some fairly powerful understandings of the social studies concepts— ideas about human adaptation to the environment, perspective, social conflict, and change. But students' understandings of historical and scien-tific inquiry were quite limited. In the end-of-unit interviews, students described history in ways that did not focus on ways of knowing in history:

Robbie: History is about the past, learning about the past.

Sharelle: History is about like people like Columbus who lived in the past and what they did and all.

Jessica: We learn about the past to help us today, like so we won't make the same mistakes they did. Like Columbus didn't know about discrimination but now we do.

Chad: History is like all the things that happened before us. Like even yesterday is history.

Jim was the only student who, without prompting, made reference to historical ways of knowing: "History is learning about the past and historians read lots of different sources so they can learn different perspectives."

There is a similar pattern of answers when describing science. Notice how students focus mostly on the content of science rather than on its purposes and ways of knowing:

Dustin: Science is studying about plants and animals and stuff like that.

Marcus: Science is like rocks, fossils, space, animals. Learning about all those things.

Melanie: Science is about doing experiments and finding things out but it's not just using chemicals in a lab—that's a stereotype of scientists.

As a science teacher, I was frustrated by the constraints placed on the science by the needs of the social studies concepts. From a science perspective, beginning by defining and exploring the diversity of Native American cultures and their environments presented a difficult starting point for fifth graders. Without understanding ideas about plants as producers, food chains, and the cycling of matter and energy in ecosystems, it was difficult for the students to do more than collect facts about plants, animals, and their habitats. Students were not developing meaningful ideas about diversity and interdependence in a biological sense.

The social studies constraints also hampered my efforts to engage students in active, meaningful scientific inquiry. How could I engage small groups of students in meaningful inquiry about topics so huge and distant from firsthand experience—woodlands, deserts, oceans, rain forests, and plains? Books, rather than experiences with phenomena, became the primary source, and this made it difficult to challenge students to think scientifically, to raise questions, and to gather evidence. In addition, since each small group of students was working with a different data set, it was hard to have provocative scientific discussions about the central question and the evidence we had to support different positions. This lack of a shared data set also made it difficult for me to scaffold students' thinking and to model integrated ways of thinking.

We called this curriculum block "science and social studies time," but most of the time it felt like social studies rather than integrated subjects. At the end of this 3-month period, my students' learning was limited to a basic descriptive level. They could describe plants and animals that lived in the particular area their group worked on, but they could not go beyond these descriptions to explain interactions among species and the importance of diversity in ecosystems. They could not explain human impact on these ecosystems over the last 500 years except in quite superficial ways. In fact, I can't name any powerful science concepts that the students learned. In addition, they did not learn nearly as much as the Case 1 students about how scientists raise questions and figure things out.

Case 2: A Cautionary Tale—Why Wasn't Interdisciplinary Learning Enhanced?

Was my dissatisfaction with students' learning in the 1492 unit just the result of faulty planning and design, the kinks of a first try? That was undoubtedly part of the problem; I'm sure what we did could be improved upon. But I have also come to believe that, at least from the perspective of my discipline (science), it is difficult to work within an integrated theme without in some way distorting or diminishing one or another of the disciplines involved.

Earlier I listed features of scientific understanding and historical understanding that I was trying to help students achieve: connectedness and structure, usefulness, knowledge as tentative and changing, and a community with shared modes of inquiry. In planning the 1492 unit, my focus on these learning goals was unintentionally moved from the foreground to the background. Making the science fit with the history curriculum moved to the foreground. I worked hard to make the fit natural and strong and to keep a focus on rich, conceptual learning goals. But the juggling act was difficult. How I wish I could have kept the science, history, and interdisciplinary juggling balls all in the air and equally visible at once!

We had hoped to integrate the two disciplines of science and history in ways that would preserve the richness of the individual disciplines while making each more alive, textured, and nuanced by the connection to the other. But as we worked to make science and history disciplinary boundaries less distinct, we inadvertently created a bland broth that added little energy to our curriculum. In channeling our energies into interdisciplinary curriculum and teaching, we lost some of the power of our respective disciplinary approaches.

TEACHING FOR UNDERSTANDING:
DISCIPLINARY OR INTERDISCIPLINARY?

The cases presented here suggest implications that go against the grain of traditional thinking about teaching for understanding in disciplinary or interdisciplinary ways. Case 1 suggests that interdisciplinary connections can emerge from contexts in which students are studying subject matters in rich, disciplinary-focused ways. Traditional views hold that interdisciplinary learning rarely develops in disciplinary-based classrooms, but this case shows the promise for challenging this view, even though these students' interdisciplinary connections fell short of representing genuine interdisciplinary understanding. The epistemological and pedagogical orientations shared by the teachers in Case 1 suggest the unusual features of these science and history classrooms that may have contributed to the surprising interdisciplinary connections. Further work along these lines may reveal that students can be supported in developing deep interdisciplinary *understandings* in rich, disciplinary settings.

Case 2 challenges the assumption that good interdisciplinary teaching will necessarily enhance student learning, helping them develop richer, more interconnected understandings. In fact, students in Case 2 developed less sophisticated, less connected interdisciplinary understandings than students in Case 1, despite having access to the same teachers and an explicitly interdisciplinary curriculum. This case suggests that even very thoughtful and thorough interdisciplinary planning and teaching does not assure student learning. We were surprised that our carefully planned 1492 theme could just as easily have been called "The Photosynthesis of Columbus" theme for all the sense it made to students.

What do these cases suggest about teaching for understanding—both disciplinary and interdisciplinary? There are many who believe that the only way to see the world holistically is to erase (or at least blur) disciplinary boundaries, and to do so from the earliest years of schooling. The cases presented here, I think, suggest caution. An alternative view is that we best develop our students' understanding of the world and its connectedness by giving them access to a variety of powerful lenses through which to view it, and that the best way to craft those lenses is to immerse our students deeply (but perhaps not solely) in disciplinary study.

In Case 1, students explored science and history separately but in similar, conceptually rich ways and with teachers who studied together and developed shared goals and epistemologies. The students developed good beginnings of disciplinary understandings and began to use those disciplinary-based understandings to make important interdisciplinary connections. In Case 2, I became concerned about the difficulties I had challenging my students scientifically in the 1492 theme curriculum. I felt like I was denying students access to new ways of seeing and making sense of their world. When we moved on to the plants and food unit, I wanted the time and focus to teach my students about the *biology* of plants, so I dropped the 1492 theme. I wanted them to understand, use, and reflect on scientific ways of thinking. And I wanted to increase the power of those concepts and ways of knowing by basing their selection solely on considerations concerning the discipline and considerations concerning the children. I didn't want any of this to be compromised or diluted by the need to fit with a theme.

But despite this apparent retreat to disciplinary teaching, I am not advocating abandonment of interdisciplinary teaching. I continue to be intrigued by the possibilities of exciting interdisciplinary curriculum—both for motivating students and for helping them develop deeper, more interconnected understandings. My cautionary tale is that creating this kind of curriculum is very difficult, and that much interdisciplinary teaching does not really promote interdisciplinary (or disciplinary) understanding. My hopeful tale is that close examination of teaching that does succeed in helping a wide range of students develop at least strong beginning *disciplinary* and interdisciplinary understandings will enable us to make better decisions about how to organize curriculum. Case 1 provides some starting points for thinking about this issue.

So, before we jump on the interdisciplinary bandwagon, let us engage in debate and study regarding the kinds of integration that are compelling, meaningful, and powerful for students. And let us develop deeper understandings of both disciplinary and interdisciplinary learning . . . from the students' perspectives.

NOTE

The author gratefully acknowledges the support and guidance she received from her teacher-researcher colleagues in the Literacy in Science and Social Studies Project, including Elaine Hoekwater, Corinna Hasbach, Cheryl Rosaen, Constanza Hazelwood, and Kathleen Peasley. The author is also appreciative for insights into history and science integration gained from her collaborative teaching with Sam Wineburg from the University of Washington.

REFERENCES

American Association for the Advancement of Science (1989). *Science for all Americans: A Project 2061 report on literacy goals in science, mathematics, and technology.* Washington, DC: Author.

American Association for the Advancement of Science. (1993). *Benchmarks for science literacy.* New York: Oxford University Press.

Boorstin, D. J. (1987). *Hidden history: Exploring our secret past.* New York: Harper & Row.

Hasbach, C., Hazelwood, C., Hoekwater, E., Roth, K., & Michell, M. (1992). *Holistic literacy: Voices integrating classroom texts in social studies.* (Elementary Subjects Center Series No. 64). East Lansing: Michigan State University, Institute for Research on Teaching, Center for the Learning and Teaching of Elementary Subjects.

Marshall, H. (1990). Beyond the workplace metaphor: The classroom as a learning setting. *Theory into Practice, 29,* 94–101.

Pelta, K. (1991). Discovering Christopher Columbus: How history is invented. Minneapolis: Lerner Publications.

Rosaen, C. L., Lindquist, B., Peasley, K., & Hazelwood, C. (1992). *Integration from the student perspective: Constructing meaning in writers' workshop.* (Elementary Subjects Center Series No. 62). East Lansing: Michigan State University, Institute for Research on Teaching, Center for the Learning and Teaching of Elementary Subjects.

Roth, K. J. (1989). *Conceptual understanding and higher level thinking in the elementary science curriculum: Three perspectives.* (Elementary Subjects Center Series No. 12). East Lansing: Michigan State University, Institute for Research on Teaching, Center for the Learning and Teaching of Elementary Subjects.

Scieszka, J. (1989). *The true story of the three little pigs.* New York: Viking Kestrel.

7

The Subjects of Debate

Teachers' Clashing and Overlapping Beliefs about Subject Matter During a Whole-School Reform

KAREN HAMMERNESS AND KAY MOFFETT

At the heart of numerous whole-school and pedagogical reforms is a re-conceptualization of disciplinary knowledge. According to reformers who promote such reorganization, academic disciplines can and should be collapsed in order to make subjects more engaging to students and to make schoolwork more reflective of the interdisciplinary nature of most real-world problems. However, such efforts often challenge teachers' deeply held beliefs, particularly because they may be in conflict with important forces shaping teachers' lives, such as their disciplinary affiliation and departmental community (Grossman & Stodolsky, 1995; Little, 1995; Siskin, 1995). Indeed, dissension can, and often does, occur between interdisciplinary reformers and subject-based teachers about what makes for rigorous and worthwhile curriculum (Muncey & McQuillan, 1996).

Yet such conflict often stems at least as much from the *process* of change as the substance of change. The nettlesome process of school reform can sometimes obscure the common ground that may exist between beliefs about curriculum held by teachers who teach courses that cut across disciplines, and teachers who teach courses in traditional subject areas such as English, mathematics, and science. This chapter explores how a whole-school reform effort balkanized teachers' stances toward disciplinary knowledge and blocked important dialogue about interdisciplinary curriculum. We found that beneath the hype at this school about interdisciplinary studies—both positive and negative—lay common concerns about the nature of legitimate curriculum for students. Though this school was ostensibly divided over the curricular reforms, the presence of these commonalities suggested the existence of a kind of "lost conversation" (this term suggests both the sense of a lost opportunity for conversation and the idea that the school had productive conversation at one time but lost this ability).

First, we describe the high school that provides the case for this exploration and give a brief history of the course of whole-school reform there. Second, we provide an overview of interviews with various teachers and administrators in the school community—those who described themselves as advocates of the reform and those who described themselves as critics. The interviews reveal clashing beliefs about subject matter knowledge, as well as some commonalities that went unrecognized and thus unexplored by participants. Third, we adopt three sociological perspectives in order to understand the nature of this lost conversation. We examine the structural, cultural, and political dimensions of the reform at this school that may have polarized teachers and stymied productive conversations about interdisciplinary curriculum. The structural perspective examines how the organization of the school may have distanced teachers physically and philosophically and obstructed a discussion of shared concerns. The cultural perspective explores the fractured ideological climate at the school and how it may have discouraged real dialogue about disciplinary matters. Finally, the political perspective investigates power shifts, which may have exacerbated the conflict over interdisciplinary curriculum and prevented common beliefs from being considered. We conclude with a discussion of the implications of our case study for schools and school reformers involved in a rethinking of traditional subject matter boundaries.

THE CASE OF FRANKLIN HIGH SCHOOL

Description and Background of Franklin

Benjamin Franklin High School sits in a comfortable suburb of a western city. Franklin High is a large school, employing approximately 90 teachers and serving roughly 1,700 students of diverse backgrounds and predominantly middle- and upper-middle-class families. Upon the arrival in 1990 of Susan Bandon, a young, reform-minded principal, the school cultivated a relationship with the Coalition of Essential Schools (CES) and undertook reforms aimed at the development of programs and processes consonant with the CES vision. After a year of heated but respectful debate, the school piloted some interdisciplinary "academies" (with 100-minute classes), while the rest of the school retained the regular departmental structure (with 50-minute classes). About one third of teachers opted to teach in one of the three academies, while two thirds chose to continue teaching in departments. The academies are characterized by interdisciplinary curricula, team teaching, student-centered instruction, nontracked sections, and alternative assessment. Teachers in the academies are physically concentrated in a couple of buildings in the school.

According to teacher accounts, the reforms ran a fairly smooth course in the early years (1990–94). However, after the academies and other integrated courses got underway, Susan Bandon and other reformers began to push for the creation of interdisciplinary academies *across* the school. At this point, many of the more departmentally-based teachers raised questions and concerns about the reforms. According to these more critical teachers, their voices got continuously squelched by the principal, the CES coach, and teacher-reformers in a pseudo-democratic process of governance. According to the supporters of whole-school change, the departmentally based teachers felt frightened of change and the attendant workload; they argued that the critics needed to expand their repertoires to better serve the changing student population.

What began as healthy conversation and debate at Franklin turned into polarization and stagnation. Critics of the reforms banded together in their opposition to the reforms and seriously questioned the integrity of the academies. They argued that academy teachers received more resources and attention than department teachers. Sometimes they called for an end to the academies altogether. Academy teachers reported feeling attacked and discouraged endless times in recent years. Many of these reform-minded teachers have refused to talk to anyone they perceived as critical and began thinking of many nonacademy teachers as "enemies" and "creeps."

During the years of our study, the teachers at Franklin were overwhelmingly white (85%), with 10% Asian, 3% Latino/a, and 2% other. The case study teachers roughly reflected this ethnic breakdown, with 14 white teachers, one Asian American teacher, and one Latina teacher. The staff was about equally split between men and women. Most striking about the demographics of the Franklin staff for this study was the bimodal distribution in terms of age. One large cohort had taught for fewer than 10 years, and the other large cohort had taught for 25 or more years. The vast majority of supporters at the school fell into the first cohort of relatively new teachers, and the vast majority of critics fell into the second cohort of more veteran teachers. Supporters and critics existed in almost all departments in the school; only physical education housed exclusively one group (critics).

Susan Bandon paid close attention to whom she hired; she had been instrumental in bringing in many teachers in the various disciplines since her arrival. At one point, she remarked: "Hiring is by far the most important thing I do." She often plucked new teachers straight out of teacher education programs, in particular a program at a nearby elite university that stressed student-centered curriculum and pedagogy. She valued her novice recruits highly, calling them her "heroes" and saying that they provided the necessary "horsepower" behind the reform efforts.

Methodology

To understand the beliefs and perceptions regarding the curricular reforms at Franklin, we conducted interviews in 1996 and 1997 with 16 teachers, an assistant principal, and the principal. Half of those teachers interviewed classified themselves as supporters and half critics of the reform. The administrators identified as advocates, since both had been involved in initiating the reform effort and continued to promote it.

Clashing Beliefs about Subject Matter and Curriculum

Supporters.   Teachers at Franklin who were supporters of the reform effort saw disciplines as dissolvable and fluid. They believed that school subjects could and indeed should be combined, and maintained that the benefits for students lay in the possibility for recognizing connections between events, ideas, and theories of the different disciplines. They also tended to equate interdisciplinary curriculum with the kinds of inquiry-based constructivist approaches often associated with reform efforts, and expressed great enthusiasm for its potential to improve the learning of students.

Marcia Sullivan, an academy teacher, believed fervently that interdisciplinary curriculum played an important role in increasing student interest and helping all students get a rigorous education. Similarly, Rosa Muñoz, a proponent of the reforms who did not teach in an academy, vested hope in such an approach as a means to hook and sustain black and Hispanic students at the school: "I think there's improvement needed in terms of serving these kids . . . through ethnic studies or teaching history through literature. I want to give kids a voice who don't have it at this school."

Supporters also tended to judge the merits of curriculum on how much it allowed students to be the prime investigators of knowledge.

Marcia and Rosa both claimed that interdisciplinary curriculum lent itself to more active learning for students. Rosa also commented that while traditional classes stress facts and figures, interdisciplinary curriculum helped students to gain investigative and analytic habits: "A lot of teachers don't believe you should be able to know and *do*, too. My own take is that it's important to know and be able to analyze critically."

Such judgments led supporters to equate interdisciplinary curriculum with constructivism more generally. Supporters like Marcia explained that student-centered approaches such as "active learning" and "projects" lent themselves most appropriately to an interdisciplinary course. Marcia, for instance, seemed to feel that the reform's goals of "personalization" were achieved by helping students see the "relevance" of various subject matters to their own lives, and she felt that such goals were well addressed by an integrated curriculum. She noted, "Teachers have a better idea who students are" in the integrated classes.

Finally, supporters expressed exhilaration and enthusiasm about the new approaches to curriculum. Marcia appreciated the fact that some of her youngest students were learning challenging and sophisticated topics such as geometry, which otherwise might be reserved only for juniors and seniors. She explained with pride, "This has been the most challenging experience ever, for them academically." Rosa declared that the new approaches had affected how she viewed the teaching of history, and noted the excitement she felt in taking an approach that reflected "a lot of alignment in terms of my beliefs and the school vision." Many supporters also treasured the opportunity to work closely with other teachers and to learn about other disciplines. In Marcia's words, "I feel rejuvenated as a teacher. . . . It's changed my professional life. It's given teachers an opportunity to have dialogue about students and teaching that is invaluable."

In sum, supporters took what might be called a *transformative* stance toward disciplinary knowledge. They did not pay much heed to the traditional organization of knowledge, but rather expressed a need to transfigure the disciplines to meet the needs of students and realize a Coalition-style pedagogy. Indeed, they tended to conflate interdisciplinarity with student-centeredness more generally.

Critics. Teachers at Franklin who opposed the curricular reforms saw disciplines as coherent, discrete bodies of knowledge. They perceived their role as one of sharing disciplinary expertise and of cultivating such expertise in students. Critics did not rely on student engagement and activity to assess their curriculum; rather, they turned to traditions of inquiry as embodied in the disciplines to determine which knowledge made the most sense to teach. They worried about the lack of developmental sequencing in interdisciplinary curriculum and about the long blocks of time allotted to such courses. Finally, they experienced an implicit critique of their own subject-based teaching due to the wholehearted promotion of interdisciplinary studies by the reformers.

Skeptics of the reform believed that there was an important body of knowledge to learn in each field and criticized interdisciplinary curriculum for often giving short shrift to subject matter in one area or another. They were particularly concerned about the viability and appropriateness of merging disciplines in classrooms. Bob Chapin, a long-time English teacher at Franklin, commented that in a popular American history and literature class, English had gotten "lost" while history was "driving the curriculum." Furthermore, critics maintained that it required expertise to impart any kind of knowledge to students. Several vehemently opposed the principal's assertions that "anyone can teach anything" and "teachers should learn a subject along with the kids." Stephanie Alton, a highly revered, veteran social studies teacher at Franklin, talked about how it had taken her 5 years to become a competent economics teacher. She added with dismay, "I worry when we accept a level of superficiality, when we say anybody can teach anything. From my perspective, if anybody can teach it, it's not worth teaching."

Alton bemoaned the lack of such expertise on the part of new teachers working in the academies. She worried that such organizational structures did not enable new teachers to develop deep disciplinary knowledge: "These young teachers don't spend any time in the department and don't seem to know anything about social studies. I have to wonder what they're doing over there." She recalled that as a young teacher, the social studies department had provided a forum for learning not only about teaching, but about her subject matter:

> The people who helped me the most were the people in my discipline. We had an office where people talked about their practice. It was delightful. We talked about curricular things: "Here, you're teaching the French Revolution, now what's important? How are you organizing it, do you need any help?

Critics also grounded their opinions about the disciplines in tradition; they considered disciplines to be powerful, time-honored methods for structuring knowledge. Stephanie Alton noted that: "I think the disciplines are there because over a hundred years ago it made sense to organize knowledge this way." Because critics saw disciplines as evolving from historically grounded inquiry, they expressed concern at a lack of systematicity in interdisciplinary curriculum. Bob Chapin felt there was little empirical support behind the school's efforts to integrate subjects:

> I think we went way too fast. There are no studies or research about what courses integrate in a viable fashion. History and science don't really seem to integrate, for example. So why are we doing this so willy-nilly? . . . Curriculum simply becomes an accident.

Critics felt that the weight of tradition lent validity to the disciplines. Thus, they considered the disciplines a worthy and trusted base for decisions about what is worth teaching.

While supporters such as Marcia lauded the possibilities for younger students to encounter knowledge ordinarily reserved for older students, Stephanie feared that the sequencing of the courses that goes hand-in-hand with a more traditional disciplinary organization was perhaps dismissed too summarily. She expressed concern that students may require a certain amount of structure and developmental sequencing in order to build knowledge.

Critics were also skeptical as to whether the longer periods of time allotted to the interdisciplinary classes were actually useful and productive. Bob Chapin expressed frustration that interdisciplinary classes were not only not doing justice to both subjects, but that "no one really seems to care that they are not integrated." Stephanie agreed, noting,

> The most compelling reasons for the academies [is] more personalized time with kids. But if you have the kids for twice the time, I don't care how you cut the numbers, you need to be able to teach them twice as much: English and social studies. And you need to be able to teach both of those areas well.

Finally, critics felt that their own teaching, which had been for years a source of pride, pleasure, and success, was no longer respected and valued. One teacher explained, "Many people have been told that what they did was worthless." Skeptics of the reform also felt that the very basis of their work was being called into question, which was deeply unsettling and emotionally wrenching. Another veteran teacher, Sandra, explained, "I feel as if I'm doing something wrong—it's more on an emotional level. And it's hard for us not involved in the change effort. We wonder what it means for our teaching and for our future."

In sum, critics took what may be called a *respectful* stance toward disciplinary knowledge; they conceived of the disciplines as reliable approaches to the organization of knowledge because they were rooted in traditions of inquiry, and saw interdisciplinary studies largely as idiosyncratic representations of knowledge. They also believed in the necessity for expertise in a subject matter in order to be able to teach it well. Additionally, they questioned what they perceived as a lack of developmental sequencing in cross-disciplinary curricula and the efficacy of long blocks of class time. Finally, they felt the interdisciplinary reforms devalued their many years of subject-specific teaching.

Commonalities: The Conversations That Never Happened

Although supporters and critics differed greatly from each other in their beliefs about academic disciplines, some important overlaps existed in the comments of teachers from the two groups. However, these overlaps were not discussed openly. Rather, they represented a lost conversation— a missed opportunity to share about concerns, questions, and passions regarding the curricular reforms.

First, many teachers on both sides of the reform discussed the merits of strong integrated curriculum, when done well. Supporters, of course, expressed this belief often. For instance, Marcia lauded the opportunities interdisciplinary curricula offered for students to understand the influences disciplines may have upon one another: "Kids have a sense of how literature evolves from history; how short stories, novels, poetry evolved out of a particular time period."

Surprisingly, critics agreed that a quality interdisciplinary curriculum could be exciting and engaging for teachers and students. Stephanie, a vehement critic, went so far as to say "A good teacher should integrate on a regular basis." Stephanie talked in particular about how she had in the past enjoyed teaching numerous interdisciplinary courses, including "Culture and Technology" and "Environmental Studies." Ironically, the Culture and Technology course was offered in one of the academies, but Stephanie, the originator of the course, refused to teach it.

However, many teachers from both sides also felt that some forms of interdisciplinary curriculum had more merit than others. For instance, supporters admitted that some linkages were unwieldy and forced. Marcia, representing the opinion of several academy teachers, noted that, "Integration is not as easy in math and science as in humanities." Critics also agreed that some subjects had more logical connections than others. They remarked that interdisciplinary curriculum was most fruitful under certain conditions: for instance, when two disciplines naturally overlap, or when two teachers have expertise in each other's respective disciplines.

Indeed, both critics and supporters considered designing substantive, truly interdisciplinary curriculum a challenge. As discussed earlier, critics frequently expressed concern about maintaining the integrity of both disciplines in the course of interdisciplinary studies, noting the tendency for one discipline to eclipse the other in interdisciplinary curricula. Academy teachers had similar concerns. They explained that they had encountered difficulties even in the combining of history and literature (which is often hailed as a logical and appropriate pairing), noting that what often happens is that one or the other subject gains dominance over the other, as opposed to both receiving equal treatment in the curriculum.

Finally, numerous teachers mentioned that creating interdisciplinary curricula requires an enormous investment of time and energy, as well as compatibility between the teachers involved. Supporters remarked that they felt drained by the effort required to design such a complex curriculum. Sam, for instance, said, "I'm burnt out. It's hard to keep creating exciting, rigorous integrated curriculum. I'm exhausted." In a similar vein, Stephanie, a critic, remarked, "It takes an incredible amount of time and energy. It's no joke. People really need to want to do it because it's no joke."

ANALYSIS

Why the Clashing Beliefs about Interdisciplinary Curriculum?

In our analysis, we focus on two questions: Why are there dramatically conflicting beliefs about interdisciplinary curriculum held by the reformers and critics of the reform in this school? And why is there the lost conversation about the overlapping beliefs? Looking at structural, cultural, and political dimensions of the conflict, we hope to illuminate some reasons for the great divide between these two groups of teachers around interdisciplinary curriculum and understand why they never openly aired their privately held common concerns about such curriculum.

The Structural Dimension of the Conflict. Examining the structural dimension of the conflict means viewing traditional and nontraditional structures within schools as important sources of meaning, commitment, and relationships for teachers who belong to them. Huberman (1991) has suggested that substructures like departments and interdisciplinary academies inform teachers' thinking and behavior in more immediate and intense ways than do larger whole-school communities. Berger and Luckmann (1966) describe how group membership in structural pockets of organizations can shape the knowledge and beliefs of members to such a degree that this context defines their "objective reality." This reality becomes so internalized that it reproduces itself, even to the extent that it can prevent the imagining of other possibilities. In this way, departments and interdisciplinary academies can be seen as important structural units that teachers at Franklin joined or remained in due to their beliefs about academic disciplines. Participating in these contexts, in turn, further ossified teachers' beliefs about disciplines.

Siskin (1995) and Little (1995) have discussed the strong influence of subject matter departments in shaping teachers' intellectual and professional identities (see also Grossman & Stodolsky, 1994, for a review of this area). Departments can link teachers to the wider community of their academic discipline, which, as Siskin (1995) has pointed out, can have an "almost magnetic pull" for many secondary teachers. Grossman and Stodolsky (1995) have argued that, in concert with departments, subject matter itself functions as an important but underexamined context for teachers' work, shaping their beliefs, curriculum, philosophy, and even teachers' responses to reforms. Indeed, many teachers at Franklin stayed in departments because they described themselves first and foremost in terms of their subject matter and saw their subject matter as separate and unique—a source of professional identity. Intellectual activity involved inquiry into and debate about their discipline with colleagues of the same department, and participation in subject-based professional communities. In this way, while the act of remaining in departments represented a belief in the integrity of disciplinary knowledge on the part of critics, it also reinforced this belief. By spending most of their time in departments with colleagues who taught the same subject—or with colleagues in other departments—critics' respectful stance toward the disciplines became their objective reality.

Similar to departments, interdisciplinary academies can both represent teachers' beliefs about disciplinary knowledge and perpetuate them. Indeed, supporters at Franklin volunteered to work in the academies because the new structures represented a set of reforms, including a new approach to knowledge, which they espoused. However, once the academies were created, the new substructures then served to bolster teachers' transformative stances toward disciplinary knowledge by creating ideologically uniform enclaves. Academy teachers worked in the same buildings, created curriculum and academy policies together on a daily basis, and socialized together. For them, intellectual stimulation meant discussing how best to realize some of the Coalition principles, such as the interdisciplinary notion of "teacher as generalist."

The different proximal organizational contexts of the critics and the supporters—department and academy—seemed important sources of professional identity and seemed both to represent and reinforce their divergent beliefs about knowledge and curriculum. One could see these proximal organizational contexts as "socially segregated subuniverses of meaning" (Berger & Luckmann, 1966, p. 85), as islands of teachers who rarely visited each other's shores and could not imagine life on other islands.

The Cultural Dimension of the Conflict. The opposing beliefs about interdisciplinary curriculum at Franklin were also related to a clash between two cultures—a veteran teacher culture made up of people who had helped build the reputation of the school and a novice teacher culture made up of people without this historical consciousness and with a futuristic orientation toward the school. Weiss (1995) has pointed out that dissimilar perceptions of the identity of a school can engender different attitudes toward changing traditional structures and norms. The conflict over interdisciplinary reform at Franklin, then, seems to have derived in part from a divide between people with a respectful stance toward the historical identity of the school and disciplinary knowledge and those with a transformative stance toward the identity of the school and disciplinary knowledge.

Critics believed that the school's identity rested in its historical legacy as a successful school, successfully serving most students and sending many on to 4-year colleges. They identified with the strong reputation of the school previous to the redesign efforts, and viewed the reforms as threatening that image of the institution and their identification with that image. As Weiss has asserted, "[T]he institution, with all its historical baggage, tended to shape what teachers believe in, what they want, and what they know and bring to bear on decisions" (1995, p. 587).

Because critics believed in the merits of the school's history, they promoted a gradualist approach to reform—one that built on the strengths of the school, such as the vital departments and individual experimentation happening around the school. Indeed, they believed that the department or classroom was the appropriate unit of change—not the whole school. For them, subject integration represented one in a family of radical changes that paid no heed to what had come before. They discounted it at least partly because of its radicalness and association with a host of other fundamental reforms.

Advocates, conversely, had a different vision of the identity of the school: they saw the school's identity as that of a reforming organization striving toward a future ideal. Muncey and McQuillan (1993) have found that Coalition reforms are often driven by youthful, less experienced teachers with strong convictions about the need for change. As newer members of the school, many of the supporters seemed to identify less with the school's successful traditions, see it as more needy of remediation, and consider it more malleable. As has become clear, supporters took a transformative stance toward the school and its historical organization of knowledge; they considered both to be flexible, requiring reform, and in their power to change. In this way, they also lumped interdisciplinarity into the general category of "positive, progressive change" and did not examine it separately from the larger reform agenda.

In sum, critics and supporters at Franklin had conflicting visions of both the identity of the school and its organization of knowledge. Critics tended to trust in time-honored traditions such as the historically validated, disciplinary organization of knowledge. Integration of subjects symbolized a whole set of reforms that could destroy everything they had known. Supporters, however, distrusted these same time-honored traditions and adopted a futuristically oriented stance toward the institutions of school and subject matter, maintaining that revolution could best improve these things.

The Political Dimension of the Conflict.   In taking a "political" perspective, we train our attention on the conflict around school reform as caused by changes in the power structure: the figures who have authority in the school and the allocation of privileges and resources. The deep rift about integrated studies at the school may have resulted partly from the fact that many of the people now out of power once had the most authority and privileges at the school. This kind of shift in power inevitably causes resentment from those who benefited from and believed in the legitimacy of the old power structure. Indeed, many of the people objecting to the change were teachers who had more influence under the old power structure: department heads and veteran teachers. Those with seniority no longer received privileges and resources; rather, these things fell into the hands of those supporting the interdisciplinary reforms. The department heads and veteran teachers felt their influence and status slipping away, and this experience may have caused them to take a strong oppositional stance to the interdisciplinary reforms.

However, the reformers had gained power. They won approval from the principal and received resources unavailable to the critics who were not participating in funded interdisciplinary reforms. Perhaps because of this position of political privilege, the supporters did not listen much to the critics' often skeptical comments about interdisciplinary curriculum; they did not need them politically and thus they did not consider their concerns seriously. Because they felt anointed by the new power structure, they sat comfortably with their own beliefs and did not have to question them much.

Why the Lost Conversation?

Those in power, the reformers, undoubtedly played a large role in attenuating communication channels between the subject-based and interdisciplinary teachers. Their approaches to change often dichotomized the two groups, squelched dissent, and, for these reasons, stymied real discussion between them. However, the reformers were certainly not the lone culprits in this conflict. The schism between the two groups arose *relationally*—that is, it arose out of the interactions and communications between the two groups. Indeed, both groups at Franklin continuously constructed each other as opposite and separate, fueling the fire between them and smothering productive interchange about interdisciplinary curriculum. By seeing each other as so different, they also avoided taking each other's claims seriously; they essentially guarded themselves against an alternative and potentially threatening view that could muddy their vision of reality.

The Structural Dimension of the Conflict. The reformers opted for a school-within-a-school (SWAS) approach—that is, they decided to focus the change effort in a structurally separate part of the school (the academies) and leave the rest of the school virtually untouched. The notion was that the academies would experiment in ways the whole school could learn from, but the result was "structurally segregated subuniverses of meaning" (Berger & Luckmann, 1966). Indeed, Muncey and McQuillan (1996) have found that SWAS approaches tend to exacerbate philosophical differences between teachers and contribute to "us versus them" divisions. Thus, by sequestering the change effort in one part of the school, the reformers created structures that clearly demarcated the differences between the two camps, separated them physically, and ultimately stifled communication between the two groups.

However, once the new structures existed, teachers in both the academies and departments allowed the structural boundaries to widen the gap between them. By rarely leaving the boundaries of their structural subunits (departments or interdisciplinary academies), all the teachers at this school exacerbated the structural balkanization. They rarely saw each other or interacted, and thus became strangers to each other. Both substructures not only reinforced teachers' beliefs about subject matter, but also solidified their oppositional positions in the school with regard to interdisciplinary curricula. They lost the ability to see one another as colleagues with complex, and sometimes compatible, viewpoints with whom they could dialogue constructively about interdisciplinary curriculum.

The Cultural Dimension of the Conflict. The reformers at Franklin embraced the Coalition principles wholesale and did not tailor the philosophy much to the local conditions. The critics, with their vision of the school as having a proud history from which to build on, argued that the departments had been a great source of strength in the past and bemoaned the movement to overhaul them entirely. Indeed, as with the other principles of CES, the notion of "teacher as generalist" became gospel for the reformers. "Interdisciplinary" served as a code word for positive, constructivist change more generally; it belonged to a whole package of reforms that needed to be adopted all together. This conflation of interdisciplinarity with constructivism and with an equitable education for students by the reformers meant that when subject-based teachers questioned integrated studies, they were questioning the whole agenda for change. Reformers did not allow for local adaptation of an imported philosophy; instead, they saw interdisciplinarity, constructivism, and equity as all bound together and inseparable. Thus, they did not entertain discussions about the nuances of integrating disciplines and whether and when it would make sense.

Indeed, as with many reformers, the proponents of interdisciplinary curriculum at Franklin assumed that the good ideas of CES would make sense to everyone. They had little sense that by promoting the integration of disciplines, they were calling for a fundamental shift in deep-seated beliefs and behaviors on the part of subject-based teachers. Cuban (1993) and Fullan (1991) have noted that reformers often fail to recognize the profound transformations in teacher culture that their initiatives imply. By not viewing their advocacy of interdisciplinary reforms as a rather radical reculturing and not just restructuring (Fullan, 1993), the supporters underestimated the task of winning the whole staff over to the new kinds of curricula and programs. Instead of acknowledging the enormity of what they were asking of subject-based teachers, they displayed impatience and frustration with the doubters and, ultimately, stifled authentic discussion about deeply held beliefs and behaviors.

However, critics of the reform also contributed to the breakdown in communication in that they wrote off the whole reform program once a part of it challenged some of their deep-seated beliefs and behaviors. Once something alienated the skeptics from the reform, they dismissed all aspects of it, even if they agreed with parts of it. Indeed, for the critics, "interdisciplinary" became a code word for the whole reform program that threatened their habitual ways of thinking and conducting their work. It signaled the dismantling of the successful school they had helped to create over many years and with which they identified strongly.

Both supporters and critics of the interdisciplinary reforms maintained publicly unified postures with regards to their beliefs about interdisciplinary curriculum. Both conflated integration of subjects with the entire reform agenda and its implications for the identity of the school. In this way, they appeared to each other as much more certain about interdisciplinary studies than they actually were. Thus, they could not talk productively about the complexities of subject integration in particular because it represented the whole reform effort and all of the emotions swirling around it.

The Political Dimension of the Conflict.   The reformers did not appear to grasp the consequences of interdisciplinarity for department-based teachers. They did not see their power alone as augmented; rather, they believed there was more power to be had by all teachers. Muncey and McQuillan (1993) have noted that supporters often overlook the power they have gained and others have lost. Indeed, academy teachers seem to have underestimated the loss of authority experienced by their department-based colleagues and the influence of this loss on these colleagues' opinions about the interdisciplinary reforms. Because of their politically favorable position in the school, the supporters would have been wise to reach out to critics to initiate dialogue.

Furthermore, the reformers' notion of democratic decision making—as a process where majority votes mandate whole-school changes—proved problematic for skeptics of the reform. Over the course of 6 years, the school essentially moved from a hierarchical power structure—the principal, administrators, and department heads making school policy—to a nonhierarchical one. The more democratic approach took a particular form—majoritarian. This version of democracy frustrated those in the minority. The rhetoric of shared decision making rang hollow to department-based teachers, as they felt their views did not get taken seriously. Not only have their minority voices not been able to carry the day on major decisions, but they have also been unable even to influence the majority of supporters.

Although the majoritarian democracy of the school marginalized skeptics of the interdisciplinary reforms a great deal, the skeptics also failed to "work the system" and ignite more productive conversations about their concerns. Researchers of schools undertaking shared decision-making have discussed a deep disbelief on the part of experienced teachers that schoolwide policy was really in the realm of their influence (Gitlin & Margonis, 1995; Midgely & Wood, 1993; Weiss, 1995). Critics of the interdisciplinary reforms exhibited this skepticism with regards to the democratic decision-making process at the school; they saw it as largely orchestrated and manipulated by the principal and reformers. This perspective may have derived from the veteran teachers' years of experience in a hierarchical system. Their feelings of marginalization could be seen as stemming partly from an inability to shed a historically situated vision of authority, a vision that prevented them from participating actively in the democratic process (attending meetings, organizing before a vote) to push through their agenda. They did not work the democratic system to their advantage. They didn't play the game.

From the interviews with teachers on both sides of the conflict, we know that common ground existed. Perhaps if the subject-based teachers had mobilized some bipartisan support for their positions, they would have felt less victimized and spurred more genuine debates about interdisciplinary curriculum. They constructed the reformers as powerful and themselves as powerless, and thus did not spark useful debate about interdisciplinary studies. The reformers, though, also displayed a strong resistance to any kind of dissent—even if on some level they agreed with it—and thus drowned out the voices of the critics before they could ever really listen to them.

IMPLICATIONS

The case of Franklin High School provides lessons for interdisciplinary reformers and anyone in the midst of such a reform initiative. Due to structural, cultural, and political dimensions of the reform, teachers at the school split into two groups that moved further and further apart from each other. Although this philosophical rift ran wide, teachers from both groups expressed some similar beliefs about interdisciplinary curriculum in our interviews that did not get voiced as part of the whole-school debate. This kind of division and lack of dialogue could be avoided, or at least ameliorated to some extent, by an attention to the structural, cultural, and political dimensions of such fundamental change.

As Muncey and McQuillan (1996) noted, schools-within-a-school (SWAS) tend to breed structural balkanization, alienating reformers from nonreformers. Indeed, the case of Franklin reveals the power of structures to create cloistered ideological universes that reflect—but also deepen—differences. Reformers may want to avoid physically separating teachers of different persuasions about a change effort, and instead encourage interaction between such teachers. Indeed, it may make sense not to isolate change but attempt to create change across the structures of a school—even if the change initiative is somewhat less intense. For instance, reformers could encourage departments to discuss the potential for interdisciplinary courses with other departments—as opposed to calling for the death of departments altogether. The traditional structures hold a lot of meaning for many teachers, and interdisciplinary reformers would be wise to respect the power of departments and figure out how to work with—and not entirely against—them.

Along with structural balkanization, the conflict around interdisciplinary reforms at Franklin also represents something of a culture clash between experienced teachers who identify strongly with the historical success of the school and largely inexperienced teachers who believe in a future ideal of the school. Reformers often don't realize that they are calling for a supplanting of one culture with another, that the beliefs and behaviors they wish to change have deep roots. Reformers also tend to become somewhat messianic about their vision and will not accept anything less than a revolution. However, such a sweeping approach to change tends to conflate such things as interdisciplinarity, constructivism, and equity—making it virtually impossible for someone, such as a subject-based teacher, to question the integration of subjects without questioning the whole program of change. This kind of orthodoxy seriously curtails the possibility for healthy, contentious debate about topics such as interdisciplinary curriculum.

Granted, a certain amount of missionary zeal may be necessary to carry off any kind of fundamental change, but reformers ought to beware of silencing important dialogue through their enthusiasm. As Gitlin and Margonis (1995) point out, resistance may often have "good sense" to it; indeed, reformers may agree with some of the criticisms if they would allow themselves to hear them. However, critics during a reform effort also need to avoid writing off a whole reform effort and acknowledge the elements that appeal to them. Both groups can too easily dichotomize each other and erode any chance of constructive dialogue about issues of importance.

Finally, shifting power and resources from one group of teachers to another can exacerbate philosophical differences between teachers and render one group all-powerful and the other powerless. Those gaining in power may not listen well to those diminishing in power and may have trouble recognizing their own privileged position—two things that will attenuate relations between the groups. And even if the shift is only a partial one, those previously in power may be unpracticed in new authority structures and may fail to capitalize on them. Thus, a dramatic transfer in power can create misperceptions, dichotomize groups of teachers, and suffocate communication.

Interdisciplinary reformers, then, may want to avoid divesting departments and veteran teachers of all their power. Instead, giving department chairs and experienced teachers leadership roles may make sense, in order to find new ways for subject-based communities to wield their authority and use their resources. In any case, reformers would be wise to attempt to balance power in the school, as opposed to creating a radical shift that completely disrupts the traditional school community. Reformers need to pay attention to the political dimension of change and stave off the dichotomization of a school into the powerful and the weak, perpetuating the hierarchical relations they likely hope to alter. Resisters, on the contrary, need to guard against the adoption of a victim role and avoid floundering in a new authority structure. Instead, they should take a proactive stance and learn to navigate the new power mechanisms, organizing to promote their agenda.

The case of Franklin reveals the complexity of attempting interdisciplinary reform at the secondary level; traditional structures, cultures, and political forms make such change an enormous challenge. Reformers of this variety will want to tread carefully and consciously into this minefield. They should respect tradition without being overwhelmed by it, and they should concede the complexities and pitfalls of their reform program. Reformers would do well to temper their enthusiasm in order to stay open to alternative visions and constantly consider what kinds of curriculum most benefit students in their particular contexts. Meanwhile, more experienced teachers need to be able to step outside tradition in order to continue developing as professionals and serving students as well as they can. Perhaps when both groups can take such measured perspectives, rich conversations can occur that will lead to the best kinds of learning for students.

REFERENCES

Berger, P. L., & Luckmann, T. (1966). *The social construction of reality: A treatise in the sociology of knowledge.* New York: Doubleday.

Cuban, L. (1993). *How teachers taught.* New York: Teachers College Press..

Fullan, M. (1991). *The new meaning of educational change.* New York: Teachers College Press.

Fullan, M. (1993). *Change forces.* London: The Falmer Press

Gitlin, A., & Margonis, F. (1995). The political aspect of reform: Teacher resistance as good sense. *American Journal of Education, 103,* 377–405.

Grossman, P. L., & Stodolsky, S. S. (1994). Considerations of content and the circumstances of secondary school teaching. In L. Darling-Hammond (Ed.), *Review of Research in Education* (Vol. 20, pp. 179–221). Washington, DC: American Educational Research Association.

Grossman, P. L., & Stodolsky, S. S. (1995). Content as context: The role of secondary school subjects in secondary school teaching. *Educational Researcher, 24,* 5–11.

Huberman, M. (1991). The model of the independent artisan in teachers' professional relations. In J. W. Little, & M. W. McLaughlin (Eds.), *Teachers' work* (p. 50). New York: Teachers College Press.

Little, J. W. (1995). Subject affiliations in high schools that restructure. In L. S. Siskin & J. W. Little (Eds.), *The subjects in question: Departmental organization and the high school* (pp. 172–200). New York: Teachers College Press.

Midgley, C., & Wood, S. (1993). Beyond site-based management: Empowering teachers to reform schools. *Phi Delta Kappan, 75,* 245–252.

Muncey, D. E., & McQuillan, P. J. (1993). Preliminary findings from a five-year study of the Coalition of Essential Schools. *Phi Delta Kappan, 74,* 486–489.

Muncey, D. E., & McQuillan, P. J. (1996). *Reform and resistance in schools and classrooms: An ethnographic view of the Coalition of Essential Schools.* New Haven, CT: Yale University Press.

Siskin, L. S. (1995). Subject divisions. In L. S. Siskin & J. W. Little (Eds.), *The subjects in question: Departmental organization and the high school* (pp. 23–47). New York: Teachers College Press.

Weiss, C. (1995). The four "I's" of school reform: How interests, ideology, information and institution affect teachers and principals. *Harvard Educational Review, 65,* 571–592.

8

"... So That the Two Can Mix in This Crucible"

Teachers in an Interdisciplinary School-University Collaboration in the Humanities

GABRIELLA MINNES BRANDES AND PETER SEIXAS

Teachers' professional development in the context of school-university collaboration has recently been the subject of considerable interest by teacher educators and others (cf., Arends, 1990; Bell & Gilbert, 1993; Cole & Knowles, 1993; Dixon & Ishler, 1992; Erickson, 1991; Richardson, 1994). Universities have the resources to undertake systematic research, and their *modus operandi* is the critical community of inquiry whose explicit purpose is the growth of knowledge. Nevertheless, the university connection creates new challenges for schools. This chapter examines a one-year interdisciplinary teacher and curriculum development project which, while being atypical of school-university collaborations in several ways, provides an important opportunity for analyzing the complexities of such work.

The project provided eight teachers from different schools (along with school-based teams associated with each of them) with an intensive one-year exposure to new scholarship in the humanities and social sciences, which they utilized in the development of curriculum materials. All eight were attracted to the project, to one degree or another, because of its promise of interdisciplinarity or (as it was called in the schools) "integration."

The British Columbia Consortium for Humanities and Social Sciences (hereafter, the Consortium) was one site in the third year of the

American Council of Learned Societies' (ACLS) multimillion dollar Teacher/Curriculum Development Project. The ACLS is the umbrella organization for scholarly societies in humanities and social sciences in the United States. It is thus composed of representatives of the scholarly disciplines. There is no organization—including, perhaps, the university itself—whose constituent elements are more clearly and unambiguously the disciplines. And yet the *raison d'être* of the organization is to provide leadership and initiative in concerns across the disciplines.

The ACLS's first initiative into "K-16" schooling aimed to infuse "new scholarship" into the schools through two avenues. First, relatively small groups of teachers would be provided with time for study at major research universities. And second, these teachers would develop curriculum materials informed by their studies. The ACLS hoped that the impact would ripple outward through the schools through both efforts: that teachers engaged with the new scholarship would draw their colleagues into that engagement; and that the new curricular materials would be used in the schools, the districts, and beyond. At its grandest, the ACLS saw the project as a major catalyst for national school reform.

The central dynamic element in the ACLS model involved academics in the disciplines working with teachers, overlooking the potential contribution of schools of education (cf., Brandes & Erickson, 1998; Cuban, 1992). The designers of the ACLS project felt that teachers in the humanities, constrained by lack of time, resources, and contacts, needed access to the dramatic new developments that had swept through history, literary studies, and the social sciences over the past 15 to 20 years.

In British Columbia, as at other sites, the project was structurally interdisciplinary. The Consortium involved teachers of English, social studies, and drama, and professors of historical geography, English literature, anthropology, and education as well as visiting speakers in a further variety of school subjects and academic disciplines (cf., Grossman & Stodolsky, 1995; Seixas, 1993; Siskin, 1994). This configuration of subject specialties and disciplinary orientations contributed, in part, to the prominence of certain cross-disciplinary concepts from the "new scholarship" early in the Consortium work. These concepts included gender and feminism, multiculturalism, postmodernism, and the problem of interdisciplinarity itself. They provided an opening for a broad set of epistemological questions related to position, voice, power, and representation, cutting a wide, common swath across traditional fields of study.

The Consortium provided funding for the eight teachers to spend an entire school year on campus, to take courses, participate in a Consortium seminar with the professors, and to develop curriculum materials. Teachers were selected from four participating school districts on the basis of their backgrounds as well as a proposal for a curriculum project that they would undertake during the year. The Consortium also provided release time for the four professors, research money, and support for conferences.

Though the project posed challenges and opportunities for all of the participants, this chapter deals only with those faced by the eight teachers (for more on the challenges and opportunities facing the university scholars, see Seixas & Brandes, 1997). The project placed them in a challenging role as a bridge between the cultures of school and academia. At one pole of the school-university tension lay the world of the school. The teachers were expected to maintain contact with their departments, schools, and school districts during the year. The four participating districts had each contributed some funding to the project, and expected, in return, reports, publishable curriculum materials, and leadership in professional development activities.

At the other pole of the tension stood the university. Most of the teachers' time was spent on the university campus during the year, taking classes of their choice (mainly in the Faculty of Arts), participating in the Consortium seminars, and engaging in the research, meetings, and writing. In order to be successful in this dimension of the project, teachers had to be excited about the sometimes meandering, sometimes arcane discussions that characterize university discourse. And at the same time they had to maintain the critical perspectives developed over the years of their own school experience. On many occasions, the teachers encountered ideas that challenged some of the basic assumptions of their initial curricular proposals (cf., Brandes & Seixas, 1998).

In most cases, connecting the ideas of the new scholarship to the world of the classroom involved hard work. The enthusiasm for interdisciplinarity in academia was different from that for integration in the schools. In many ways, the humanities and social sciences had become broader, incorporating feminist and multicultural concerns. At the same time, thorny epistemological and methodological problems (often subsumed under the rubric of postmodernism) arose precisely because of the new attempts at inclusivity. Entering the university-based project, the teachers had to be able to enjoy, or at least to tolerate, the postmodernist professors' delight in destabilizing knowledge. They were being invited, moreover, to join the academic forays into interdisciplinarity without recent immersion in the disciplines upon which the professors—consciously or not—depended. The assumptions, motivations, and knowledge that lay behind the boundary-crossing of subjects in the schools, and disciplines in the university, was thus significantly different in the two sets of institutions.

From their position in the project, the teachers faced three chal-

lenges. First, coming from the culture of the schools, they had to participate actively in interdisciplinary academic explorations. Second, they
needed to mine this scholarly work for its utility in relation to their often
multisubject curriculum projects. Third, their responsibilities as leaders
of curriculum change back in their districts demanded that they act as a
bridge between the discourses and cultures of school and university. We
explore these three challenges through composite pictures of the teachers
in the first part of this chapter. In the second part we extend the analysis
by offering in-depth accounts of two teachers' participation in the project.
Data upon which this study is based include teachers' project applications, transcripts of interviews at the beginning and end of the project
year, transcripts of seminars during the project year, teachers' written
curriculum projects, and retrospective interviews conducted 1½ years
after the completion of the project.

CHALLENGES

Teachers Engaging in the "New Scholarship"

When the teachers arrived on campus, they effectively shifted from their
day-to-day focus on teaching to an interdisciplinary academic exploration, including both regular undergraduate courses and a project seminar.
Before the teachers' year on campus, the four professors composed a list
of topics deliberately reflecting issues across the humanities and social
sciences (e.g., constructing history, multiculturalism, gender theories).
They also assumed responsibility for the first two seminars by selecting
readings on "feminism" and "postmodernism." Teachers' reactions to
this beginning were not entirely positive, and they very soon articulated
a need for more participation in shaping the direction and substance of
the seminars. Teachers' responses to the courses and seminars were different from those of regular students, either undergraduate or graduate.
Behind the interdisciplinary studies always lay the question: How does
this relate to the subjects and students and classes that I teach?

Sally regarded the year as an opportunity for intellectual pursuit that
full-time teaching did not allow her to do, yet she never left her role as a
teacher entirely behind. She had majored in history with a minor in geography, subsequently completing a postdegree program in teacher education. Her teaching responsibilities included both social studies and humanities classes in a large suburban secondary school. She approached
the courses she took with a different set of questions and understandings
than she had as an undergraduate:

I'm finding now that I'm looking at the classes from a different perspective. How can I use this in my classroom? And as I take notes, I'm actually writing notes on the page of ideas of how to work it into my classes.

Sally saw the question of interdisciplinarity as a pressing one. Though she had attempted to bring insights from social studies and English into integrated units in her own teaching, she did not see her prior accomplishments as fully integrative:

Right now [my humanities lessons are] social studies with a little bit of English mixed in. I think we have a lot of programs in my district anyways that we call humanities, which is just English and social studies taught by one person.

Like other teachers in the group, she hoped that the academic explorations of interdisciplinarity would shed light on these problems.

At one extreme was another teacher who was less willing to meander along intellectual pathways which might—or might not—lead back to her classroom. Patricia had completed her teaching certificate 9 years earlier, after earning a B. A. in English and theater. For the past 2 years, she was the Fine Arts department head at a large new suburban school organized around a program in self-paced learning. After 3 weeks of the project, Patricia reflected:

I had thought . . . that the seminar would be much more product-oriented. I was a little disappointed to find out that that wasn't the case. . . . I'm getting something out of this, but what is my team getting, what are my students ultimately going to get out of this?

The seminar generated resentment from Patricia from early on, particularly because she could not see its utility in the classroom.

There were other teachers who appreciated the academic focus in the seminars. Ramesh, whose first degree was in science, had come back to a program in special education and English. Starting teaching in 1987, he moved from teaching special education to social studies, English, and humanities. He acknowledged the dual goals of his participation in the Consortium, but his emphasis was different. His starting point was that he would spend the year "seeing the world as a scholar but at the same time writing and using what I learned in the scholarship" toward ends at school.

I think this year I have an amazing opportunity to express who I am and exercise that voice. I know I have something to say. And to fill, at least the way that I perceive a lot of gaps in Western ideology.

At the end of the project year, Ramesh was grateful to the project for giving him access to scholarship on issues surrounding multiculturalism. He felt that he could articulate a number of key issues that he "just couldn't piece together before." For him, seminar discussions and literature on deconstruction, postmodernism, and feminism were tremendously helpful. He said that he had previously lacked the conceptual apparatus and vocabulary to deal confidently with issues in English education, in part because his undergraduate degree was in science.

Tom, like Ramesh, enjoyed the academic pursuit but brought another perspective to the seminars. Following a B.A. in English, he had taught English, English as a second language, social studies, and humanities over 23 years. He criticized the first seminars not for being too theoretical and divorced from classroom issues, but for being not rigorous enough. The very vocabulary and concepts that Ramesh found empowering were experienced by Tom as constraining and ideologically driven. Though there were some courses he took and ideas he encountered that he respected, he was most critical of the seminar.

I suppose it may have started with being given a vocabulary at the beginning which clearly indicated this is the way we will talk about things here. This is what we will learn. These are the words we will learn to describe reality and here they are because you don't know them and now you're going to know them and use them.

Tom maintained his critique of postmodernism throughout the seminar discussions and organized a highly successful session built around readings that challenged the relativistic aspects of postmodernist thought. Thus, as critical as he was, he was fully engaged in the intellectual issues raised in the context of the seminar.

However, participants varied in the value they placed on these scholarly pursuits and their relevance for them as teachers. Some considered the concepts, language, and frames of mind presented in the academic context as critical components of their professional growth. They linked their engagement with the "new scholarship" to their ability to conceptualize and articulate curricular materials. However, other teachers thought these discussions were too theoretical and removed from the realities of the school. They found it harder to create links between discussions in the seminars and the preparation of curricular materials that would be used in schools. All the teachers were excited by the opportunity to be students again. However, they varied in the degree to which they were willing to commit time and energy to these pursuits, when they considered the expectations placed upon them to create curricular materials and lead teams in their schools.

Bringing "New Scholarship" into the Schools

The Consortium's collaborative framework included many potential avenues for school change, including ongoing scholarly ties, access to resources for teachers, conferences, and the formation and strengthening of school teams. But the most tangible vehicle for impact on the schools during the project year was the teachers' creation of the package of curriculum materials. There was a clear expectation that the curricular materials would reflect issues from the "new scholarship," which had been discussed in the seminar. Having discussed the interdisciplinary, epistemological questions that grew out of these concerns, the teachers had to bring them to the schools. It was almost unilaterally on their shoulders to shape these questions for the students in their classrooms in a developmentally appropriate way. Clear understandings and clear articulations were prerequisites to undertaking this task.

As much as Sally saw merit in theoretical academic discussions, she—like Patricia and others—continuously sought to make connections between the topics in the seminars and the realities in school, with an eye to the curricular product she was expected to produce:

> Well, I wanted us to spend some more time talking about how these ideas and these concepts could be used in the classroom. And I just felt that when you're talking about topics like postmodernism, I mean these are big huge things to grasp that it would have been nice to have been able to spend fifteen minutes to say okay, how could you introduce this to your grade nine classroom?

Ramesh, on the contrary, felt relatively unconstrained by traditional ideas about curriculum materials for teachers, and developed texts that might be used in the context of a university class in teacher education, but which would be unlikely to be picked up by teachers outside of a formal program. He struggled through much of the year, realizing how far he was from translating ideas that he personally felt as transformative into something that would have an impact on the schools. In the end, he chose not to write lesson plans, but composed a series of reflections on reconceptualizing multicultural education, interwoven with powerfully written autobiographical narratives.

But measured against the huge goal that he had set for himself at the outset—to develop a new framework for education for a multicultural society—his accomplishment was only a bare beginning. Thus, the overriding message from his second interview is one of incompleteness and frustration along several dimensions. The one-year project was too short a time. He had school change in mind but, as he said, "I couldn't do it this year because this is the year that it took me to develop."

> In September, I could critique, I knew that there was something wrong, but I couldn't critique it because I didn't have the language for it. And to think that it took me a year to develop the language of scholarship to be able to critique something. Then simultaneously to propose something that was new . . .

A contrasting case is offered by Tom. As noted above, he engaged the ideas and debates in the university seminar as fully as did Ramesh. Unlike Ramesh, he began the project year with a clear sense of what he wanted in the way of a curriculum project, a unit surveying world religions through architecture. Though he changed it along the way, he always felt that he was on track toward a package that would be directly usable by teachers. Though Tom heartily embraced the debates about postmodernism and the new scholarship, these had relatively little impact on his curriculum product. He explained:

> You have the knowledge that so many people in the world have different points of view of the world and you understand a little bit about them. But I can't apply certain things [from the seminar] that I might apply in another context . . . certain tools and strategies for looking at why people believe in what they believe in. It's kind of complicated . . . it's too sensitive of an area.

In talking about the development process, he contrasted the culture of the Consortium with that of the schools, particularly in respect to the time it provided to talk to colleagues. The deliberative pace of the year on campus allowed him to mull over the meanings of scholarly developments. He knew his colleagues back in school would face the ideas in very different conditions.

The curricular materials that teachers developed took a wide variety of forms and orientations. Some teachers used the Consortium resources (time, people, the academic context, school teams) to create materials designed specifically for their own schools, and others created materials with larger audiences in mind. Some teachers saw their role as compiling materials their teams generated, whereas others used the opportunity to explore their own ideas. Moreover, while all of the curricular materials paid considerable attention to the notion of subject integration within the humanities, the degree to which they incorporated the "new scholarship" varied, perhaps as a consequence of their differing goals.

Working for School Change

Alongside Sally's hopes of seeking the integration of the humanities curriculum in her school, she faced the argument from both social studies and English colleagues that "at university" students take separate courses. Sally discussed some of the problems in promoting change in the subject-organization of schools, noting the broad parallel between the interdisciplinary work of the professors involved in the project, and the challenge facing teachers in her school:

> You're getting professors from different disciplines working together. . . . For projects like humanities to work within the high schools and junior high schools, some of that needs to be reflected into universities.

The push both at the district level and among the participants in the project toward integrating the subjects of English and social studies was not without opposition. Sue circulated a flyer entitled "English Teachers and Humanities" (1994) published by the BC English Teachers' Association, on whose executive committee she sat. It complained of "no general definition of what a Humanities programme is or should be" and expressed concern that Humanities courses might end up with social studies curriculum dominating English "as a consequence of its linear, content-based structure. . . ." Leaders of the English Teachers' Association, cognizant of reader response and related pedagogy in their subject, had the view that much social studies teaching was governed by a drive to transmit historical information (or "content"), and that this imperative would dominate attempts to integrate the two subjects.

As it turned out, the Consortium proved to be a difficult location from which to press for integrating school subjects. The concept of interdisciplinarity, as it was approached at the university and in the seminar, bore an uncertain relationship to the considerations that lay behind the integration of English and social studies in the schools. In the university, interdisciplinarity was an attempt to generate epistemological complexity and depth; in the schools, integration was an administrative response to students' experiences of a fragmented and alienating school timetable, targeted at students' social and psychological needs. Once again, university discourse seemed distant from the needs of the school.

In an idealized model of this professional development project, there would have been an easy fit among personal professional growth for the teachers, curriculum materials development, and broader school change to accommodate and respond to the new scholarship. The reality was different. The teachers faced varying degrees of resistance to change in their schools. Some teachers, team members, and administrators were keen to hear about new frameworks and curricular materials, whereas others saw the project primarily as an opportunity for professional growth for the teachers themselves. Teachers varied in the scope and nature of the changes they hoped to effect, and in their skill (and luck) in bringing together cross-subject school teams. In sum, teachers found themselves throughout the year negotiating between their new, temporary location at the university and the realities of the schools to which they would return.

TWO TEACHERS—A CASE STUDY

In this section, we offer extended accounts showing how two teachers managed the tensions between school and university. We continue the focus on the three central challenges for teachers in the project: the need to deeply engage the new scholarship in an interdisciplinary academic setting, the problem of bringing that scholarship into curriculum products for humanities classes in the schools, and the difficulties of initiating school change from a collaborative project with a strong base at the university.

Sue

Sue had been involved in curricular reform in her school prior to the project year. Her application to the Consortium was motivated in part by a desire to sort out issues that troubled her in the change process. The questions that drove her participation were posed from her strong identification as an English teacher. She had majored in English, she "love[d] creative writing," taught courses in writing and drama, and served, as noted above, on the executive committee of the provincial English teachers' association.

Yet she was also involved in designing and teaching an integrated humanities program in her school and saw the Consortium as an opportunity to further that work. She had concerns about the issues of subject integration in the humanities in the schools. She observed, "The notion of humanities is kind of slapping together English and social studies." She acknowledged that she saw these problems in part from the vantage point of an English teacher: "from . . . an English teacher's perspective . . . history really seems to take over."

She referred here to social studies teachers' concerns with covering particular topical content. She worried that social studies teachers would accuse their English colleagues teaching humanities: "You didn't cover the Russian Revolution!" She thought that the ties between English and social studies had to be thought out more thoroughly, and that the Consortium would give her the time and the collegial contacts to do so.

At the outset of the project year, Sue quickly became immersed in the intellectual pursuits of the university. While showing few signs of it at the time, she later said she had been "overwhelmed" by the intellectual and logistical demands at the outset of the project. She was stimulated as she entertained challenges to her assumptions about interdisciplinarity. But at the same time that she was getting oriented on campus, she felt the demands from her district. In October of the project year, district personnel began asking Sue to speak about humanities at various schools in the district. She found it somewhat frustrating to be asked "to go and present to department heads in our district when we . . . didn't ourselves know what it was about, what was going on." If the purpose of the project was to provide an opportunity for reflection and study about these problems, then it was no surprise that Sue felt unprepared for this task one month into the year.

Sue put considerable effort into communicating with everyone, and she spoke freely both about the substance of the seminars and about their dynamics with both teachers and professors. She also spoke enthusiastically about scholarly aspects of the project:

> I really think that it was important to have . . . the new scholarship [as the focus] and taking a look at what was happening in different disciplines so I wouldn't change that because I think that's really what made this project . . . unique and was such an important part of this.

Similarly, Sue took on the writing of curriculum materials as a personal challenge. In her first finished product, she worked with Sally to develop a novel study package based on a piece of historical fiction, *Catherine, Called Birdy* (Cushman, 1994) for grade 8. The package challenged students to grapple with questions of historical evidence and the nature of historical fiction. Initial discussion questions asked, for example, "Is it possible to know whether a historical novel is accurate? Does it matter? How do we reconcile conflicting historical and literary accounts?" Sue recalled the succession of her feelings "never really having done something like this before, actually writing curriculum." She "just felt so good . . . getting something like *Catherine, Called Birdy* on paper."

Beyond her own school, Sue had strong ties to her school district's professional development activities. In May of the project year, she and another teacher organized a one-day session for teachers in the district. In part because the push toward integrating English and social studies was a district priority, there was a strong response. Sue was always conscious of the project's potential impact in the schools, even if it took the form of a "binder of lesson plans":

> I felt a lot of expectations from the district and I think that was
> kind of reflected in the planning and doing of the [conference on
> the] 24th which I'm really happy that we did, but it was quite a bit
> of pressure to give workshops. And I always felt in the back of my
> mind that I had to have this really concrete binder of lesson plans
> at the end of all of this . . .

Though she saw the year initially through the frame of the curricular problems of her school, over time she began to judge the quality of her school and district activities in part on the basis of their scholarly merit. At the end of the year, she reflected: "I just feel like I have a really solid foundation in some of the vocabularies, the words, the theory, the concepts. . . . So that gives me a lot of confidence to know that that's something that I came through this year." She spoke of working on her historical fiction novel package with the question in mind, Does this reflect current scholarship? Her lessons did indeed challenge students to consider issues of historical epistemology and historical empathy in ways that built upon recent scholarship. Two years after the project, Sue continued to mobilize that work as a source of ideas and approaches for high school teaching. She continued to take university classes, chosen on the basis of their relevance to her teaching; and she continued to draw on concepts, conversations, and courses from the year in the project.

In sum, Sue felt and expressed the tensions that all of the other teachers felt. Her year at the university was a welcome opening as well as a new departure, which she explored fully, without losing sight of the school projects that had gotten her involved in the first place. Returning to the district, she assumed new positions in professional development activities. Her leadership was exercised both in the traditional subject of English, as department head in a new school, and in a subject-integration initiative, in her contribution to the establishment of a local Humanities Teachers Association.

Dan

Dan had taught for 27 years. Having spent most of his career in the elementary grades (after completing a degree in history and geography), he had moved to the secondary school 3 years before the Consortium project, to a teaching load evenly divided between English and social studies. He described himself as a political activist ("I eat up anything political"). Years of experience representing teachers locally and provincially had developed his skills at handling politics both at the small-group level and in broader arenas of political change.

Like Sue's, Dan's staff was grappling with the problem of how to handle the district's push toward combining English and social studies. Dan's initial impetus for the curricular project was the need to create a course to fit the combined English and social studies in grades 8 and 9. "We have a curriculum integration notion as English and social studies teachers. . . . Humanities to us means pulling English and social studies together." In the schools, however, he noted the resistance that "humanities" courses encountered:

> The social studies teachers are afraid the English teachers aren't going to teach map skills terribly well, and the English teachers are absolutely certain the social studies are going to bomb on teaching poetry. . . .

A school team had already begun work on this problem, prior to the inception of the Consortium. Seeing the possibility of more substantial support than the team had worked with up to that time, Dan applied to be a participant in the project. Dan articulated the tension built into the project:

> [T]here's a real tendency, I see it in myself and I see it in my other colleagues in the project for us to . . . rush to the practical very quickly . . . and I have to rein that in and say no. . . . [On the other hand] I just have to move ahead of some [academic] people into the practical, I'm finding. And that's creating a little tension for me. . . .

He conceived of the school-university collaboration as a reciprocal give-and-take. The teacher's role, he said, "is to become more knowledgeable in our [subject] areas . . . but also to bring the knowledge of practice into the university so that the two can mix in this crucible." Dan emphasized the teachers' contributions to the seminars and to the professors' understandings of teaching and learning.

Dan engaged the seminar fully, organizing and leading a session analyzing the impact of a "right-wing discourse" of privatization on Canadian public decision making. Though he dismissed some aspects of postmodernism as "drivel," he found the concepts of voice, representation, and appropriation—drawn from some of the postmodernist literature—to be powerful tools for both the analysis of literature and the consideration of social studies issues. He also used them to analyze the collaborative dynamics of the school-university relationship itself. Believing strongly in the value of teachers' experience and voice, Dan expressed concern that "very often we teachers find our own history made invalid."

His most extensive use of the concepts of voice, representation, and appropriation came as he worked on his curriculum project (*Meetings of Cultures and in Cultures: Contact and Conflict,* designed for the integrated grade 9 course). This project was organized thematically around issues of culture contact and conflict, and it included a study package for the novel *Copper Sunrise* (Buchan, 1972). Frequently studied in British Columbia schools, the work deals with the extinction of the Beothuk people of Newfoundland. Dan provided short excerpts from six other accounts of the extinction of the Beothuk, written between 1915 and 1995, with questions probing issues of evidence, interpretation, and voice. Their inclusion grew out of seminar discussions on historical evidence and epistemology. As Dan described it:

> The historical thinking is another really big part of our project and writing a supplement to deal with history . . . using documents . . . was something we decided to do after the seminar more or less encouraged us in that way.

The courses he chose (on the basis of school and curricular concerns) contributed as well. As he said, "Some of the ideas I already had, but [the academic work] gave me a framework to use, it was directly applicable."

The choice of *Copper Sunrise* led Dan through a tortuous path: at first he thought the novel would be both convenient (it was readily available in schools) and appropriate. Dan's political sensitivity and concern with representation and voice led him to consult with local First Nations people about the novel study. Later, he received their forceful rejection of the work, since it centered on a book about First Nations people written by a nonnative. Faced with a dilemma, Dan discussed possible responses—including throwing out the novel study—with both his school team and Consortium members. He finally decided to rework the package, strengthening its critical components, to create "an antiracist, postcolonial novel study package." He added a preface, noting the origins of the author, and characterizing *Copper Sunrise* as "an early attempt to examine the violence and racism of the colonial period." He called attention to Buchan's portrayal of natives as entirely passive, with the only resistance to their slaughter coming from a white boy. Further, he asked teachers to consider how they would prepare perhaps unidentified native students in their classes to deal with the racist slurs unchallenged in the novel.

Here, the issue of voice, taken up theoretically in the seminar in relation to literature and history, surfaced as a political dilemma in all its real-world complexity. And Dan noted, "I think probably I couldn't be doing what I'm doing now, which is back-tracking and back-filling on what could have been a mistake without that sensitivity that I've gained through the year." Being at the university-based Consortium and not working under the conditions of school life, Dan had the time required to write, consider, consult with others, and rewrite.

From the outset, Dan understood some of the complexity of the school-university interaction. At several important junctures he made contributions based on his extensive experience of the classroom and the school politics. He found in the academic discussions, readings, and research, new perspectives that significantly enhanced his ability to create a rich learning resource. Provided with the time to sort through various aspects of complex political and curricular issues, he was able to harness them for his curriculum project.

CONCLUSION

There were at least two agendas for school change at work in the Consortium activities. One originated with the teachers, principals, and district personnel. At the outset, they associated the word "humanities" with recent provincial reform efforts that tied social studies and English into a "humanities strand" of the curriculum. Many schools were experimenting, variously, with rescheduling, team teaching, or having one teacher teach both English and social studies to one group of students.

A second agenda originated with the ACLS. Ambitiously, it aimed to infuse recent scholarship in the schools. While the new scholarship included interdisciplinarity, a vision of interdisciplinarity was not the central idea. Also at work were the conceptions of scholarship brought by the local professors. While their positions varied considerably, the postmodern questioning of disciplinary epistemologies loomed large across their intellectual landscapes. Initially the ACLS proposal had put forward the notion that, if the teachers were immersed in scholarly activities and maintained contact with their teams, then scholarship would somehow be transformed and transmitted to the school. This conception of change would come up against the complex structures and cultures of the schools. There could be no simple transmission, particularly given the nature of the ideas comprising the new scholarship.

As a result, the participating teachers were stretched between two cultures, two ideologies, and two very different institutional contexts for change (cf., Fullan, 1993, p. 21). Most importantly, they had to negotiate two different perspectives on knowledge and interdisciplinarity. In schools, knowledge was organized into subjects: Bells indicated changes from one subject to another; there was time pressure to teach the prescribed curriculum before the end of the school year; and there were report cards, parent-teacher conferences, and staff meetings to monitor progress.

Conditions for the teachers were quite different at the university. They chose the courses they took, they had access to university faculty and libraries, and they had the luxury of time to explore, to read, and to reflect. Yet, coming from the culture of the schools, academia was in some respects a foreign country, posing challenges of its own. Moreover, the Consortium placed the teachers as the bridge between school and university. They felt the pressure to use their time and resources at the university to produce curricular materials that would both fit into their schools and reflect the new ideas in which they were immersed.

Not surprisingly, all the teachers viewed writing the humanities curriculum materials as a challenge. The greatest difficulty came because their work would be measured by two very different sets of standards. On the one hand, they faced colleagues in the schools who would ask whether the humanities teacher with the English background could teach map-reading skills, or whether the one from the social studies department would take seriously the teaching of writing. On the other hand, they faced professors pursuing questions like, "How does a map write the world?" The negotiation between these two discourses was in many ways the core of the project, though nobody was in a position to articulate it in these terms at the outset.

But there were other important outcomes. Looking back on the year of Consortium work, all of the teachers agreed that they had grown personally through their participation in it. Evidence of its impact on schools, districts, and the province as a whole is far more spotty and questionable. Several of the packages of curriculum materials achieved wide circulation through the B. C. Teachers' Federation's Lesson Aids branch, and were among their most frequently ordered materials (Top ten BCTF lesson aids, 1997). One of the teachers returned not to the classroom, but to a district curriculum leadership position, from which he continued to circulate ideas that had been central to the project. Another became a new department head. Further, some of the individual professional relationships bridging school and university survived into subsequent years.

But, given the ACLS's large aims, funding for one-year constituted a significant flaw in the project's conception. Though the districts and the university maintained a series of conferences and workshops, there was no infrastructure in place to develop further the collaborative relationships initiated in the project year. If the year demonstrated anything, it was that a workable, ongoing intellectual collaboration involving both schools and universities is an extraordinary challenge. While there are many manifest reasons for undertaking such a collaboration, the depth of difference between the two educational cultures requires extended exchange, negotiation, and building of trust.

In this chapter we have focused almost exclusively on the teachers as bridges between the two cultures. But it should be clear from our analysis that we see a shared responsibility for making school-university collaboration work. With all of the limitations on the impact of this project, there is also much to learn from it, particularly that enriching and expanding the intellectual community in which teachers take part, is worth continuing effort.

REFERENCES

ACLS. (1992). *The ACLS elementary and secondary school curriculum development project: A description*. Unpublished manuscript.

Arends, R. I. (1990). Connecting the university to the school. In B. Joyce (Ed.), *Changing school culture through staff development* (pp. 117–143). Washington, DC: Association for Supervision and Curriculum Development.

Bell, B., & Gilbert, J. (1993). *Teacher development as professional, personal and social development*. Paper presented at the annual meeting of the Canadian Society for the Study of Education, Ottawa, Canada.

Brandes, G. M. (1995). Teachers' perceptions of the interplay between theory and practice in a professional development context. In R. Hoz & M. Silberstein (Eds.), *Partnerships of schools and institutions of higher education in teacher development* (pp. 207–218). Beer-Sheva, Israel: Ben Gurion University of the Negev Press.

Brandes, G. M., & Erickson, G. L. (1998). Developing and sustaining a community of inquiry among teachers and teacher educators. *Alberta Journal of Educational Research, 44*, 38–52.

Brandes, G. M., & Seixas, P. (1998). Subjects and disciplines: Asymmetries in a collaborative curriculum development project. *Teachers and Teaching: Theory and Practice, 4*, 95–114.

Buchan, B. (1972). *Copper sunrise*. Richmond Hill, Ontario, Canada: Scholastic-Tab.

Cole, A. L., & Knowles, G. J. (1993). Teacher development partnership research: A focus on methods and issues. *American Educational Research Journal, 30*, 473–496.

Cuban, L. (1992). Managing dilemmas while building professional communities. *Educational Researcher, 21* (1), 4–11.

Culler, J. (1997). *A very short introduction to literary theory*. New York: Oxford University Press.

Cushman, K. (1994). *Catherine, called Birdy*. New York: Clarion.

Dixon, P. N., & Ishler, R. E. (1992). Professional development schools: Stages in collaboration. *Journal of Teacher Education, 43*, 28–34.

Erickson, G. L. (1991). Collaborative inquiry and the professional development of science teachers. *Journal of Educational Thought, 25*, 228–245.

Fullan, M. (1993). *Change forces: Probing the depth of educational reform*. Bristol, PA: Falmer Press.

Grossman, P. L., & Stodolsky, S. S. (1995). Content as context: The role of school subjects in secondary school teaching. *Educational Researcher, 24*, 5–11.

Richardson, V. (Ed.). (1994). *Teacher change and the staff development process: A case in reading instruction*. New York: Teachers College Press.

Seixas, P. (1993). The community of inquiry as a basis for knowledge and learning: The case of history. *American Educational Research Journal, 30*, 305–324.

Seixas, P. (1999). Beyond "content" and "pedagogy": In search of a way to talk about history education. *Journal of Curriculum Studies, 31*, 317–337.

Seixas, P., & Brandes, G. M. (1997). A workshop in uncertainty: New scholarship in the humanities and social sciences as a basis for professional and curriculum development. *Journal of Curriculum and Supervision, 13*, 56–69.

Siskin, L. S. (1994). *Realms of knowledge: Academic departments in secondary schools*. Washington, DC: Falmer Press.

Top ten BCTF lesson aids. (1997, November–December). *Teacher: Newsmagazine of the British Columbia Teachers Federation, 10*, 3.

9

Restructuring Knowledge

Mapping (Inter)Disciplinary Change

LESLIE SANTEE SISKIN

Subj: I need ideas!!!!!
Date: 11/20/96 11:40:16 PM
Please forward all info that you might feel would help in devel-
oping thematic units for 9th graders in the following topics:
"Morals and Values," "Decision Making," "The Power of Nature,"
"Mythology & Change."
Are there any other thematic units that you might feel 9th graders
should be exposed to?

Subj: math thematic units
Date: 6/17/95 6:59:35 PM
Does anyone have any good math thematic units?

Across the United States and indeed, around the world, high school
teachers like those above are calling out for "ideas" and "good thematic
units" as they struggle to implement the widely advocated yet largely
unspecified educational reform of interdisciplinary studies. Although the
ideal of an interdisciplinary reorganization of curriculum has been advocated at least since the Progressive agenda of the early 1900s, the topic
exploded onto the reform agenda of the 1990s, warranting a special issue
of Educational Leadership in 1991, a special strand at the 1996 conference
of the National Association of Secondary School Administrators, and a
"highest priority" designation by members of the Association for Supervision and Curriculum Development (Brandt, 1991). But while it seems
that everyone is talking about "interdisciplinary" studies these days, it

has become apparent that we are not necessarily talking about the same thing, and that there are a vast variety of different kinds of efforts going on in different places, using different kinds of strategies, employed by different people for different purposes—who often seem to be talking at cross-purposes.

People are talking in a new medium as well, for the calls for interdisciplinary restructuring are often linked to the new structures of the Information Age—the explosion of information signalled by computer technology and the Internet. The specific examples of people talking about, and undertaking, this work that I examine here are taken from 292 online postings from high school teachers, which appeared on Internet bulletin boards maintained by America Online (AOL), by the American Federation of Teachers (AFT), and by the National Educational Association (NEA) between November 1994 and November 1996. Additionally, the Websites of 45 individual teachers or schools that were found in a search of "interdisciplinary studies" and "high schools" are used. (All identifying names, and spelling errors, have been removed.)

This is not, then, a case of exemplary models of innovative teaching, or of cutting edge restructured schools—in many cases we do not even know the schools in which these teachers work. But they are examples of high school teachers who are attempting interdisciplinary work and who are turning to the field, most often for practical help in what is very new, unfamiliar, and uncharted terrain. This chapter examines the kinds of messages these teachers are sending, and the kinds of movement across the disciplinary boundaries these messages represent. In so doing, I offer a preliminary map of what is, and what is not, happening under the reform rhetoric of interdisciplinary studies.

INITIAL OBSERVATIONS

This current project draws in important ways on initial observations from two earlier studies. The first was a study of subject departments as a context for teaching (Siskin, 1994), which was done through the Center for Research on Context (McLaughlin & Talbert, 1993). There we began to understand the importance of subject matter, and of the department within comprehensive high schools—and to be able to distinguish between the two, delineating characteristics of each that turned out to matter to teachers' professional identity and practice (Grossman & Stodolsky, 1994; Little, 1993; McLaughlin, 1991; Siskin, 1994). Subjects mattered, not only to content, but to who teachers saw themselves to be, and how they understood teaching and students. Moreover, subject affiliations were reinforced by department structures that divided schools, and played an active role in dividing up resources—at least in the large comprehensive high schools.

The second was a study, through the National Center for Restructuring Education, Schools, and Teaching, of 10 small high schools that provided a very different context for teaching (Siskin, 1996). These were cutting-edge schools that proposed to "reinvent" the high school, and interdisciplinary studies were seen as a critical component of that change. Drawing on the principles of the Coalition of Essential Schools (Sizer, 1992), they planned a shift from a hierarchical, departmentalized structure to one of collective responsibility, and a move from subject content-coverage to interdisciplinary projects. Yet even in these schools, in the absence of departments, subject matter mattered in important ways:

- subject identities and understandings remained strong, and while teachers sought to reach across to other disciplines, they simultaneously felt compelled to honor or protect their own disciplinary values;
- the work of working together and of defining meaningful interdisciplinary work was much more difficult than teachers had anticipated;
- interdisciplinary teams worked more smoothly in English/social studies pairings than in attempts to combine all four core subjects, or to pair math/science (and indeed, math emerged as a particular problem, with efforts to "integrate" math often scaled back or slowed down);
- problems were likely to be interpreted as local, or even personal ones—as unclear vision, or an individual who was not sufficiently committed, or skilled, or easy to work with.

There were, however, two competing hypotheses. The first was that the task was simply too much too fast (these schools were trying to find a building, hire teachers, recruit students, find another building, create a governance structure, deal with a new superintendent . . . all in their first year). The second possibility was that there was just something inherently problematic with the interdisciplinary demands . . . or with math.

In sharp contrast to the local explanations, one teacher went so far as to suggest that the very structure of interdisciplinary, project-based learning was intrinsically tied to the epistemological assumptions of the humanities—and in conflict with those of science and math:

It seems to me that the basic design of the pedagogical theory of Coalition schools is based on a model that comes from humanities and social science, primarily humanities. You read Sizer, what he has to say about the humanities is cogent and interesting. But he really has very little to say about mathematics or science. . . . And the assumption is that learning is something which you go from superficial ideas to deep ideas . . . and you integrate more of your experience in your thoughts and your expressions, and you interact with people intensely in order to find out what they really think, and what they really think about what you really think, and so on. It's assumed that you always know something, and that you can always have an opinion. And that whatever it is, you can say something about it, because there's something in your experience that you can reflect upon. And you go from poorly integrated ideas to better-integrated ideas. Now, there are a lot of things in mathematics and science that really don't work that way.

In the highly influential Horace's School, often cited by advocates of interdisciplinary change, Sizer (1992) tells the story of proposing to a high school faculty that they could reduce by half the number of students they teach—if they would just teach the same students two subjects. But the chemistry teacher, who was "enthusiastically nodding and agreeing" with the first half of that equation, "balked" at the second, and "broke into tears" (p. 43). For while both subjects use numbers, what they do—and think should be done—with those numbers is quite different, and as she kept repeating, "I'm not a math teacher." But in the small schools I was studying, with so much going on, and so much of it so new, it was impossible to disentangle which things, or subjects, "really don't work that way."

The questions about what was happening then led to this current effort to "map" the state of interdisciplinary studies, to locate what things were or were not working on a larger scale, and in a broader range of high schools. Rather than going to specific schools, however, this study went out across the Internet, as teachers venturing into interdisciplinary studies in their own sites also ventured into the new medium of virtual conversation.

DISCIPLINE AND FURNITURE

The first pattern to emerge across these messages, as in those that open the chapter, is the predominance of calls for help, and for help of a particular kind. These are teachers who accept, or even embrace, the category of interdisciplinary teaching—and then search for the appropriate content to place within it. They call out for good thematic units for ninth-graders, or for math, for projects that mix science with other subjects. One marks her desperation by adding six exclamation points to her call for "Help!!!!!!" as she searches for "ideas or projects or just how to combine the two [World History and English]." Another, crying out for science projects, ends his message, "Any ideas or warnings or support?"

The calls for content, and cries for help, become particularly dramatic when the task has been assigned, or "handed" to teachers:

Subj: schoolwide interdis. projects
Date: 6/2/96 9:06:29 PM
I have just been handed the task of writing curriculum for a school-wide ninth-grade project. I am looking for some ideas. This is the first time our school has done this on such a large scale. In addition, I also am looking for ideas for a SCHOOL-WIDE project. (The caps should indicate some level of my apprehension at this tall order.) I'm thinking of something that would involve giving back to the community. Any ideas? Please e-mail me at (XX). Many thanks ahead of time.

Subj: Math and Science Projects
Date: 12/26/95 7:53:09 PM
I need help with ideas that would form legitimate projects to integrate science and math at the high school level. I teach in a high school that will soon be visited with an edict from the state for teachers to design multidisciplinary projects that would accomplish this. It is a formidable task because all students would be expected to complete this task prior to graduation. Hopefully we can devise a task that would accomplish these goals and not become simply another project to be completed by the student and graded by the teachers.

It is a formidable task indeed. But the search for ideas, for content, is only part of the task that confronts these teachers. Kliebard (1986), in his studies of curriculum change and stability, described an 1829 report that "recognized two main functions of education, 'the *discipline* and the *furniture* of the mind'" (p. 5). It is the moving of *furniture* that surfaces most prominently here—questions of which pieces are necessary, or where they might be found. The messages focus on content, on projects, or on tasks. Elsewhere I have described this as a "nondisciplinary type" of interdisciplinary effort, where thematic units focus on *what* disciplines know, often at the expense of *how* they know (Siskin, 1996). For example, one teacher, on a quest for materials for a 10th-grade unit on King Arthur, seeks information on how to make shields from tagboard. Questions about disciplinary ways of knowing, methodological approaches, or epistemological underpinnings that might complement or conflict in these new thematic arrangements are largely absent, as the furniture of the subjects gets moved from room to room.

The absence of such questions may be a function of this medium— these teachers may be having such conversations with real colleagues rather than virtual ones, and indeed these quick messages out to unknown colleagues are not well suited to the lengthy conversations such questions entail. But our time in schools suggests that teachers have taken, or have been given, little time for such talk even among their school colleagues. It is only when they are well into, and up against, teaching or evaluating interdisciplinary units that such differences begin to surface— as when Sizer's chemistry teacher begins to confront what it would actually mean to teach math. Even then, though, the difficulties are often interpreted as personal baggage rather than disciplinary difference.

Here it seems almost as if the call went out to grab a partner, find a theme, and begin the interdisciplinary dance. Indeed, in two instances, that's literally what happened. A physics teacher offered the example of a dance theater company, which visits high schools and universities to perform "The Science Project," in which the dancers combine doing experiments with dancing the forces, and fears, of physics. A math teacher tied the geometric study of lines to line dancing, where she takes the furniture from another subject, and "sees" it though the disciplinary lens of her own:

> Subj: Coordinate Line Dancing
> Date: 1/14/96 12:23:09 AM
> To the casual observer, it's just a dusty classroom floor. As for me, I see the square-foot tiles forming the coordinate system upon which human geometric models will dance! . . . How about some transformations? Instruct the human points to translate 3 units to the right, rotate 90%, or reflect about an axis. . . . As a followup project, perhaps students can be given the option of "choreographing" their own transformational dance. My students thoroughly enjoyed this activity. It gave them a chance to see mathematical connections where they least expected to see them. I think it also inspired them to look for ways to incorporate their creative talents in the mathematics classroom.

There is much creativity, and variation in these postings—but pairing dance with science, or dancing math patterns, are in fact quite rare. Instead, what we see are systematic patterns of interdisciplinary activities across particular borders: English partnered with social studies, science partnered with math. Music, art, and vocational studies are represented far less frequently.

DEPARTMENT EFFECTS

That differential participation of particular subjects, I argue, is not a matter of content, or even epistemological or methodological compatibility, but rather a department effect—one that traces back to the organizational and political positioning of the disciplines, and that affects who even gets invited to the dance (Foucault, 1980; Goodson, 1987; Siskin, 1994).

A number of the efforts to restructure schools into interdisciplinary teams aim explicitly at undoing the strength of subject departments—naming as problems the fragmentation of faculty, the uneven status and power bases, or their buffering resistance to change efforts. This strategy may, as Andy Hargreaves and Robert Macmillan (1995) found in the study of one such restructured school, simply reinscribe the same "balkanization" problems onto new units. Often, however, what we see is a new problem: a team structure replaces the department one, but provides only some teachers with secure places on the team (Dow, 1996; Meister & Nolan, 1998; Siskin & Little, 1995; Spies, 1994). Thus we have the "core" teams, composed of English, math, science, and social studies teachers, while the "specials" circulate individually around that core:

Subj: TEACHING CONCEPTS
Date: 5/29/96 12:26:21 AM
Our school is just beginning to integrate block scheduling and interdisciplinary instruction. We are hoping to form several core teams (Math/Science/Language Arts/S.S.) in the 9th and 10th grade levels. Developing concepts (Critical Attributes, etc.) that can work with all four content areas is the most challenging aspect for me. Some of us have come up with outlines for the concept of Relationships and also Patterns. I need help with the concept of CHANGE and also COMMUNITIES any other ideas for concepts would be greatly appreciated. Please E-mail me.

Subject: Electives
Date: 11/08/96
From: (XX)
I am working on a school reform committee where presently 18% of the faculty is double blocking. Another 12% has agreed to sign

on for the 4 x 4 next year. We are at a standstill with a few departments. . . . Vocal and instrumental music, industrial arts, business,
journalism, and AP classes, to name few. These teachers believe the
4 x 4 will greatly reduce their numbers for next year and/or elimi-
nate their classes . . . (where do you put these courses in the 4 x 4?).

The questions of "where you put these courses" or whether they will
continue to exist at all under new configurations raise serious concerns
for those teachers outside the core (Gehrke & Sheffield, 1985). Art teachers fear they will be displaced by science teachers who incorporate
da Vinci into biology lessons, or by history teachers who show slides of
Picasso's Guernica.

As interdisciplinary expansions intersect with budgetary constric-
tions, that fear becomes particularly evident, and the evidence to support
it accumulates across case studies of model schools that partner with cultural institutions, or bring in artists in residence (but only bring them
in part way, and for short periods). Still, one music teacher online sees
integrating subjects as "the ticket to survival of Arts (music) education
in this country" and passionately proclaims that "we must not allow education to be controlled, supported, and encouraged by bean counters,
back stabbers and socially isolated technoheads now manipulating the
bleak future." Another music teacher declares that "this is war friends"
and ends her message "Music teachers without a job. . . . Kids without a
program!" Interdisciplinary studies look quite different from the perspective of those pushed to the periphery of the new core, and what had
looked like an expansive reorganization begins to look like a contraction
of curriculum, and perhaps of careers for those teachers who see themselves "outside the core, then out the door."

If art teachers fear being displaced, the place of vocational teachers
in this new dance is even more questionable, for these are teachers who
have long seen themselves as "second-class citizens" (Siskin, 1994), whose
work lies "on the margins" of high schools (Little & Threatt, 1992), or
even in "other worlds" (Little, 1995; see also Goodson, 1987). Their subjects remain on the margins of these conversations, if, indeed, they make
it onto the dance floor at all. The AOL "teachers' lounge" board, for example, is organized by subject: English, math, science, social studies, art/
photography, and music are here. Health/PE is included but less popu-
lated; perhaps surprisingly, geography and adult literacy have their own
areas. Vocational studies, however, is entirely absent from AOL's categories. The AFT board separates school-to-work/vocational studies from
the general Teachers' Message Board. Despite recent efforts to integrate
academic and vocational studies, to organize curriculum from "school-
to-work," that division still seems firmly in place in these online commu-

nities. Among the academic subjects, however, we can see old divisions shifting, and new ones forming.

MAPPING THE CHANGE

There is a persistent impulse to "map," to spatialize the divisions among disciplines, and place on firm ground what is inherently unstable—the shape, contours, and borders of the fields of knowledge. After all, these are "fields" of study, "areas," or "territories." Ellen Messer-Davidow and David Shumway, who have done substantial work in this area, declare in their first book in the series, *Knowledge: Disciplinarity and Beyond,* that the "present volume should be seen as something like a map" (Messer-Davidow, Shumway, & Sylvan, 1993, p. 1). Tony Becher (1989) found in his studies of "academic tribes and territories" that university faculty "produced clear and detailed conceptual maps" of their areas:

> Economics was said to have one common frontier with mathematics and another with political science; some trade relations with history and sociology; and a lesser measure of shared ground with psychology, philosophy, and the law. Biology was portrayed as being bounded on one side by mathematics and the physical sciences (especially physics, chemistry, and physical geography) and on the other by the human sciences (in particular by psychology, anthropology, and human geography) (p. 36).

Producing such a conceptual map on paper, however, is quite another task, especially when change and movement are what we want to chart. While mapping the messages allows for a broader overview of just what is taking place underneath the umbrella term of "interdisciplinary studies," it does have two important limitations.

First, focusing on the surfaces and simple outlines of the subjects glosses over the rich details that we find in closer, smaller, studies of teachers' work across disciplinary boundaries (Dogan & Pahre, 1990; Dow, 1996; Hannay, 1995; Little, 1993; Roth, 1994; Siskin & Little, 1995; Wilson & Wineburg, 1988). But, as Borges's famous story of the detail-oriented mapmaker reminds us, if we try to capture the details, we lose the conceptual power and convenience of the map.

Second, the subjects of study are shifting not only in their relations to each other, but also within themselves: U.S. history, which back when I took it, ended with the breathless May race to cover World War I, World War II, and the UN before finals, now has 25 years more to cover—in the same amount of time. And at the same time, it has been pressed to include people, events, and topics previously ignored, and new theoretical approaches to include them.

Even math, which consistently has been identified as one of the more stable (even static) of school subjects (Grossman & Stodolsky, 1994; Siskin, 1994) is altering its form and its features, incorporating fractals and manipulatives, or integrating algebra and geometry. In the Webpage of one math teacher, she has constructed an elaborate set of links to other sites: to an interactive site on Fermat's spiral, to a collection of curves, to a math quote of the day and a problem of the week. Indeed, she makes her own interdisciplinary connections—to the history of math, biographies of mathematicians, and even to her own "favorite place in the world," which links to the city of London. As Kliebard (1986) concludes, after exhaustive study of earlier efforts at curricular change: "the one fortress that proved virtually impregnable was the school subject. . . . But subject labels alone may be misleading. . . . The subjects survived but in an altered form" (p. 269).

With those limitations noted, I want to borrow a mapping strategy from Donald Campbell's (1969) depiction of disciplinary knowledge in his argument for a "fish-scale model of omniscience." What Campbell argues is that "the present organization of content into departments is highly arbitrary, a product in large part of historical accident" (p. 331). These accidents formalize more or less overlapping collections of subject matter and methodology into institutionally bounded territories. Departments, in his illustration, are represented as clusters of overlapping circles, which represent distinct subfields or disciplines; departments with higher consensus, or tighter paradigms, cluster more tightly.

In this model, "*psychology* is a hodgepodge of sensitive subjective biography, of brain operations, of school achievement testing, of factor analysis, of Markov process mathematics, of schizophrenic families, of laboratory experiments on group structure in which persons are anonymous, etc." (p. 332). A department collection, then, may have within it subfields with their own quite different connections to different neighboring disciplines; some psychologists pull toward sociology, some toward biology—and sometimes a field spins off to find a new home in another discipline, or to create a new field such as psychobiology.

Using the imagery of these overlapping circles to map the phenomenon of school subjects and interdisciplinary messages allows us to visualize the broad patterns of movement (see Figure 9.1): the distancing of the four academic core subjects from the arts and vocational studies, and the connecting of subfields within the core.

The spinning off of subfields to form a new specialization area is what we seem to be seeing in the English/social studies pairing—which at first glance looks to offer the most enthusiastic, and sustained linkages across these online messages, and across closer case studies of interdisciplinary teaming (Little, 1995; Meister & Nolan, 1998; Siskin, 1996; Spies,

FIGURE 9.1: Mapping the School Subjects

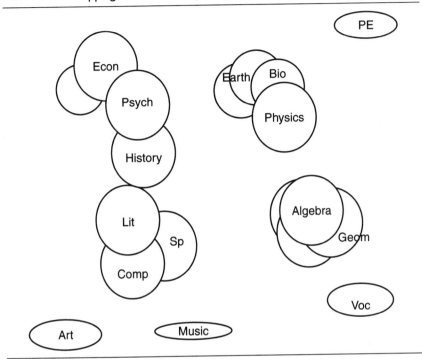

1994). On closer look, however, what emerges as the predominant pattern is actually English-as-literature combining with social studies-as-history:

Subj: help
Date: 2/5/96 2:48:18 PM
We are about to begin a pilot program to integrate the social studies and english departments in our building. I am looking for some excellent sources, lesson plans, and ideas to help with the first year. The class needs to cover US history and American Literature. If you can help me . . . I would greatly appreciate it.

Subj: Re: English/social studies
Date: 2/19/96 10:01:51 AM
I am looking for good ideas to teach history and literature using *The Great Gatsby*. This is for students with average reading ability. Please e-mail to me or post response.

As is the case across the postings, most of these exchanges are about rearranging "furniture," but there may be less epistemological or methodological conflict here, since literary studies and history are fields with a common ancestry, a long history of border crossings, and a lot of ground in common—biographies, New Literary History, even the public popularity of the historical novel (Ian, 1987; Messer-Davidow, Shumway, & Sylvan, 1993; PMLA, 1996). I don't mean to elide the important differences between these disciplines, but rather to contrast these subtler shadings against the greater distance of English from the other social sciences. In Little's (1995) study of interdisciplinary teams, for example, teachers linking literature and history express "concern" about the differences in their approaches, or about the pace of coverage in the two subjects—but as one English teacher puts it, "I can make all kinds of connections, but I don't want to teach econ and government" (p. 185). That distinction seems to be widely shared, and may explain the shifting boundaries that are now pulling literature and history back together under the new collective label of "humanities," while the other social sciences maintain their distance, and what was an interdisciplinary massing of social studies breaks apart.

INTERDISCIPLINARY IMPERIALISM

If literature and history appear to be spinning off a new partnership, the movement across the space separating math from science is quite distinctive in character. The messages here are qualitatively different: requests for thematic ideas for math, calls for units that link math with science, or questions about how to bring math teachers fully into the team. As in the small schools study, integrating math into integrated studies appears to be particularly problematic.

The boundary between math and science has quite a different history from that separating literary studies from history, and, indeed, math was long thought to reside closer to music than to "natural philosophy." J. L. Heilbron (1993) writes of the movement toward quantification, back in the 1780s, which might have brought the two fields closer together, but instead sparked "a mathematicians' mutiny, with morals." In another kind of boundary work, Shumway and Messer-Davidow (1991) point out that the first distinguishing move of the Royal Society was to close its borders to women in the 18th century, and to hold them closed until the middle the 20th century. The boundaries around math, then, have a long and successful history of being well guarded against encroachments from outsiders.

Whatever the reason, this pattern of difficulty in assailing the borders around math persists in this online data. While the frequency of messages attempting to link math with science is second only to the number of English/social studies pairings, here the calls for help far outnumber the helpful replies, and the asymmetry of the relationship is far more pronounced. What we often see here is what I called in that earlier study "interdisciplinary imperialism": the appropriation of math skills in the service of science projects and purposes. Math teachers are often, not surprisingly, less than enthusiastic about seeing their subject viewed as providing the calculating and graphing tools for other people's content.

Yet in the exchanges where people do describe the projects they are attempting, it is mathematical means for science ends that predominate, with math methods being used on science's data, for science (especially physics) projects. A physics-algebra combination will "put together a project dealing with functions and basic physics principles where the students build pinewood derby cars." Another teacher offers as a helpful suggestion a project which

> involves analyzing the concentration of a colored solution using the Spec 20 Spectrophotometer. Absorbance of light by the solution and concentration of the solution are a linear relationship. I teach chemistry and algebra, and brought the equipment into my math class and had the students analyze water samples for iron. We used the TI-82 to work with the data. A lab like this helps answer the question, "Where will we ever use this stuff?" Ask your chemistry teacher if you have a spectrophotometer and how to use it.

While such projects may use both chemistry and algebra, it does not take a spectrophotometer to analyze which dominates the mixture. Indeed, even a teacher who self-identifies first as a math teacher cites as the primary objective the need "to better prepare students for success in science":

> Subj: Math prep for Science
> Date: 2/29/96 11:33:19 PM
> Dear colleague,
> I am a High School Math teacher co-certified in science. Please help me on a project to make some math-science connections for our students. I am attempting to construct a series of stand-alone modules that a math teacher with little science background could use to better prepare students for success in science by reducing or removing the math hangup factor.

Interpreting these moves as appropriation rather than affiliation, or simply not seeing how the ends of math can be reasonably served through the means of such interdisciplinary relationships, many math teachers are reasserting the uniqueness of math as a subject, the inviolable sequential structure of the curriculum, and the strength of the boundary that separates them from the sciences. Across the messages, there are no arguments for how these interdisciplinary connections work well for math, no helpful ideas for how to integrate the subject; no one offers any "good math thematic units." As the teacher in Little's (1995) case study so aptly stated: "The study of mathematics is by itself, it stands alone" (p. 179).

A number of science teachers, left without the participation of their mathematics partners, take up the interdisciplinary stance within their own departments. Here they attempt to forge stronger links among the separate disciplines clustered under the school subject called "science," which is itself a radical and challenging task:

> Subj: Science Teaching/Interdisciplinary
> Date: 3/12/96 4:32:38 PM
> We at (XX) H.S. . . . are seeking curriculum ideas, materials and comments (pro & con) about teaching elementary concepts in all four science disciplines in the 9th and 10th grades. It would be followed by choices of 1/2 credit semester courses in 11th and 12th grades. Any ideas or warnings or support?

> Subj: Integrated Sci 9th & 10th
> Date: 4/4/96 3:03:48 PM
> Some time ago, several messages were posted regarding interdisciplinary science courses in the developmental stages. People were seeking assistance in developing their curricula. I am now seeking assistance and wonder if any of the people who were then seeking assistance would now give it (or anyone else for that matter). I would be interested in forming a network of High School Science teachers who are trying to achieve the same goal: a good 9th & 10th grade integrated science class. Interested? Contact me by e-mail: (XX) Thank you!

CHALLENGES

While integrating science may seem minor compared to integrating the whole academic core, it is no small challenge. Yet across all these bulletin boards, there are remarkably few teachers who challenge the idea that this interdisciplinary reform work is what they should be doing:

> Subj: science & social studies
> Date: 8/4/96 8:42:56 AM
> I have been given the task of (co)developing a gifted seminar program for 9th graders that will integrate science and social studies. Any ideas and/or help would be appreciated. Thanks.

> Subj: Re: science & social studies
> Date: 9/5/96 3:48:49 AM
> Yes. Ask the people who gave you this task just why this integration is desirable at ninth grade level.

No one takes up the challenge of explaining just why this particular integration would be desirable, nor do we know just who the people are who have given this task. Another teacher does, however, offer an argument for integration—at least within the sciences:

> Subj: Re: Interdisciplinary science
> Date: 11/25/96 10:04:45 PM
> An integrated approach seems better. I know there are problems with credit issued, but scientists now work in teams and solve problems from an integrated approach. Why do we continue to teach students only one science at a time, when few scientists work this way now? We need a skill and problem solving approach for young people today. How to do science is more important than factoids!

The reference here to the idea that integrated approaches are more like, and better preparation for, work in the "real world" is one that is often offered by advocates of interdisciplinary studies. In this online conversation, however, it is quickly challenged by a "real" scientist:

> Subj: Re: Interdisciplinary science
> Date: 11/26/96 12:49:53 AM
> I'm one of those scientists who work with others on interdisciplinary problems, often in groups. We rely on each other for the appropriate "factoids" and wouldn't invite anybody in who didn't have some detailed expertise to offer. Problem solving is our livelihood and joy, but you have to have a detailed background to apply to complicated problems. Give the kids lots of facts and skills and THEN integrate if you ever want them to do science.

Interdisciplinary studies are often embraced, at least in the United States, rather automatically as a "good" thing, and there are remarkably few people disputing the possibility or purposes of integrating school subjects, or even questioning whether high school is the right time to integrate them. "After all," suggests Timothy Austin in a recent forum on the topic, "Interdisciplinarity suggests collegiality, flexibility, collaboration, and scholarly breadth—the academy's equivalents to parenthood and apple pie" (PMLA, 1996, p. 272). Still, the movement is sometimes challenged offline, as in Gardner and Boix-Mansilla's (1994) provocative comment—one that quickly circulated across a number of disciplinary borders—that "shorn of disciplinary knowledge, human beings are quickly reduced to the level of ignorant children, indeed, to the ranks of barbarians" (p. 199). Like the "real" scientist above, they suggest that what is needed for true interdisciplinary work is first a detailed background in content knowledge, and a strong grounding in disciplinary thinking.

The move to interdisciplinary curriculum was challenged, too, in Kean's (1993) vivid depiction of "trying to build a better Beowulf," an effort that left her "grappling with a monster nobody warned me about—a national education reform movement that is half Barney and half Grendel, a creature with the cuddly body of progressivism and the sharp teeth of capitalism" (she is, I hardly need to add, an English teacher). She questions the practical purposes of teaching literature to develop workplace skills, and the kinds of curriculum that result, subtitling her essay "The New Assault on the Liberal Arts." On perhaps even fewer occasions, the purpose and politics of the movement itself is directly questioned, as it was in Roth's (1994) "second thoughts" after trying to teach science and social studies, an experiment which left her frustrated and questioning: "Why is 'integration' placed so prominently in national and state reform documents?" (p. 44).

CONCLUSIONS

The question of why integration is being taken up by politicians, businesses, and educators is not answered in these online messages; indeed, the question is not even asked. Instead, these messages pose the more concrete and immediate questions of what connections can be made across subjects, what content to include, what pieces of furniture can be moved. And while it is not clear here what the ultimate benefits might be, it does seem that teachers are bearing the cost of having to reinvent curriculum without sufficient local support to guide their work. Most of these messages represent teachers who need help knowing even where to begin this difficult work—and none of them names local professional development opportunities, consultants, or school teams as having the capacity they need. Instead, they call out for help from more distant colleagues, from someone who has tried this before, for anyone who might have "good ideas" or "good thematic units."

The replies that do offer ideas and units demonstrate that some teachers are finding room to experiment under this reform, and the variation in their responses, along with the enthusiasm of their descriptions, hold promise for reinvigorating teachers, and inspiring creativity and engagement in their students. High schools, long thought to be the educational organizations least open to change, here find room for dancing physics, for line-dancing geometry, or for linking American literature to American history. Set against the massive apparatus of disciplinary divisions and departmental fragmentation, this is no small accomplishment.

But these online messages suggest two cautions to that optimistic interpretation. First, the pattern of what connections are being asked for and offered suggests that these connections move the content, or furniture of the disciplines, from classroom to classroom with little consideration of the disciplinary perspective, or ways of knowing, that the disciplines provide. Disciplines not only mark off certain topics as worth studying; they also provide the theoretical, methodological, and analytic tools that make that studying possible. Without serious consideration of those disciplinary perspectives, two outcomes are likely: (1) teachers who misconstrue collegial conflict as personal pathology rather than disciplinary difference, and (2) curricular units that deliver substantively less meaningful learning for students.

The second reason for caution comes from the patterns within the variation among these messages, patterns that suggest that the movement of ideas they represent varies systematically by subject. Interdisciplinary studies look quite different from the perspectives of different disciplines. In these messages, as in the case studies of schools available in the literature, the division between the academic "core" subjects and the "specials" appears to be widening, and the political differences appear to be exacerbated. Patterns within the academic subjects, too, confirm the tentative insights of the smaller case study reports: literature and history move most readily into partnership; humanities and American studies appear as newly integrated, or reconnected, topics of study. What will become of the older interdisciplinary collection of the social sciences remains to be seen. Science and math, which are so frequently assumed to be a logical connection, find connecting far less satisfying, and find few ways to connect that do not reduce one subject—usually math—to the status of mechanistic means to serve science's ends. Without the concrete help that could make this partnership make sense to both partners, math once again "stands alone," and math teachers are seen as resistant to change.

The mapping of such changes, then, suggests both that there is movement across disciplinary divisions and that such movement is more difficult than many reformers, and teachers, had anticipated. If there are schools that, as one message asserts, "will soon be visited with an edict from the state for teachers to design multidisciplinary projects," then that challenging task will require more than mandates. What this map suggests is that teachers will want substantive, concrete help inventing the new curriculum, that they will need time and encouragement to think through not only the furniture but also the discipline of their subjects, and that this thinking and talking will require taking into account the political, as well as the intellectual, differences among the disciplines that take up this new interdisciplinary dance.

REFERENCES

Becher, T. (1989). *Academic tribes and territories*. Milton Keynes, England: Open University Press.

Brandt, R. (1991). On interdisciplinary curriculum: A conversation with Heidi Hayes Jacobs. *Educational Leadership, 49*, 24–26.

Campbell, D. T. (1969). Ethnocentrism of disciplines and the fish-scale model of omniscience. In M. Sherif & C. Sherif (Eds.), *Interdisciplinary relationships in the social sciences* (pp. 328–348). Chicago: Aldine.

Dogan, M., & Pahre, R. (1990). *Creative marginality: Innovation at the intersections of social sciences*. Boulder, CO: Westview Press.

Dow, A. (1996). *Status Quo? Post-Fordism, knowledge and power at Gallipoli High School*. Paper presented at the annual meeting of the American Educational Research Association, New York.

Foucault, M. (1980). *Power/knowledge: Selected interviews and other writings, 1972–1977*. New York: Pantheon Books.

Gardner, H., & Boix-Mansilla, V. (1994). Teaching for understanding in the disciplines and beyond. *Teachers College Record, 96*(2), 198–218.

Gehrke, N., & Sheffield, R. (1985). Are core subjects becoming a dumping ground for reassigned high school teachers? *Educational Leadership, 42*(8), 65–69.

Goodson, I. (1987). *School subjects and curriculum change* (2nd ed.). London: Falmer Press.

Grossman, P. L., & Stodolsky, S. S. (1994). Considerations of content and the circumstances of secondary school teaching. In L. Darling-Hammond (Ed.), *Review of research in education* (pp. 179–221). Washington, DC: American Educational Research Association.

Hannay, L. M. (1995, April). *Curriculum change in secondary schools.* Paper presented at the annual meeting of the American Educational Research Association, San Francisco.

Hargreaves, A., & Macmillan, R. (1995). The balkanization of secondary school teaching. In L. S. Siskin & J. W. Little (Eds.), *The subjects in question: Departmental organization and the high school* (pp. 141–171). New York: Teachers College Press.

Harraway, D., & Kunzru, H. (1997, February). You are borg. *Wired,* 156–209.

Heilbron, J. L. (1993). A mathematicians' mutiny, with morals. In P. Horwich (Ed.), *World changes: Thomas Kuhn and the nature of science* (pp. 81–129). Cambridge, MA: MIT Press.

Ian, M. (1987). *The teaching of English from the sixteenth century to 1870.* Cambridge: Cambridge University Press.

Kean, P. (1993, May-June). Building a better Beowulf: The new assault on the liberal arts. *Lingua Franca, 1,* 22–28.

Kliebard, H. M. (1986). *The struggle for the American curriculum.* New York: Routledge & Kegan Paul.

Little, J. W. (1993). Professional community in comprehensive high schools: The two worlds of academic and vocational teachers. In J. W. Little & M. W. McLaughlin (Eds.), *Teachers' work* (pp. 137–163). New York: Teachers College Press.

Little, J. W. (1995). Subject affiliation in schools that restructure. In L. S. Siskin & J. W. Little (Eds.), *The subjects in question: Departmental organization and the high school* (pp. 172–200). New York: Teachers College Press.

Little, J. W., & Threatt, S. (1992). *Work on the margins: The experience of vocational teachers in comprehensive high schools.* Berkeley, CA: National Center for Research on Vocational Education.

McLaughlin, M. W. (1991). *What matters most in teachers' workplace context.* Palo Alto, CA: Center for Research on the Context of Secondary School Teaching.

McLaughlin, M. W., & Talbert, J. E. (1993). *Contexts that matter for teaching and learning: Strategic opportunities for meeting the nation's educational goals.* Palo Alto, CA: Center for Research on the Context of Secondary School Teaching.

Meister, D., & Nolan, J. (1998, April). *Out on a limb on our own: Uncertainty and doubt in moving from subject-centered to interdisciplinary teaching.* Paper presented at the Annual Meeting of the American Educational Research Association, San Diego, CA.

Messer-Davidow, E., Shumway, D. R., & Sylvan, D. J. (Eds.). (1993). *Knowledges: Historical and critical studies in disciplinarity.* Charlottesville, VA: University Press of Virginia.

National Council of Teachers of Mathematics, Commission on Teaching Standards for School Mathmatics. (1991). *Professional standards for teaching mathematics.* Reston, VA: National Council of Teachers of Mathematics.

PMLA. (1996). Forum. *PMLA, 111*(2), 271–311.

Roth, K. J. (1994). Second thoughts about interdisciplinary studies. *American Educator, 18*(1), 44–48.

Sherif, C. W. (1978). Climbing disciplinary walls and learning how to borrow. *Women's Studies International Quarterly, 1,* 229–224.

Shumway, D. R., & Messer-Davidow, E. (1991). Disciplinarity: An introduction. *Poetics Today, 12,* 201–225.

Siskin, L. S. (1994). *Realms of knowledge: Academic departments in secondary schools.* London: Falmer Press.

Siskin, L. S. (1996). *Starting small: Report on the Campus Coalition Schools Project's second year.* New York: National Center for Restructuring Education, Schools, and Teaching.

Siskin, L. S., & Little, J. W. (1995). *The subjects in question: Departmental organization and the high school.* New York: Teachers College Press.

Sizer, T. (1992). *Horace's school: Redesigning the American high school.* New York: Houghton Mifflin.

Spies, P. (1994). Learning teams: The necessary design of secondary schools for the 21st century. *Teaching and Change, 1.3,* 219–237.

Wilson, S., & Wineburg, S. S. (1988). Peering at history: The role of disciplinary perspectives in the teaching of American history. *Teachers College Record, 89,* 525–539.

About the Contributors

Sam Wineburg is a Professor of Educational Psychology in the College of Education and an Adjunct Professor in the Department of History at the University of Washington.

Pam Grossman is a Professor of Curriculum and Instruction in the College of Education, University of Washington.

John I. Goodlad is Co-director of the Center for Educational Renewal at the University of Washington and President of the Institute for Educational Inquiry. In addition to advancing a comprehensive program of research and development directed to the simultaneous renewal of schooling and teacher education, he is inquiring into the mission of education in a democratic society to which such renewal must be directed.

Scott Beers is a Ph.D. candidate in the Department of Curriculum and Instruction, College of Education, University of Washington.

Veronica Boix Mansilla is a Research Coordinator at Project Zero at the Harvard Graduate School of Education.

William C. Miller is a social studies teacher at Concord Middle School, Concord, Massachusetts.

Howard Gardner is the Hobbs Professor of Cognition and Education and Co-director of Project Zero at the Harvard Graduate School of Education. He is also an Adjunct Professor of Neurology at the Boston University School of Medicine.

Judith Rényi is Executive Director of the National Foundation for the Improvement of Education. The foundation, established and supported by the National Education Association, empowers public education employees to innovate, take risks, and become agents for change to improve teaching and learning in our society.

Frederick L. Hamel is a doctoral candidate in Curriculum and Instruction at the University of Washington, and is a secondary English teacher at Bremerton High School, Bremerton, Washington.

Arthur N. Applebee is a Professor of Education and Director of the Center on English Learning and Achievement at the State University of New York at Albany.

Robert Burroughs is an Assistant Professor in the Teacher Education Division of the College of Education at the University of Cincinnati.

Gladys Cruz is the director of one of twelve Bilingual Education Technical Assistance Centers funded by the New York State Education Department. She has also conducted research for the National Research Center on English Learning and Achievement at the State University of New York at Albany, where she is currently completing a Ph.D. in Curriculum and Instruction.

Kathleen J. Roth is an Associate Professor in the Department of Teacher Education at Michigan State University.

Karen Hammerness is a Research Associate in the Stanford Teacher Education Program at Stanford University.

Kay Moffett is a postdoctoral fellow and Instructor and School Partnership Coordinator in the Stanford Teacher Education Program at Stanford University.

Gabriella Minnes Brandes, Ph.D., is a Lecturer in the Department of Language and Literacy Education at the University of British Columbia.

Peter Seixas is an Associate Professor in the Department of Curriculum Studies at the University of British Columbia.

Leslie Santee Siskin, Ph.D., is an Associate Professor at the Harvard Graduate School of Education.

Index